Renaissance and Reformation England

1509–1714

THE HARBRACE HISTORY OF ENGLAND

PART **II**

THE HARBRACE HISTORY OF ENGLAND

Charles M. Gray

University of Chicago

Renaissance and Reformation England

1509-1714

Under the General Editorship of John Morton Blum

Yale University

Harcourt Brace Jovanovich, Inc.

New York / Chicago / San Francisco / Atlanta

ISBN: 0-15-535108-7

Library of Congress Catalog Card Number: 72-97674

Printed in the United States of America

Preface

General history books are useful for giving shape to complex periods covered by innumerable specialized works. They are also useful because they permit all the interconnections of history to be seen as they appear to a single historian. For the same reason, such books are never neutral. They speak in one particular voice among many possible voices, and they should be taken as cues to listen for other voices, both those of other historians and those of the sources. New general books are necessary from time to time because history is a collaborative enterprise, and equally because it is a highly individual one. New information and reinterpretations gained by the collaborative effort will inevitably lead to new attempts to generalize.

At the same time, general history cannot and should not merely sum up the changing picture of a period on the many fronts where historians are making changes. In the end, it must be the author's own picture, gained by sifting and evaluating the work of others—and sometimes by looking past that work to the things in history that engage his particular interest and the connections that satisfy his own sense of coherence.

The picture of England in this book is new in the sense that everything individual is new. It is offered in the hope that some students will find that it makes this period of English history understandable from their viewpoint.

I wish to thank Professors Paul Seaver and Perez Zagorin for reading the manuscript and making helpful suggestions. My other principal debt is to my students at the University of Chicago, who have heard much that is contained in this volume in the form of lectures, and who have assisted in its evolution from my earlier presentations of Tudor-Stuart history.

Charles M. Gray

Introduction

To the Middle Ages England owes many distinctive and lasting features of her national life: her premodern pattern of settlement and cultivation; the momentous reality of being a single nation under a central government, despite a deeper localism than modern people can easily imagine; the common law, which, because it has spread to divide the world with Roman law, is England's oldest title to be called another Rome; parliamentary government and along with it the understanding that English monarchy was limited by law and mixed with other elements (a commonplace medieval understanding which England and her progeny, most notably the United States, succeeded in translating into a variety of modern constitutional dialects); a language, finally, from whose fecundity more literatures than one would spring. To the Industrial Revolution of the later eighteenth century, England owed the opportunity for power and empire and the challenge to adjust her institutions and her spirit to an environment for which nothing in man's experience had prepared her. To England's transitory glory, the opportunity was seized; the challenge was met with contributions to civilization which the fall of empires cannot sweep away.

This volume falls between the medieval achievement and the modern transformation. Materially, England in the sixteenth and seventeenth centuries was largely continuous with medieval England. The population, which had been drastically reduced by the Black Death, recovered to the level of the early fourteenth century only about halfway through the sixteenth; thereafter, a population growing beyond the highest earlier point created problems for a modestly expanding, but still essentially medieval, economy. Even so, the maximum medieval population was not so much as doubled by the end of the seventeenth century. The order of magnitude of later population growth, and of the economic development that accompanied it, was much higher. Neither in magnitude nor in much of the quality of everyday life was the society of the sixteenth and seventeenth centuries unrecognizably new by medieval standards. With benign effects and inefficient ones, the shadow of medieval institutions hung over the period ambiguously called postmedieval or early modern. Ways of doing public business and of organizing social relationships and economic production in the local communities where people passed their lives carried the burden and the blessing of an impressive paternity. If, however, one takes a more inward view—into the minds of men when they are articulate and into the infinite nuances of attitude and response with which the articulate and the inarticulate alike confront experience—one is bound to see a new culture, a break with the Middle Ages. No break in history is clean, and the civilization of the Middle Ages was anything but homogeneous and unchanging; nevertheless, one constellation gave way to another, and perhaps the sixteenth and seventeenth centuries were quite as new as the configuration that succeeded them, to the accompaniment of much more dramatic external change, in the eighteenth and nineteenth centuries.

Historical constellations are unfixed, moving things. They consist in successive major alterations in ways of thinking and feeling—and inevitably of doing, even when custom and technological limitations make for the kind of discrepancy between outward conservatism and inward revolution that we perceive in our period. Successive and simultaneous breaks with the past are related to each other causally, antagonistically, and dialectically. They add up to the unity of a culture, but the sum is always changing with new additions, and the unity consists more and more in diversity, in tension as well as harmony, in enrichments pregnant with future possibilities as well as consolidations of the new to exclude the old. As the new culture of the early modern period consolidated, the values and styles of the Middle Ages found less room; as the culture of the postmedieval period grew richer, the seeds of later modernization were accumulating. One should look for the ways in which the industrialization of England and the institutional and intellectual adaptations to it were made possible by the cultural alterations of the sixteenth and seventeenth centuries. On the other hand, one should never look at history with too insistent or too ambitious a teleological eye. The culture we are concerned with in this volume needs no justification beyond itself. It was latent with future achievements, but they were realized by the impoverishment of the rich synthesis of ideas and values that was worked out in the intermediate period of English history.

A eulogist might almost rest his case on the age's capacity to produce William Shakespeare, on the one hand, and Sir Isaac Newton, on the other. The history of sixteenth- and seventeenth-century England may serve to show that the genius of these great men and of many more was not ineffable, although that history will also show that greatness cannot be entirely explained by the phenomena that explain it in part. Whether or not their pretense to have recovered the Gospel can be justified, the sixteenth and seventeenth centuries were the Apostolic age of English Protestantism. Protestantism sprang in the fervor of youth, suffered enmeshment in politics, bred its own schisms and heresies, cooled to the post-Apostolic tone of the eighteenth century, and furnished ingredients for the revival of religious enthusiasm and Christian disputatiousness in the nineteenth. Among the manifold trials of Protestant England was the most grievous civil disruption in English history—the Great Rebellion of the mid-seventeenth century, when Europe's main Protestant monarchy was temporarily abolished and soldiers who called themselves saints discovered how difficult it was to found a Gospel republic. With hindsight, a hundred years' worth of clouds can be seen as portending that storm. When the rains of revolution were spent, men's zeal to avoid another outburst contributed to a cooling of religious and political zeal, to the search for more pacific and constructive interests, to the displacement of a collapsed political revolution by a real scientific one, to the last cultural phase of the intermediate period and the first of the modern.

There is hardly a better reason for saying that our period represents a cultural break than that its inhabitants supposed that it did. Even before the Reformation announced its break with past corruptions, the Renaissance had proclaimed new standards for learning and new ideals for the practical world. The two main movements of the sixteenth century were not only new, but consciously so. At the same time, both looked backward, to pasts glowing enough to be confused with the future; they were movements for rebirth and reformation; their past and their future were classical civilization and the Apostolic age of Christianity. With complications, the attitudes of the Renaissance and Reformation were transmitted from the sixteenth century to the seventeenth. Their sense of era was included in the transmission, though about that, too, complications gathered. In some ways, perspectives grew less backward-looking; the moderns dared challenge the ancients, and progress into the future in some measure displaced revival. A consciously antimedieval period turned into a consciously modern one, while reinforcing in both practice and consciousness its alienation from the Middle Ages to which England owed so much.

Contents

Illustrations

Maps

Renaissance and Reformation England

1509–1714

CHAPTER ONE

Dynasties make convenient dividing lines, but not the most significant ones. This book begins with the accession of Henry VIII in 1509, rather than with the transition to the Tudors in 1485, for the lineage of kings matters less than the shape of history. Henry VII ruled well, in the best tradition of his forbears and of his Yorkist rivals; bringing broils to rest, he made "normalcy" work. Henry VIII upset the world he inherited. The Henrician Reformation and the ensuing Protestant Reformation mark one of the clearest breaks in English history. His ecclesiastical revolution alone gives Henry VIII a title his father could not claim, that of a true innovator.

In another sense as well, the son's title exceeded the father's. Henry VII had come as a challenger, as inheritor by a devious descent of the Lancastrian claim to the throne. However just its cause, the Red Rose had sprouted in a soil of usurpation. Henry VII made his bid, succeeded, and consolidated his success by good policy. And with good policy he married; Henry VIII was begotten by Lancaster on York. In the son's veins the divided streams of the blood royal ran again as one. The wound was closed, the tragedy concluded with joy and reconcilement, the taint of usurpation expunged. Of course, a last-ditch Yorkist need not concede Henry VIII's title; had he had a less symbolically perfect mother, he would probably have come to the throne no less smoothly on the strength of his father's

Renaissance England

achievement. But the symbolism of Henry VIII's parentage appealed to imaginations. Propagandists were ready to point out the beauty of it all. From the sixteenth century's own point of view, there is reason to draw a line between Henry VII and Henry VIII. Better than the last antagonist in an old quarrel, this son of auspicious birth was suited to inaugurate an age.

A feeling of sunburst attended Henry VIII's accession. The new king was just under eighteen years old. Whatever he might turn out to be, he was fantastically endowed with "image." His tall, strongly muscular frame figured forth a race of heroes: He looked the part of Mars, and in the playground warfare of the joust, as in other athletics, he filled the part superbly. Yet he was no dull bruiser: bright, well-educated, talented in music, outgoing and cheerful, he was a youth to charm the world, fit to enjoy a bountiful estate. The ceremony of his midsummer coronation was as resplendent as the king himself. That rite had been preceded by a royal wedding, whereby Henry VIII took to wife Catherine of Aragon, relict of his brother Arthur. It was a season of ritual and holiday. The old king, now pompously laid to rest, was remembered for his worth, but little missed. The parsimony of his later years had left a sourish aftertaste. The new king gave promise of a more liberal, more spirited reign. Youth had come into its own.

Renaissance Culture:
The Humanist Movement

The English Renaissance did not begin at a specifiable time. Yet it is appropriate to let Henry VIII's accession serve as the starting point for a chapter more concerned with the Renaissance than with that monarch's deeds. The king was young and promising: fresh currents of thought and aspiration stirred the learned and touched the laity. The king was heir to hard-won success, freer than his father to relax, spend, and enjoy: new moral and aesthetic ideals, already at work over the last decades, were gathering toward predominance. A new culture was coming into its own. The young king seemed to be cut after the pattern of Renaissance ideals. His all-around accomplishments, his ease of bearing, the intelligence and cultivation that graced his handsome, soldierly frame—the formulators of new values were looking for such qualities. From a king such virtues might spread into the commonwealth.

Renaissance culture, in the sense we shall define it, was of prevailing importance in England through the sixteenth century and well into the seventeenth. It makes sense to speak of the English Renaissance as running from about 1500 through, say, the career of John Milton (1608–74). It makes sense to see the late Elizabethan and Jacobean periods, the Golden Age of English literature, as the climax of the English Renaissance. On the other hand, a purpose is served by contracting this time span. Beyond the middle decades of the sixteenth century, Renaissance values were in vigorous competition with other new growths. The competition was not all inimical: sometimes the relationships between Renaissance culture and other tendencies were symbiotic. However, by the late sixteenth, early seventeenth century English civilization had taken on complexities that the preceding period lacked and that the European sources of Renaissance culture did not entirely furnish. Earlier in the sixteenth century, the ideals of the Renaissance were "in the driver's seat": they were in competition with older values over which they tended to prevail. They set a tone, standing for the new and the creative.

The Renaissance is identifiable at the core with the humanist movement, the liveliest current in Italian intellectual life from the fourteenth century and in European intellectual life at the turn of the sixteenth century. The Renaissance was preeminently the product of scholars and men of letters, yet the movement argues that ideas can have practical influence. The humanists would be no more important in history than other intellectuals had they not spoken to needs felt beyond the study and shown new possibilities of life to people whose main concern was not with literature.

The humanists' literary interest was in the authors of classical antiquity. The Italian humanists, especially, were responsible for the recovery of many classical texts. All humanists sought to read the ancients aright and to learn and to teach the pure, long-corrupted style of classical Latin. They also sought to acquire and impart the orientation toward literature that they attributed to the Greek and Latin authors. They were not classical scholars in the modern sense, although they founded the tradition from which classical scholarship has sprung. Nor were they mere grammarians and stylists. To appreciate their importance, it is necessary to consider their attitudes, which formed a distinctive outlook on the world, although not a formal philosophy. The influence of the humanists reached beyond the Groves of Academe because they had something to say about life.

The humanists thought learning and letters relevant in the affairs of this world. Such an orientation toward literature, as well as a mellifluous style, they perceived in the ancients. The humanists thought the ancient authors (and such of the moderns as could catch a spark of their eloquence) could be forces for practical good. In short, the humanists were the opposite of academic. Idealists with a practical eye, they were impatient of studies carried on merely for the sake of intellectual exercise or for technical interest alone. They quarreled with scholasticism, the standard medieval and postmedieval academic fare, because it seemed idle and impractical. The role they most exalted was that of the moral teacher, the man who could dispose others to noble acts and to inward tranquility. They were preoccupied with eloquence because they believed that love of virtue could only be communicated through skill with language, and that only by language well-used could the good man in the world persuade others to noble courses. To the humanists, the end of literature was didactic, and its means emotive. Teaching in the highest sense, they believed, aimed not at the communication of information or technique, but at a quickening of the heart.

The varieties of literature the humanists admired seemed to subserve their ideal; those they practiced were made to subserve it. Poetry was to clothe virtue in beauty, to heighten its color and sweeten its appeal. According to the taste and fancy of the humanist, history was superior to poetry because it is truer, or inferior because its lessons are less clear-cut. Either way, history was meant to teach by the example of famous men and to put starch in those who felt the spur of fame. Oratory was the antique art on which the precepts and worship of eloquence were based, the Roman orator Cicero the chief prophet of the humanist creed. The humanists wrote orations in their closets for fun and gave an oratorical sound to their other forms of writing. They encouraged ritualistic speechmaking on public occasions and taught style to those who needed to make speeches. Informal modes of literature with good antique pedigrees, such as the dialog and the letter, were assiduously cultivated. Such forms lent themselves to the exploration of moral questions, to a certain casualness of manner (which had the virtue of teaching without seeming to do so too heavy-handedly), and to satirical aspersion on the enemies of light and grace.

At heart, humanism was a sober, edifying movement. If our description of it evokes the stuffed shirt and the headmaster, that is fair enough. Its best products transcend such associations, but run-of-the-mill humanism was heavy with the limitations they suggest. Humanism was too practical to sympathize with the speculative mind and too centered on man to care much for nature. It was often too stiff and serious, too "old Roman," to respond to the unstudied beauty of popular culture or to the mere zaniness of life. It took its morality from the sages, its examples from the great, questioning too little whether ultimate goodness will always stand with the official virtues and looking too little at the backsides of its approved heroes. It is only in retrospect, however, that these limitations of humanism appear. In their day, the humanists held up new, inspiring goals.

Humanism and the Aristocracy

English humanism's most important social function was to provide the governing class with new values. Humanist doctrine had an intrinsically aristocratic bent. The ancient literature it was founded on was the product of a small upper class. The standards of learning and accomplishment that the humanists upheld presupposed leisure and wealth. Their concern for moral action in the world was inevitably focused on the classes to whom practical influence was open in late-medieval Europe. In such countries as England, that meant the landed aristocracy. Humanism gave the sixteenth-century English ruling class a more sober and strenuous conception of its role, and educational standards appropriate to that conception.

Although the king's political position, compared to that of the magnates, was strong in the early sixteenth century, England's social constitution remained profoundly aristocratic. Save for what the Crown and Church held, most of the country was owned by a rent-drawing upper class, comprising the titled nobility and those known as gentlemen. Preeminent status went with landowning, which, in an overwhelmingly agrarian society, meant the major share of economic power. Those who gained great wealth by trade usually tried to turn it into status by acquiring land. Although gentility did not pass to a rich purchaser with the deed, caste feeling was not so rigid as to prevent its springing up in the children. The landowning class was in several senses a governing class. The English tradition of central government did not prevent landlords from enjoying fragmentary political authority within their estates—and certainly not from seeming to be "authority figures." In addition, the king's government used lords and gentlemen to carry on its business in the localities.

In the sixteenth century, the dependence of royal government on the aristocracy increased because the Tudors did not create a nonaristocratic bureaucracy to carry the greater burdens that a more vigorous state and new legislation entailed. Justices of the peace—chosen from the gentry and serving without pay—acquired new functions and became increasingly crucial for local government. At the center, the king's service became more attractive to gentlemen, for the monarchy's prestige was greater, and the decline of territorial magnates reduced opportunity in the service of other lords than the king. The professional element in medieval government—clerical bureaucrats compensated by Church patronage—faced increased lay competition in the early sixteenth century, at which time the clerics remained important; they were largely washed away, to the competition's benefit, after the Reformation. In sum, the Tudor reassertion of royal power gave the upper class a firmer place in the structure of authority. By prevailing standards this development was good, for society was conceived as a hierarchy mirroring God's hierarchical world. Wealth, splendor, nobility, and real political power should go together; they should be supereminent in the royal image of God and in the Church, but proportionably enjoyed by the lesser stars to whom ordinary men looked up.

Humanism brought a message to the aristocracy; it supplied its practical and psychological needs. The gentle class came into the sixteenth century equipped with an ethos and a style, something an elite needs to give it identity and justify its privileges. But the old class code was straining against reality and becoming less convincing. The tradition of the aristocracy had been basically military: the original justification of its preponderant wealth and freedom from toil had been that such privileges were necessary to sustain a class of soldiers. Even in the earlier Middle Ages, there was a large element of mythology in the upper class's military identity. Landowners were often, in fact, more preoccupied with wealth, family, politics, hunting, and hospitality than with fulfilling a soldierly role. But being expert in fighting and endowed with the appropriate physical and moral virtues was a useful object in life, as well as a satisfying one, when other skills were not so much in demand and when there were not strong cultural pressures to be something more than battle-ready. As late as the fifteenth-century civil wars, a gentleman who was only a soldier could be confident that he was enacting the time-honored part of a gentleman. By the later Middle Ages, the aristocracy's military identity had been overlaid and complicated by the code of chivalry, an ethos that, at bottom, was an idealization of the military tradition. Soldiering remained the gentleman's vocation, but military skill and courage were woven into an elaborate context of moral and aesthetic ideas. Although constructed from the military tradition, full-blown chivalry was also a critique of that tradition. Gentlemen needed to be something more than soldiers, and accumulating cultural pressures told them they ought to be. Richer accomplishments were demanded; men needed to see themselves in richer dreams to be satisfied of their gentility.

The chivalric ideal was in many ways as insubstantial as a dream. Acted out, it often issued in silliness. Knowing how to fight and doing so fearlessly were real accomplishments, as justifiable as the political ends that called for fighting. Chivalry, nourished on romantic stories, told the soldierly man that his natural virtues had value only in the service of an evanescent image—the noble, questing soul. Such a man of dreams would worship women, and for the indefinable honor and unattainable love of one special woman face death against all comers. In a lifetime of adventures, no aspersion on his honor (or hers) would go unchallenged. Yet, in this reconciling world of fantasy, honor would carry no chip on its shoulder. Its obligations would always coincide with justice and charity, gentleness and courtesy would smooth the warlike brow and sweeten the fierce heart.

Although Don Quixote is probably the only man to have put this ideal into serious practice, it helped to give the aristocracy a style and *esprit de corps*. Real refinement of manners, as well as the stylized etiquette that sometimes serves instead, was encouraged both by the cult of women and by the men's club cult of honorable quarreling and courteous reconciliations. Some acquaintance with music and poetry was incumbent on a gentleman, if he was to please the ladies and understand his romantic scenario. Make-believe in essence, chivalry stimulated the creation of a make-believe reality. The sport of jousting, surrounded by elaborate pageantry, absorbed much of the martial energy and passion for honor that would otherwise have gone sour in gentle breasts. Chivalric orders (in effect, clubs or lodges of men born gentle and bred in the accomplishments of their class) provided attention-consuming ritual and, in the manner of clubs and lodges, wrote the credo of knightliness into their statements of purpose. A make-believe reality, however, can contribute to a leisure class's identity. Gentlemen can be recognized, in their own eyes and others', by the pseudoactivities they are eligible by rank and know-how to engage in. Fantasy activities were accompanied by real beauty. More conspicuous consumption and more art adorned the upper orders than in the earlier Middle Ages. The glow of a charmed life led by superior people was more visible to the world.

The military ethos of the aristocracy and its chivalric overlay were not adequate, however, to the conditions of the sixteenth century and to the class's long-term needs. A governing class, becoming more so, needed to think of itself as a governing class. It needed to acquire skills suitable to its role. Solider food than chivalry was required to give gentlemen the sense that their superiority was real, their function equal to their privileges, their attainments related to a real function. Humanism provided such food. It conceived the aristocrat primarily as a public figure, a magistrate or a counselor to princes. It put classical learning at the center of the attainments to be desired in a gentleman. Learning in itself was a spiritual good for all men, the more so because to the humanists it was the road to moral effectiveness. It was the truest mark of superiority in anyone, not something that clerics and scholars might specialize in and gentlemen leave alone. Learning's intrinsic worth was only magnified by its practical usefulness to men with jobs to do in an increasingly complicated society.

Humanism had much to give the aristocracy, but the aristocracy had a good deal to give in return. Renaissance culture, in England as elsewhere, was in a major aspect the product of such give-and-take. As described above, humanism looks rather gray—an earnest faith, a projection of the schoolmaster. But if you associate high color with Renaissance culture, you are to many intents correct. An exchange of energy between humanism and the traditional style and values of the aristocracy accounts for much of the period's tone. Humanism put classical learning and an elevated moral tone at the center of its picture of the ideal gentleman. But the books devoted to painting that picture worked the traditional aesthetic of gentility into the composition. The finished gentleman was to be soldier and athlete as well as scholar and magistrate. He was to be at home in love as well as in letters. Gracefulness was not to be lost as sagacity was gained. Grace, indeed, was essential if wisdom and virtue were to be effective in the real world. An analogy was seen between the eloquence that made good ideas persuasive and the qualities in a nobleman that would enable the sage and statesman in him to "come across." He must fit into a world where military prowess was still expected of a gentleman, a world where a touch of the chivalric character still identified an aristocrat and where not everyone would swallow Roman virtue raw. He must, in short, be frighteningly all-around.

Two books especially document these themes. The greatest gentleman's manual of the Renaissance was an Italian product: Baldassare Castiglione's *Courtier*. First published in Italian in 1527, it was known to Englishmen in the original in the early sixteenth century. Later (1561) it was translated by Sir Thomas Hoby into one of the major monuments of Tudor prose. *The Courtier* stands witness to Italy's generative role for European Renaissance culture, for it perfectly illustrates the synthesis of humanism and aristocracy. Its casual, graceful style symbolizes its emphasis on manners and traditional gentlemanly accomplishments, yet its message is deeply serious. The ideal courtier must have all the charm and *savoir faire* that the word "courtier" suggests, but the object of his life is to become a leader of men and adviser of princes. Antique wisdom and valor are to be built on courtly foundations. Ultimately (a famous concluding passage tells us), the courtier will only be fulfilled by developing his attributes still further. On learning, eloquence, and political sagacity, he must build philosophical and mystical insight into the nature of things. *The Courtier*, starting as a book of manners, looks outward to statesmanship and thence to contemplation. The last step involves translating the courtly ideal of the accomplished lover into the Platonic ideal of fully sublimated love. At all levels, aristocratic tradition and classicism meet.

The most important English gentleman's manual was Sir Thomas Elyot's *Governor* (1531). The very title signifies that the upper class was coming to be seen and idealized as a ruling class. More sobersided, less artful, and less exalted than *The Courtier*, *The Governor* makes the same general point: the physical, military, and aesthetic virtues of traditional aristocracy are important, but thorough humanistic learning and moral self-development must crown the making of a gentleman. These latter qualities alone render a gentleman worthy of his status and fit for magistracy.

The influence of such books as *The Courtier* and *The Governor* is hard to gauge exactly. Prescriptions for perfection are not likely to be literally applied. But all signs suggest that the well-born were hungry for literature addressed to themselves and that humanistic literature was the ascendant species. The introduction of printing made books more available and sped the circulation of ideas. In the earliest days of printing, a good deal of chivalric literature was brought out, which suggests a market for books in which gentlemen could seek their identity. As the sixteenth century progressed, these new-style gentleman's manuals and classical literature tended to supersede romance. Gentlemen were dreaming new dreams and buying books on self-improvement.

However directly the gentleman's manuals altered upper-class aspirations, educational standards rose dramatically in the sixteenth century. Classes below the gentry were also affected by heightened educational expectations and improved facilities. Progress was made at many levels—at the level of basic literacy, on the middle ground of book-based popular culture and utilitarian knowledge, and at the heights of learning. In the long run, it is as important that solid education spread beyond the aristocracy as that it spread within it. But no segment of the "educational revolution" carried more historical weight than the aristocratic.

By 1500 the battle for basic literacy was not won within even the top class. It was shortly to be. The modern expectation is that the rich and socially distinguished will attain more than basic literacy and will receive more bookish education than the average man, even if that education does not turn them into scholars. This expectation first became realistic in the sixteenth century. A substantial part of the gentry went further. The English universities in the Middle Ages were clerical institutions. They remained so in the sixteenth century but added the important function of providing higher liberal education for significant numbers of gentlemen. The law schools operated by the Inns of Court (the lawyers' guilds) in London became, like the universities, more than professional agencies. It became fashionable for young gentlemen to enroll in the Inns, some to learn the socially eligible trade of a lawyer in earnest, more to acquire the smattering of law that a country magistrate could use, and others for little more than to be educationally and socially "finished" by good company and residence at the center of culture and power. As not every Inns of Court man grew learned in the law, so not every high-born university man advanced to distinction or to a degree. The universities, like the Inns, were in part social centers, places where it was creditable to be seen and where people of the right sort were to be found. To some extent, they were substitutes for the noble households where, by old aristocratic tradition, boys were sent to live, serve, and acquire class style. But using universities even for a social purpose says something about upper-class aspirations: centers of learning, for the first time, had snob value.

For many scions of the gentry, universities had real value. Whether osmotically and informally or through the prescribed steps to a degree, many members of the governing class approached the humanistic ideal through university education. More (for university attendance was still far from an automatic incident of upper classness) got solid literary education through tutors and grammar schools. Such secondary education was wholly humanistic—there was nothing else for it to be. If boys were to have book-learning at all, that learning would be classical. Before the program and attitudes of Renaissance humanism held sway, secondary training had centered on the Latin language and on the ancient arts of grammar, rhetoric, and logic through which the language was analyzed and manipulated. The effect of humanism was to raise standards of proficiency, to introduce better textbooks and a richer diet of reading in the ancient authors, to bring Greek into the curriculum, and, above all, to make "good letters" a more sought-after commodity.

In many ways, sixteenth- and seventeenth-century English history is a success story for the aristocracy. Although families moved in and out of that class with exceptional rapidity, and the balance within the class between its greater and lesser members wavered and shifted, the aristocratic niche in the social hierarchy remained firm. As time went on, the aristocracy's weight in politics grew at the Crown's expense. Noblemen and gentlemen came to dominate the central administration and twist it to their own purposes. Parliament became a mouthpiece of the gentry more completely than in the past, and, at the same time, it became more independent and more critical of the monarch. Eventually, in the seventeenth century, a large faction of Parliament and the gentry took up arms against their king. Although these developments are complex and far-reaching, the aristocracy's educational progress was by any reckoning a crucial factor in its success. By becoming better educated, it made itself more worthy of the claims that contemporary social theory made for hierarchy and deference. Gentlemen became more confident of themselves and better qualified for a political role. The more educated in the humanistic mode they were, the better they learned the part that humanism set for them.

Earnest, patriotic, politically ambitious, versed in history and in the moral and political debates to which classical education exposed them, they were not necessarily prepared to be the most tractable of subjects.

Alteration of a class's character is always slow. The aristocracy's educational gains, and indeed the general consolidation of its strength, came to fruition only in Elizabeth's long, stabilizing reign. But the impulse behind the upper class's retooling was alive from the beginning of the sixteenth century. The spark was struck by humanism rubbing against this class's needs.

Christian Humanism

Religion is the second major area in which humanism reached out from its scholarly center into the fabric of history. One of the distinguishing features of the Renaissance in Northern Europe was its preoccupation with religious questions and with the state of Christendom.

On the surface, humanism had no quarrel with Christianity. The Christian religion and the Catholic Church presided with the immeasurable weight of tradition over the world in which humanism grew up. Although the Catholic Church was soon to be challenged by the Protestant revolution, there was no challenging the hegemony of the faith itself. That faith remained the principal determinant of men's values and of their conception of the world. By and large, new intellectual tendencies took the Christian framework for granted, insofar as they did not make a conscious adaptation to it. Humanism was high-thinking and morally earnest. One would not expect a movement of that tone to conflict with Christianity in any immediate way. Humanism did not profess to be a religion or a substitute for religion, and its everyday moral values were no different from those that a church profoundly supportive of the social order endorsed.

At a deeper level, however, there was tension between humanism and Christianity. As a form of secular learning and of literary taste, humanism was harmless, but it was too serious to be quite so innocent. Could a man believe passionately in the wisdom and virtue of the ancients and still believe that Christianity had contributed something uniquely valuable? Although classical and Christian moral standards were close enough for purposes of everyday good behavior, was not the spirit of Christian ethics really very different from that of men whose idea of goodness was limited by the horizons of this world? If a man took Cicero too seriously, could he love Christ as he ought?

At one level of reconcilement, the basic one, humanism gave a modest and comforting answer to these questions. Of course Christianity brought something new into the world—not only the true religion, but a higher morality than antiquity had known. The ancients show the way up the lower slopes of human perfection, as far as man's reason and his natural strength can carry him. The rest of the ascent is only possible with Christ's guidance, and this path leads to a perfection that the ancients could not imagine. Even so, the lower slopes of human perfection must be traversed: there is no higher perfection, for most men at least, until the more elementary stages of moral training are mastered, with the help of the wisest and best men who have traveled that lower road unaided. Nature leads into grace; grace presupposes nature.

Thinking in such a way, humanists could live at peace as Christians. But not all humanists were content merely to distinguish their sphere from that of divinity and to assert that the two spheres were compatible. Some humanists took a deeper interest in religion and in the religious implications of their attitudes. Historians apply the term "Christian humanism" to the work of those men. England was at the center of the Christian humanist movement, and its impact on her religious history was lasting.

Christian humanists proposed not so much to separate and reconcile the spheres of humanity and divinity as to integrate them. To their way of thinking, humanistic training would not simply lead a man to a certain point, beyond which religion must take control. Rather, the techniques and orientation instilled by humanistic training would guide men toward a true understanding and a living realization of their faith. The upper slopes of the mountain of human perfection were, to be sure, Christ's territory—a realm of grace, revelation, and ethical values beyond the ancients' reach—but the meaning of Christ's message would be best understood by those who had been shaped by the humanistic framework of ideas. Christian humanism had something distinctive to say about religion and a great deal that was critical to say about the contemporary Church.

Humanism, in general, was possessed by the imagined beauty and grandeur of days long past. By Christian standards, the ancients had a limited prospect of human possibilities, but within their limitations they were king-size. Their eloquence, wisdom, and nobility had long been lost. The present hope was that the ancient virtue might be recovered, that modern men might clear away the rubble that centuries had deposited around the ancient fountains and drink their pure water once more. Renascence—rebirth—was the hope of Renaissance humanism. The Christian humanists transposed belief in the purity and grandeur of the remote past from the secular realm to the sacred. The original Gospel of Christ, the early history of the Church, and the authors of Christian antiquity were the fountains of the faith. Like the fountains of secular literature and civility, these had been long-obstructed. Christianity, too, was in need of rebirth.

The humanists' skills and academic prejudices were conducive to the belief that they could have a purifying and restorative role in religion. The New Testament is in Greek. With their new-won knowledge of that language, some humanists were impelled to study the Word of God in the original. They saw themselves as uniquely qualified, by their philological skill and by the art of close reading they had practiced on the classics, to understand what the Bible really said and meant. Neither the standard Latin version (the Vulgate) nor a mass of current religious opinion supposedly based on the Scriptures could be trusted.

Moreover, the humanistic approach was at open war with contemporary academic theology and its intellectual and educational milieu. The late-medieval theological expert was a technician in the analytic tradition known as scholasticism. Higher general education—from which theological study, as the most prestigious professional course, took off— was heavy on logic and was dominated by the categories of Aristotelian philosophy. Whether or not they became theologians, the products of such training were conditioned to a dry, jargon-ridden style of expression and to interests of a subtle, intellectualistic cast.

All the themes of humanism gathered in enmity against the scholastic mind. As linguists and men of letters, the humanists saw the scholastics as butchers of the Latin language. They saw them as moderns wrapped up in the little problems of their specialties, ignorant and heedless of the great minds and voices of antiquity. To the humanists, scholastics were intellectuals for the sake of intellectual exercise, not serious men whose learning bore on life. They were spinners of webs from their own undistinguished innards, webs that both veiled the eye of common sense and hid the literary sources of true nourishment.

To the Christian humanist, scholastic theology cast the baleful shadow of the scholastic mind over holy places. It substituted its dry tomes for the inspired and inspiring founts of Christianity: the Bible and the Church Fathers. (In the former, God spoke directly; in the latter, the piety of the early Church could be quaffed in good Latin.) Scholasticism seemed to overload the plain meaning of the Christian faith with interpretation, to overintellectualize a truth to which the simplest unclouded heart should be able to respond. Obsession with dogma and endless debate over its fine points seemed to stultify men whose mission as divines should have been to communicate the heart of the matter and to show how the faith could be lived. In their own conceit, the humanists would make better spiritual guides. In addition to their ability and determination to go to the fountains, they would not forget that the end of learning is to teach (not to teach other professors) nor that the fruit of true belief is good living.

One man has the unchallengeable claim to be remembered as "Mr. Christian Humanism": Erasmus of Rotterdam (*c.* 1466–1536). Dutch by birth, he belonged to all Europe through his reputation and his unique sense of self. His relationship with England, however, was so close as to make him virtually the leading figure of English humanism. Erasmus paid several long visits to England and spent one five-year period "in residence." Even apart from his religious studies, he was the most eminent humanist

Desiderius Erasmus: The central figure of Christian humanism and the chief influence on English humanism. The artist, Hans Holbein, painted portraits of numerous English political and intellectual figures of the early sixteenth century. (Archives Photographiques, Paris.)

of his or any day, *nonpareil* in classical learning, in the accomplishment of his Latin style and the fecundity of his pen, in the force of personality and purity of conviction with which he stood for all that humanism meant. He was the cynosure of the English humanists who had the benefit of his company and correspondence. But although he was the great influence on English humanism, he also took something from it. Erasmus impressed the Christian side of his humanism on Englishmen; at the same time, English influence contributed to that side of Erasmus's lifework.

Such influence proceeded to some degree from John Colet (1466–1519), one of the purest examples of a Christian humanist. Scion of the rich urban elite, his father a sometime lord mayor of London, Colet was one of the first Englishmen to study in Italy. His later career in the Church led to the distinguished post of dean of St. Paul's Cathedral in London. Dean Colet was responsible for a major step toward bringing the standards of humanism into education: the foundation of St. Paul's School in 1510. For the school, Colet drew up rules expressive of the humanistic ideal of education. With his first headmaster, William Lily, he also wrote a Latin grammar for it. *Lily's Grammar*, as it came to be known, was a pillar of education and the basic textbook for Renaissance England. Earlier in life (1496–1506), Colet had made his major contribution to Christian humanism by lecturing at Oxford on the Epistles of St. Paul. These lectures exemplify the Christian humanist program of close Scriptural study: looking to St. Paul was looking to the first, most indisputably authentic Christian theologian. Although Colet did not fall into unorthodoxy, he caught an emphasis and spirit in St. Paul that did not sit easy with the prevailing mood of the Church. Such was the way of Christian humanism.

Erasmus's religious *magnum opus*, an edition of the Greek New Testament with aids to its study, was the principal fulfillment of the humanist hope that the Bible might be better known in its naked purity and attended to with sharper ears. To the chorus against scholastics (and against mere ignorance and inadequacy among churchmen) Erasmus joined his resounding voice. From such foundations, shared with many humanists, Erasmus developed a religious stance with more specific "punch" than the foundations imply in themselves. It was more a religious stance than a dogmatic position, but in its way it was radical.

Erasmianism was worked out just as the Protestant Reformation was beginning. There are affinities between the two. Protestantism, like Christian humanism, turned in wrath on the contemporary Church and on the accumulation of "lying tradition" that obstructed the true Gospel. It, too, looked back to the fountains, exalted the primitive Church, prayed for its renascence, and elevated the Bible over all human voices that had presumed to speak for God. Some men became Protestants because they were imbued with Christian humanism. To such people, the Protestant revolution against the Church was the daybreak that Christian humanism prophesied. Yet Erasmus himself—called upon in his eminence to take a stand and half-expected to welcome the new dawn—repudiated the Protestant movement. Although his decision is sometimes taken to reflect on his courage and clear-sightedness, it should not be interpreted that way. Ultimately, Erasmus aimed at something different from Protestantism: it does better justice to both the "punch" and the distinctness of Erasmus's cause to see it as a movement for reformation in its own right, a *tertium quid* alongside Catholic conservatism and Protestant revolt. As it turned out, Protestantism and Catholicism divided the field of history. There was no overt "Erasmian reformation." Christian humanism had to be content with the underground success of infiltrating and influencing both Protestant and Catholic camps. Nowhere did it enjoy such semisuccess as in England. The first phase of the English Reformation in some ways approached an Erasmian reformation, and in its Protestant days the Church of England derived its unique character from the Christian humanist book.

Christian humanist eloquence hammered at many aspects of ecclesiastical culture, joining with long-standing popular anticlericalism to weaken respect for the Church as it was. In that way alone, it contributed to the day when many people could look on Henry VIII's measures, or even Protestantism, as a better choice than the shopworn Church of Rome. But where its thrust was most radical, Erasmianism went a step beyond castigating betrayal of those Christian ideals that the orthodox mind must uphold and is bound to find betrayed in this world: from seeing that the Church was not what it should be, Erasmianism stretched toward what to some is blindness and to others deeper insight: uncertainty—rather felt than expressed dogmatically—as to whether the Church as a sacramental institution, Christ's very body under Christ's Vicar, has real meaning apart from its visible performance. To waver on that point is to lose one's grip on the deep content of Catholicism, while approaching Protestantism only superficially. Although Protestantism repudiated the Catholic understanding of the Church far more explicitly, it did so from a point of view incompatible with Erasmianism—to expose the sinner's absolute dependence on Christ's saving grace. Erasmus could not accept the Protestant insistence that man is confined to trusting God in helplessness, without the slightest contribution of his own free will to his salvation. That reaction was Catholic enough in itself, but from Erasmus it was ultimately the reaction of a moralist—of a man worried about Protestantism's tendency to undermine moral motivation, but of one for whom it was equally difficult to put full faith in a mystical Church that could not move its people to live by Christ's pattern. On the surface, however, Protestantism and Erasmianism had common enemies. Both attacked monasticism, and both bore down on the cultistic or superstitious side of late-medieval Catholicism. Their reasons for such enmities were not identical, but they overlapped, and the overt attitudes of Protestantism and Christian humanism were hard to discriminate. Confusion and interplay between the two distinct, yet sometimes convergent, strands was to be a theme of Reformation history.

As the effects of secular humanism on education and upper-class ideals were slow to bear fruit, so Christian humanism scarcely swept England at the beginning of the sixteenth century. Rather, it was a leaven at work, part of a larger atmosphere of dissatisfaction with the Church. Neither the Christian humanist point of view nor the wider discontent was apt to raise an immediate storm. In many ways, official England was the Church's loyalest son, while ordinary religious life trudged on in the paths of custom and orthodoxy. In the 1520s and 1530s, when Protestantism had to be reckoned with and politics awoke a mighty ecclesiastical storm, Christian humanism showed its strength. It continued to do so for a long time.

Sir Thomas More and "Social Humanism"

England's most distinguished native humanist became a Catholic saint. Although he shared the humanist disquiet at the Church's condition and participated in the humanist belief that classicism and Christianity could live in harmony, he was not at one with the Erasmian drift of Christian humanism. He valued just those mystical and dogmatic aspects of Ca-

Sir Thomas More and family: Sir Thomas More's search for the perfect community was fulfilled in real life in his family. (Kupferstichkabinett, Basel.)

tholicism that meant least to Erasmus. A Catholic conservative, he wrote against the Protestants. He died a martyr. Henry VIII's scholarly friend and eminent servant, Sir Thomas More (1478–1535), transcended his age to become St. Thomas More.

A rare abundance of intellectual and moral gifts made Thomas More almost the perfect man of humanistic dreams: he shone at the center of the circle of English humanists. He was an accomplished Grecian and a superb Latin writer, a master of all the favored forms—letter and dialog, polemic and history. He was against obscurantist resistance to the "New Learning"; the humanists' cause was More's. He was not an aristocrat but from a middle-class family turned lawyers and officials; his graces were not those of the knightly-courtly stamp. They did not need to be, for nature and education had given him a more inclusive charm. Good humor, affability, readiness, wit, a naturalness and ease of manner that made it seem as if his extraordinary intelligence and goodness required no effort— all were qualities that humanism prized. The qualities also testify to something the best education could not have bred into the aptest material: an integrity that bespoke the saint within an effective man of the world.

More did not stand off from the world. He entered the law and then the king's service, in which he finally rose to the high office of lord chancellor. The humanistic ideal of public service was fulfilled in him as in no one else of comparable scholarly and literary standing. Yet More did not embrace the world with all his heart. He was more skeptical than most humanists as to how the learned and virtuous could escape corruption when they mingled with the political world, or how they could elevate ·that world through their persuasiveness. He acted on humanist premises more heartily than he believed in them. Ultimately, More's integrity was that of a man strong enough to surmount conflict, rather than that of a naturally harmonious soul.

More's tensions were, in fact, more radical than those involved in the choice between a literary or a political life. He longed for the contemplative life of a monk, for the thin, burning air of God's mountaintop above the pleasant breezes of Parnassus. He renounced the unalloyed delights of learning and dwelt in the cities of the plain. All the while, he practiced the mortifications of a monk in secret. Underneath his worldly costume he wore a hairshirt; the most companionable of men lived lonely with his God. Amid a brilliant society, but not of it, he belonged at heart to the community of the religious. That community eluded him on earth; God was to send him the lonely way of martyrdom into the community of saints.

More's death we shall witness in its place. For the present, we must look at his work and the side of English humanism that it illustrates. More's famous dialog. *Utopia* is the masterwork of what may be called "social humanism." Like its author, the *Utopia* is complex. It embodies some of the general themes of humanism and the main theme of social humanism, but it cannot be reduced to the commonplaces of either. Before discussing the *Utopia*, we must say something of social humanism in general.

We have already noted the hierarchic character of Tudor society and social thought. The image of society as a hierarchy was inextricably linked with the metaphor of society as an organism. Society was conceived and idealized as a closely woven whole, each man and each class having a part to play in the life of the social body and each having a claim on the community. The king and aristocracy were meant to rule. Insubordination on the part of lesser members would only destroy the organism. In this way, the sense of organism reinforced the sense of hierarchy and gave social thought a conservative bent. On the other hand, the organic theory favored distributive justice and regulatory law; lesser members of the body were nonetheless parts of it. If the humble could not work and live, the body would be diseased: parts that ought to be contributing to the whole would rot away into crime and vagabondage, disturbing everyone's peace and sapping respect for law and rank. The poor had their place and should stay there, but the better-off should stay put, too. The latter should discharge the duties of their places, including a responsibility to the poor. They should refrain from taking more than their share and avoid the greed and climbing that would spur discontent. If people refused to behave like members of an organic, hierarchic commonwealth, the government should make them.

Such were the truisms. Economic reality in the sixteenth century provided plenty for conventional social ethics to criticize. Unemployment and misery were visibly increasing. The main cause of these developments was that the luxury of relative underpopulation was becoming a thing of the past—a long past whose grisly beginning was the Black Death, which brought cheap land and high wages to its lower-class survivors. England's population reached the pre-Black Death level sometime in the first half of the sixteenth century and then forged dangerously beyond it—dangerously, because the economy was unable to generate enough new activity to absorb new hands. Until about halfway through the seventeenth century, the unemployed and underemployed sector of the population grew, and the life of wage-dependent people deteriorated. The days of the first two Tudors were fairly prosperous. The pressure of population on an endemically underdeveloped economy was not so severe as it later became, and by the standards of the age development was brisk. England's big export industry, woolen cloth, expanded significantly in an atmosphere of comparative freedom from regulation and monopoly.

It takes hindsight, however, to realize that the problems of the early Tudor economy were less acute than they might have been. Contemporaries saw suffering to which they were not accustomed. They blamed it humanly and legitimately on bad men and inadequate government. The science of economics is a blessing the sixteenth century lacked. It changes from a science to a dismal religion when it hardens men to misery and obscures the ways in which individuals and governments might do something to abate that misery. The wholly moralistic viewpoint of sixteenth-century social critics at least escaped the pitfall of indifference.

The critics concentrated their fire on one special target: the large-scale conversion of arable land to sheep pasture. Such conversion is usually called "enclosure"; actually, it is only one type of enclosure. "To enclose" means what it implies: to build a fence around a previously unfenced piece of land. If a landlord wanted to convert land hitherto let out to farmers in open-field strips into a sheep ranch, he would normally "enclose" it after getting rid of his tenants. That was the type of enclosure that aroused complaint in the early sixteenth century. Another species was the fencing of wasteland or rough pastureland hitherto unfenced and open to regulated use for grazing, fuel-gathering, and the like. The landlord's motive for enclosing such wasteland might be to pasture his sheep or, say, to create a hunting park. This second kind of enclosure also drew complaint because it deprived poor men of the incidental use of rough land. A third kind of enclosure was the breaking-up of open-field systems in order to give each tenant a consolidated farm instead of scattered strips. Again, fencing of individual holdings normally accompanied consolidation. This third species was common in the sixteenth and seventeenth centuries, too. It often resulted in less than justice for the very poor, but since it was otherwise as much for the tenant's sake as for the landlord's it was less objectionable.

Social critics exaggerated the amount of large-scale conversion to pasture and failed to appreciate its economic advantages. The amount of land affected was actually not very great; tenants evicted from converted land were a small fraction of the unemployed; conversions large enough to depopulate whole villages had tapered off before the voice of indignation arose; the phenomenon was confined to the midland counties, where optimum land-use required a shift in the balance between arable and pastureland; and, finally, wool production fed a growing native industry.

Still, the critics saw something real. They saw rich landowners doing the economically rational thing for themselves, while caring nothing for the evicted. Although most enclosure was legal (a matter of not renewing run-out leases or buying unexpired ones), legality is often unclear, and the rich man is likely to get the better of the poor in bargaining or in litigation. If the country needed more sheep, it could have secured them through small farmers' responses to the market. In fact, tenants constantly shifted from one land-use to another, and their decisions had a greater effect on the supply of different agricultural commodities than the entrepreneurship of a landlord class that was not very enterprising. In short, the encloser was an apt enough villain for a morality play whose real indisputable message transcended him: selfishness was abroad in the land.

Selfishness is not a surprising condition, nor unique to early Tudor England. Whether they enclosed or just raised their rental incomes when they could, landlords had not suffered a simple moral decline. Rather, circumstances had so changed that the results of normally self-interested conduct contrasted all too sharply with the ideals of social theory. Landowners looked responsible when, year in and year out, they took the "old accustomed rent" and let small holdings to a relatively large number of poor tenants. The main reason for their admirable behavior may have been that they had little opportunity to do otherwise. With more people and, as the sixteenth century went on, more money competing for rental property, owners had a greater chance to bargain for higher rent. The rental process favored the one who could farm profitably and pay a good dividend to the lord, while it disfavored the poor man who, by a combination of petty agriculture and labor, could earn only subsistence after meeting a low rent. Such was the pattern of the sixteenth and seventeenth centuries as a whole. In the early part of the period, however, traditionalists and idealists were not accustomed to this pattern.

Why should they condone it? The moral point held: the favored few of a drastically unequal society would rather take advantage of new circumstances than bear a loss for the sake of stability and brotherhood. The landowners would rather maintain and increase their own wealth than allow the well-off farmer to flourish on a somewhat uneconomic rent and the marginal tenant to stay in his cottage. In a complex sense, perhaps moral standards had declined. Were the rich not more interested in getting richer than they had once been, more obsessed with advancing their families to grandeur, more intent on living in a magnificent style defined by ever-rising standards of magnificence? The cult of aristocracy and Renaissance notions of high style made gentlemen feel poor if they could not live in a better manner and unsuccessful if they could not secure and improve the standing of their families on the ladder of prestige and power. In addition, the decline of a superaristocracy gave hope to lesser landowners that they might increase their holdings and win for themselves a share of the expanded room at the top. If better education made landowners surer of their right to privilege, it also made them more able to keep track of their wealth and to calculate the means of increasing it. Habit and sentiment weighed heavier with the old-fashioned landlord who never got on top of his affairs than with the man who had improved his mind, learned some law, or caught the knack of transposing studiousness from the schoolbook to the account book.

Meanwhile, money-making flourished in the middle-class sector of the economy. To the guardians of social morality, the hard-driving businessman was no hero. Merchants were useful, but they should not be too ambitious to break out of their class, and they should not be tempted by greed into violation of a conservative business ethic. They were best off in guilds and trade associations, which, although monopolistic, were also regulatory. A restricted number of merchants in privileged associations would feel secure enough to refrain from ruthless avarice; brotherhood would dissuade them from cutthroat competition and generate community ethics; the corporate body would regulate its members to assure the quality of goods. Stable prices were healthy prices, not because long-run stability was understood as a sign of good markets and sound money, but because charging no more than the customary price signified a moral man.

The relative openness of trade in the early sixteenth century was beneficial to the economy, but social critics had no way to appreciate the virtues of laissez-faire. They saw what they saw and judged appropriately. They looked out on a more expansive economy than people were used to and saw the sort of behavior that usually goes with rapid expansion: hard-bargaining, "interloper" businessmen were competing with more conservative merchants and artisan-tradesmen. Perhaps such businessmen communicated a greedy spirit to those from whom charity and noblesse oblige were expected. There was outright wrongdoing of the sort that greed and opportunity will always encourage—market-cornering; money-lending in violation of the taboo against usury; illegality, when laws controlling wages, prices, or quality were disregarded. In addition, the structure of the dominant cloth business encouraged market fluctuations that were painful and unjust, for the merchant-entrepreneur, who carried almost no capital investment, could curtail his jobbing abruptly, while the poor weaver, who typically worked in his country cottage with his own equipment, was put out of work.

Although social critics were narrowly agrarian in their prejudices, they cannot be blamed for seeing only evil in change. In the long run, they were right for the wrong reasons. England's one-product export economy "overheated" in the course of a long boom, and at the midpoint of the six-teenth century it collapsed. The misery of an ensuing serious depression vindicated social criticism and redoubled its voice. After the crash, business was conducted more conservatively with the government's encouragement. The cloth trade recovered and expanded again, but more slowly and with-out so many fly-by-night operators. Although it did not realize the poten-tial that freer trade and a more entrepreneurial spirit might have brought out, the Elizabethan economy was more stable and diversified than that of the first half of the century. Poverty was accepted more readily, and private and public charity assuaged the pain that no longer seemed preventable. Social theory remained the same and social ethics continued to be preached, but the voice of outrage was muffled.

The humanist contribution to social criticism was not original. The concept of society as an organism was commonplace in the Middle Ages—its deepest layer the Christian insight that men are "members" of each other. The plea for commonwealth was first of all the cry of Christian conscience—at its mid-century height, of Protestants. What humanists added was the reinforcement of eloquence and "practical idealism." Their belief in the educability of human beings could be converted to a vision of a shaped and ordered society. The influence of humanists in and around the government added to its determination to govern—to use its accepted power to regulate. Humanism was not much concerned with abstract political theory: most of its influence was used to strengthen the confidence of strong governors and to remind them of their duty to weed and prune the garden of the realm. The numerous laws against enclosure are only the most prominent examples of regulatory medicine applied to the diseases of the commonwealth. Trivial laws also reveal the active, well-meaning, but interfering spirit of government that humanism encouraged: thou shalt not wear clothes above thy station, thou shalt practice thy archery and refrain from dice, and so forth.

The shadow between the ideal and the real was heavy. Government without a professional local bureaucracy and without police or modern communications was not efficient. Forces generated by the interplay of private interest and uncontrollable conditions were too strong to be more

Amaurotū vrbs.

Fons Anydri.

Oſtium anydri.

ROMA.

Frontispiece, *Utopia:* Like England, Utopia was an island. As this illustration shows, its organization by cities was more like the ancient world than like England. (Rare Book Division, New York Public Library.)

than peripherally regulated. We have seen that the economy was relatively uninhibited by government in the early sixteenth century, although regulatory theory was vocal and respect for the state was conspicuous. Elizabeth's governments looked after the garden better—for example, by legislation to strengthen the apprenticeship system and to reinforce the traditional structure of industry and by establishing a long-lasting system of public poor relief. It is doubtful whether Tudor regulatory measures would have been a blessing if they had been efficiently applied. They were economically innocent, inconsistent with each other, and, in the end, all too biased in the ruling class's favor. Are the concepts of organism and hierarchy incompatible ideals? Is a hierarchic society with a social conscience not likely to end by regulating the strong in principle but the weak in reality?

Despite the shadow, Tudor social thought made a permanent contribution to what we may call the "socialist tradition." Humanism cooperating with religion brought a new articulateness and zeal to the old ideal of an integrated community—a social body whose members are not strangers to each other's needs, where a man can find his place and live as meaningfully for the whole as for himself. By restating the old ideal and applying it to disturbing new conditions, Tudor social critics helped translate that ideal into the modern world.

Thomas More's *Utopia* is the work that has survived from the literature of social humanism. *Utopia* consists of two books: the first contains a straightforward attack on contemporary social evils such as enclosure; the second describes an imaginary commonwealth, Utopia, which means "nowhere" in Greek. Utopia is a commonwealth indeed. Poverty is unknown, for there is an even distribution of necessities and worthwhile comforts; greed does not obtrude, for the inhabitants have no irrational craving for worthless gold or the idle display it purchases in other countries; a stock of genuinely good things is kept full by a very moderate amount of labor, for everyone works and the deployment of effort is well-organized; the genuine commodity of leisure is as well-used as it is abundant, for education has put reasonable and satisfying pleasures within the reach of everyone; training reinforces the law and enlightened law works as an educative discipline; individual well-being is fully integrated with cooperativeness.

The obvious relationship between the two parts of *Utopia* is contrast: on the one hand, England's false values and needless injustice; on the other, the healthy social organism that can be imagined. The contrast is heightened because Utopia is not a Christian country: the Utopians know religious truth only as far as clear-minded people can without God's direct revelation. It is legitimate to see Utopia as an idealized projection of the humanistic view of antiquity. Like the Utopians, the ancients lacked the immeasurable advantage of Christianity, but they used their God-given intelligence and moral energy well. Christian men should not scorn their example. Then look at how far short Christian England has fallen of the society that unaided reason might build!

Beyond its basic structure and argument, *Utopia* is an elusive book. How literally did More mean to recommend the institutions of the Utopians? In one sense, that is to ask how radical was his social thought. Did he see money, private property, inequality of rank and privilege, and other institutions of English society as insuperable obstacles to justice and harmony? Or did he think that institutions are indifferent in themselves, that virtue, instilled by better education and backed up by regulatory law, could achieve a just society within the traditional setting of English institutions? The laws and customs of Utopia might be the most reasonable ones possible, but "reasonable" could be double-edged for a man with More's outlook. Reasonableness might be the goal of a non-Christian society, the necessary condition for a decent society where Christian truth and inspiration are lacking. A Christian society, More might have said, could be just and charitable without following a wholly reasonable pattern.

Despite the range of possibilities, there can be no doubt that More took his Utopia seriously as a possible model, if not the necessary one, for the kind of community that England failed to be. It is more doubtful whether he had hope for his ideal. Can the education and statesmanship that humanists put such faith in really reform? Will the addition of Christianity, even if it is preached in relation to life—as Christian humanism hoped it might be—enable a society to overcome the sin in its members and intergraft them into a healthy body? Is Utopia indeed "nowhere," a fantasy that ignores the perversity in human nature? In the real world, is the best hope defensive warfare—the Fabian move, the occasional reform that good men unafraid to dirty their hands may achieve? Or is even that hope too encouraging? Is the Christian Utopia a monastery, the attainable commonwealth a mystical body?

Such questions arise from More's masterpiece, as from his life. A humanist and a deeper Christian than most humanists; the greatest expositor of the ideal for an organic society; a hard-hitting judge of reality against that ideal, perhaps a more radical judge than most social humanists and socially minded preachers; an idealist with a sharp intellectual's sense of the clouds enveloping sunny utopias; and yet a man of action, busy and effective throughout his later years on the everyday surface of politics and law—More wove together many themes—he was a commonwealth in himself. Doubting, complex, witness to the tangle of thought and emotion in his age's intellectual life, More was to die in the most single-minded of postures, as a man who could do no other than suffer for his certain faith.

Earlier in life, he had given an impulse to social humanism, a movement from which a great deal was to be heard in thinner voices than his. Although social humanism had practical results, its ideals did not always escape the Scylla of this world and the Charybdis of internal contradiction; More was warier of such vortices than other navigators.

Early Henrician Politics and the Ministry of Thomas Wolsey

The first part of Henry VIII's reign was like an ironic play performed against the backdrop of Renaissance culture. The young king bore out the ideal of aristocracy by combining intelligence and cultivation with the physical prowess and courtly tastes of knightly tradition. He summed up the majesty of the state in his person, for he was both genuinely forceful and mindful (so grand was his passion for pageantry) of the figure a king should show his people. Yet Henry VIII failed the ideals of public conduct that humanism held up. In his own political character, he was a spendthrift and a warmonger; the expensive ritualism and bellicosity of the chivalric type outweighed the cerebral and responsible qualities of the humanistic, both in the king himself and in most of his noble companions. Unlike his father, Henry VIII had no taste for the actual job of "governor." (There could hardly be fun and games enough to satisfy his boundless energy, but he was no man for paperwork.) Partly because he was lazy in the realm of public affairs, he allowed a great minister, Thomas Wolsey, to share the spotlight with him throughout most of his early reign.

Like the king, but in a very different way, Wolsey both embodied and failed the best aspirations of his age. He was an able statesman, whose essentially responsible policies checked the king's desires, yet his greed for power and possessions undercut the character of a Christian statesman in which his profession as a churchman and his sense of self cast him. Henry VIII and Wolsey were co-stars of a comedy, for despite his faults the king was too bright and strong to be upstaged. Although politically complementary, Wolsey was at home with his master's lifestyle. They made a team. But the last act turned into tragedy for Wolsey, while Henry survived to play a heavier part.

Henry VIII's first aggressive act as king was to make war on France. He was resolved to do so virtually from the moment of his accession. His motives were hot-blood, dreams of glory, and opportunity. Was France not the traditional enemy? Was the King of England not King of France by right and was he not honor-bound to vindicate his title? Were civil wars not now happily concluded, Lancaster and York rejoined? Was it not time to resume the proper business of an English king, turning valor long misspent at home upon the upstart Valois? Who since Harry the Fifth had been so like Mars as the present Harry? Who was so fit as this English king to replay Crécy and to stage another Agincourt? As for opportunity, the peaceful and businesslike reign of his father left Henry VIII well-heeled enough to spurn good sense. Diplomatically, he had to wait for his opening, but it was not long in coming.

To depart from the stand-offish foreign policy that served England's interests meant to plunge into the tangle of European politics—an evil web to get caught in. Humanists were stingingly critical of the spirit that prevailed among the European states in the early sixteenth century. There was an "international humanism" that corresponded to the social humanism discussed above. A passage in the first book of More's *Utopia* states its theme; Colet touched on it; Erasmus developed it at length. International humanism hoped for sobriety in the conduct of states as in the lives of men. Peace should be the first goal of policy. The chief interest of every ruler is to promote the welfare of his subjects—to shield them from war, to save their resources from the waste of reckless enterprises, to nourish their prosperity with peaceful commerce. Christian princes should aim at making Christendom a community of brother-states. Surely a gospel of peace implies that princes should look beyond their own glory and the narrow interests of their people to the well-being of fellow Christians.

Idealists have probably never had a better case against the power brokers than international humanists had against the states of their time, for irresponsibility was unusually rife. Henry VIII's itch to challenge the French was only a parody of the spirit that prevailed everywhere. More gratuitous, since England was isolated from the maze of moves and countermoves that other European states found difficult to escape, and more innocent, in that its motive was derived from a boyish romanticism, Henry's intended policy still partook of this widespread tone.

The leading actors in Europe at Henry VIII's accession were Ferdinand, King of Spain; Maximilian, the "Roman" emperor and principal German power; Louis XII of France; and Pope Julius II, whose political importance was derived both from his office and from the temporal states of the Church that bestrode Italy. The personalities, motives, and excuses of these potentates were various, but all of them were given to self-aggrandizing ambition, to schemes more intricate than meaningful, and to easy treachery. Northern Italy, where the native states were too small to compete with the "great powers," was the main prize the potentates squabbled over. France was perhaps the most blatant aggressor; her ambitions in Italy were the most persistent threat to other interests there. The prize was rich and famous, and the interests, especially the Pope's, real enough. The peace of Christendom may have meant a little more to the powers than their critics thought, but the European rulers were on a merry-go-round from which it was hard to dismount. In most of them there was a touch of Henry VIII's fever. With better-organized states than medieval warlords had had, they retained a good deal of the chivalric character: adventurism; preoccupation with personal glory; the tendency to put dynastic projects ahead of national aims; the assumption that war, after all, was the business of kings and gentlemen. When they were not mischief-making knights, they were hard-boiled Machiavellians. The blend was worse than either type alone.

Henry VIII's plan to reopen the Hundred Years War was briefly delayed by an unusual configuration of the major powers. On the Pope's initiative, the powers had ganged up on Venice. This union of Christian princes to fight an Italian border war was broken when the Holy Father and his faithful sons saw fit to redirect attention to their larger problems. His anti-Venetian appetite satisfied, the Pope undertook in 1511 to organize a Holy League against the French. The faithful sons, including chastened Venice, would now join brotherly arms to drive France from Milan, the rich Italian duchy that she had held since 1499. Henry VIII was as welcome to this most Christian alliance as he was eager to join it. As was only right, the Pope recognized the King of England's title to be King of France. Under the banner of the Lord, Henry sallied forth to take his own.

Henry brought home some glory and some real estate. As an adventure, the wars of the Holy League were far from a total loss. As a national enterprise, the fling cost more than it was worth. Henry staged two invasions of northern France. In August 1513, in personal command of his host, he chalked up a famous victory, the so-called Battle of the Spurs. Public relations imagination was required to make that minor engagement a synopsis of Crécy and Agincourt. Still, it was a happy joust, and it was followed by the conquest of Tournai, a good-sized episcopal city. By adding Tournai to the port of Calais, England for the time being doubled her foothold in France. At home, a more important military event than the king's gests abroad was taking place. Scotland, France's traditional ally, seized the occasion to strike across the border. On Flodden Field (September 1513), the flowers of the Scottish forest were weeded away by the English Earl of Surrey, and the threat from the North was neutralized for some time to come.

The auspices for Henry's dreams looked fair, but then the Holy League began to melt away. The French had been badly hurt in Italy. Rethinking their particular interests, the allies were as ready as usual to betray each other and the Pope's great cause as well. Although disappointed and aggrieved, King Henry had no prudent choice but to mount another bandwagon, this one headed peaceward. He got good terms from France and, true to the dynasts' courteous usage, let Venus smooth what Mars had rumpled: Henry's pretty sister Mary went in marriage to moribund King Louis XII. (When the Holy League was thriving, Mary had been engaged to Charles of Burgundy, the Emperor Maximilian's grandson—heir apparent to Spain and the future Emperor Charles V.)

During the wars of the Holy League, Thomas Wolsey proved himself the indispensable public man. Wolsey was of middling origin. That his father was reputedly a butcher gave aristocrats something to titter about, but his career was not abnormal. Academic success started him on an ecclesiastical career. Like other able churchmen before him, Wolsey found his way to court as a chaplain, and there his practical talents were put to use. He was remarkable for the brains and drive that carried his career to exceptional heights, but he reached them as a late bloom of a common species.

Henry VIII lusted for battle; Wolsey knew how to organize a war. After the war, he rose to greatness on the parallel tracks of ecclesiastical and secular preferment. In 1514 he became Archbishop of York. Canterbury escaped him because his patron, William Warham, another clerical civil servant of the old school, was long-lived, but Wolsey made up for that by assuming a cardinal's hat in 1515. That same year he was made lord chancellor, a high dignity and a vital judicial office. In 1518 he became the Pope's legate in England—representative of the Holy See and, as such, supreme over the Church in both archdioceses. Great as his offices were in dignity, power, and income, they are no measure of his political role. From the end of the war until his fall, Wolsey was in effect vice-king.

Wolsey had the stuff of a great administrator. If in the long run his triumph was not administrative, it is because he was burdened with too many roles. He suffered from a fault too likely to afflict an indefatigable, competent, domineering man of affairs: inability to delegate authority. Busy on many fronts, he was not always on top of routine business, and his energies were not channeled into administrative reorganization. He was not vice-king and vice-pope to be a chief clerk and bookkeeper. The roles of diplomat and judge engaged his deepest interest and embodied his own grand image of himself. As a judge, he was creative and controversial. As a domestic statesman, he fancied himself protector of the poor against the strong, of justice against oppression—an apt role for a prince of the Church. As the world goes, his pretenses were justified: for example, he staged a major drive to check enclosure.

In foreign affairs, Wolsey succeeded fairly well in his aims: to keep the peace in Europe so far as England could, to keep England out of expensive military adventures without disengaging her from the web of continental diplomacy. He has been accused of turning England into a papal satellite partly because he had hopes of becoming Pope himself. That charge is exaggerated and unfair if it implies betrayal of English interests. As the world goes and his age went, Wolsey's diplomacy was not ignoble. He was not insensitive to the humanists' critique of contemporary politics nor to their dream of a united Christendom.

Wolsey's life, of which his diplomacy was only a part, is emblematic of the good and bad in a passing era. He was not the first churchman to be worldly to the core. His very worldliness—his love of wealth, display, and high society, to which his pompous palace at Hampton Court still stands as a monument—made him effective in the political environment he moved in: he was a man after Henry VIII's heart. Nor was Wolsey's magnificence ill-suited to his image of himself as a pillar of Christendom, a figure of the Church's authority and responsibility, overarching kings and nations. Yet Wolsey's power and style bred rancor in his countrymen. The aristocrats to whom he was an upstart were the politicians over whom he was a triumphant competitor. The humble whom he championed were bound to see him as a rich and distant potentate, too big for a subject's britches and too princely for a churchman. Anticlerical clichés seemed proved by his example. Although he was concerned with its needs, Wolsey had too much else on his mind to lead the Church toward revival and reform. He paid dearly in reputation for a position whence, by his lights, he did Christendom some service. The Catholic Church in England was to get the final bill for his career.

The diplomatic history of Wolsey's hegemony can be briefly summarized. The rapprochement with France that had ended the war dissolved by stages. Louis XII's death broke the marriage alliance. The new French king, Francis I, was a young blood of Henry VIII's stamp, from whom rivalry and troublesome ambition could be expected. For the moment, however, Wolsey steered clear of war. In 1518 he was the principal architect of a peace pact and a collective security arrangement among the leading powers, a hollow triumph for Wolsey's intentions. In 1519 Maximilian died and his grandson Charles came into the last piece of his stupendous inheritance, the Hapsburg territories in Germany. Already Duke of Burgundy and King of Spain, he was elected emperor, as it was now customary for the head of the Hapsburg house to be and despite French efforts to prevent it. Charles V's huge agglomeration of possessions was a threat to France, and intermittent war between the Hapsburgs and Valois was to dominate the political landscape for decades. England tried to play a balancing role, committing herself to neither side, talking business with both. To the period of negotiation (1520) belongs the celebrated pageant of "The Field of the Cloth of Gold," a "summit meeting" between Henry VIII and Francis I near Calais. The conference was a wonderful excuse for the royal brothers to compete in jousting and conspicuous hospitality. Meanwhile, English policy was moving toward alliance with the emperor, the traditional alignment and the one that served papal purposes, since France was again dangerously strong in Italy. In the early 1520s England made a very minor military contribution to the allied cause. (Enthusiasm for war and willingness to foot the bill were at low ebb at home.) A serious French defeat in Italy brought on a "diplomatic revolution" in 1525–26: England now adjusted the balance of power by collaborating in an anti-imperial coalition.

This realignment was Wolsey's last unencumbered diplomatic job. The final years of his ministry were burdened by the great matter of our next chapter. Heirless save for one sickly daughter, troubled in conscience (so he said) by his marriage to his brother's widow, and in love with a lady-in-waiting, Henry VIII was soon to seek a divorce. He was lucky, one would have thought, to have a master diplomat and cardinal of the Church to see him through.

CHAPTER TWO

In 1517 a great heretic arose in Germany—"a wild boar in the vineyard," in the words of the bull *Exsurge domine* by which Pope Leo X excommunicated him in 1520. Martin Luther's protest in 1517 concerned the technical subject of indulgences, but over the next three years he had worked out the fundamental break with Catholic tradition that later came to be called Protestantism. Indeed, Luther's thought and religious experience had been preparing the way for a radical departure before the indulgence controversy.

Protestantism was precipitated by the Roman Church's external and manifest deficiencies, but it was ultimately an intellectual revolution rather than a reaction to imperfection—a more thoroughgoing break from the framework of Catholic thought than Christian humanism and other strands of dissent. To many people Protestantism was profoundly liberating, but in a sense that easily eludes the modern liberal imagination. It was not directed against authority as such; for example, early Protestant political theory reinforced the duty of submission to the secular state. Although they subverted the Catholic understanding of the Church's authority, the Protestants did not put freedom of religious opinion in its place. The liberty they proclaimed was Christ's release of mankind from the bondage of "works"—which is, finally, to say, from self-enslavement.

The
English Reformation

Christianity teaches that because of their pride men claim a capacity to make satisfaction for their sins and to "justify" themselves before God; but in their hearts, they know they lie, for their wills are slaves to sin and their souls are bound to the anxious service of an empty quest. Christ has made total satisfaction for man's sin; "justification" is the gift of his pure love; man's only response is to rest his faith in God's unconditional mercy. At bottom these teachings are the common ground of the Christian faith. With good reason, the Protestants accused the Catholics of spurning God's grace—of turning free men's grateful worship into the idol-service of a man-made Church and of reenforcing the demand for a more positive human role in man's deliverance than "faith alone." But Protestants, too, as Catholics saw, threw away something of the grace whose all-sufficiency they celebrated: they failed to grasp the full sense in which the Church can be conceived as Christ's gift at its richest—his ongoing life in the world, into which men can be engrafted and through which they can participate in the inexhaustible work of grace. Both sides parodied each other's thinking and their own. In the end, the great schism in Western Christianity perhaps only testifies to all men's incapacity to accept God's love in all of its dimensions. Over two centuries of English history, the shadow of the schism hung heavier than any other reality.

Henry VIII's Divorce
and the Break from Rome

Luther's ideas soon became known beyond Germany, partly because several German princes took up his cause, giving it a political dimension. Although Protestantism had some influence in England during the 1520s, the great majority of people remained immune from heresy. A friendly but cautious interest was more widespread. Anticlericalism, Christian humanism, and strains of popular heresy, some of it remotely descended from Wycliffe, made for a certain receptivity. There were stirrings enough to awaken officialdom. At the end of the decade, the first English literary controversy between Catholic and Protestant pitted Sir Thomas More against William Tyndale. Tyndale, the most important early Protestant apostle to the English, was a vigorous publicist and translator of the first English Bible of the Reformation. (Access to the Scriptures in the vernacular, whereby the truth of the Protestant interpretation and the saving promise of God would come through to Everyman, was an important plank in the Reformation platform.)

Henry VIII himself was quickly off the mark as a Catholic apologist. In 1521 he published (and dedicated to Pope Leo X) a little volume entitled *A Defense of the Seven Sacraments.* Although an unoriginal statement of Catholic orthodoxy against the background of Luther's attack, the book did Henry credit as a prince of varied talents and as the good son of the Church that he had been in politics. The Pope rewarded him with a new title, "Defender of the Faith," thenceforward a jewel in the string of titles known as the "style" of English monarchs.

Around 1526 Henry VIII made up his mind to press for a divorce from Catherine of Aragon. Properly speaking, he sought a judgment that he had never been validly married to Catherine, not a divorce in the modern sense. Such a judgment was to be obtained by showing cause in an ecclesiastical court. The appellate hierarchy ended in Rome, where a disputed, politically charged suit by a king would inevitably be decided.

Henry's motives for wanting a divorce were various. If the king was driven by an inextricable mixture of passions and calculations, he was only human. He was worried, rationally enough, about the future of the Tudor dynasty. Catherine had now all but passed the age of childbearing. A sad history of stillbirths and infant mortality left her one sickly daughter, the future Queen Mary. There was no rule against female succession to the throne, but there were no precedents for it either, save for the unencouraging one of the Empress Matilda. A promising boy would have nothing to worry about; a daughter might well be challenged by someone with ambition in his heart and royal blood in his veins. Should Mary predecease her father, the king would face extinction of his line, and the nation would face a feud among Tudor and non-Tudor claimants. With dynastic civil war not far in the past, it would be naive to expect the king's senior cousin (the King of Scotland and a foreigner) to mount the throne in perfect peace if there were no lineal heir. The king needed a legitimate son and, if possible, other children in line for the position. (One bastard he had, but a bastard would probably have been challenged.)

Besides, the king was in love. The girl he was in love with, Anne Boleyn, would not give herself to him. Such modesty was probably unusual in ladies-in-waiting when their impassioned suitor was the monarch. Anne (or her high-born relatives, the Howard clan, whose head was the Duke of Norfolk) presumably saw that amorous cards well-played might make her a queen. Yet Henry was not quite the dupe of a comedy, driven mad by a crafty wench. He was a vigorous man in his mid-thirties. Although not wholly faithful, he had been an affectionate husband to Catherine, his political bride. But Catherine had not only disappointed him as breeding stock; she was several years his senior and had lost her attraction. Out of love with his wife and badly in love with a much younger girl, the king might have yearned for a new marriage without the additional lash of frustration.

Finally, Henry claimed his conscience bothered him because he was married to his brother's widow. Henry's conscience was probably as apt to be lubricated by convenience as are those of other people, but perhaps the specter of sin really did scare him. The basis for his misgivings was the same as his main legal contention advanced against the marriage when the divorce suit was launched: marriage to a brother's widow was against the ecclesiastical law. (That law contained several prohibitions against marriage to persons with whom one was connected by "affinity," meaning an in-law relationship, as opposed to consanguinity.) Because of the prohibition, it had been necessary to obtain a dispensation from the Pope before Henry married Catherine. There was no doubt that the Pope had wide powers of dispensation from rules generally binding on Catholics. It was also clear that the Pope's dispensing power was not absolute; some rules were so fundamental that no exceptions could be made. Marriage taboos (of which there were many of no real moral significance) were on the whole within the dispensing power, but for marriage to a brother's widow there was a catch. That prohibition appeared to rest directly on the Scriptures (Lev. 18:16, "Thou shalt not uncover the nakedness of thy brother's wife: it is thy brother's nakedness"; and Lev. 20:21, "If a man shall take his brother's wife, it is an impurity; he hath uncovered his brother's nakedness; they shall be childless"). It was arguable that rules of ecclesiastical law with a clearly Biblical basis were too fundamental to be dispensed. If Henry's conscience was really disturbed, it was because he thought he had gone against Leviticus and that the sinfulness of doing so could perhaps not be expunged by a papal dispensation. Leviticus predicts that violators of the taboo will be childless. Although Henry and Catherine were not literally childless, the king may well have feared that God's anger was behind the trouble they had had in producing viable offspring.

The divorce suit was started in hope. The king had good political reasons for suing, and he had good relations with the Pope. In Wolsey he had a great ecclesiastical operator. After protracted negotiation and litigation, however, the suit failed. Part of the explanation is political. In 1527 Rome was sacked by out-of-control imperial troops, and Pope Clement VII fell captive to Charles V. Charles had no political reason to be kind to Henry and every personal reason to support Catherine, who was his aunt. And it was not feasible for the Pope to act contrary to the emperor's wishes.

But these accidental circumstances are by no means the whole explanation of the divorce's failure. Henry did not have a compelling legal case. If certain twists beyond the central question of marriage to a brother's widow were omitted, the most convincing line of reasoning suggested that the Pope could dispense in such cases as Henry's. The principle that rules based on the Bible are indispensable was sound enough, but in the instance of the passages from Leviticus there were complications—another passage from the Old Testament (Deut. 25:5) positively commanded men to "take" their brothers' childless widows and breed children with them, and there were various Biblical examples of people who had done so. The best conclusion, supported by precedents, was that God's prohibition on marriage with a brother's widow was far from absolute and hence that the Vicar of Christ could dispense with it if he saw sufficient reason. Although a Pope free from political pressure might have obliged King Henry, he would have risked the charge of putting expediency above his judicial duty. In addition, although he might have avoided it by deciding for Henry on a technicality, the Pope could hardly be expected to deal a blow to the dispensing power of the papacy.

After extensive legal and diplomatic jockeying, and a shift in the political wind whereby the Pope was partially liberated from imperial control, Henry won an apparent victory. The Pope consented that the divorce suit should be determined in England by two commissioners acting in his stead, Wolsey and Cardinal Campeggio, a prestigious Italian canon lawyer and papal official. It looked as if the Pope had delegated his powers to a court from which the king might expect favorable results. Actually, Campeggio was instructed to stall. As long as the drawn-out trial reached no conclusion, the Pope was free to rescind his commissioners' powers and to recall the case to his own court. It was understood that a recall would be equivalent to denial of Henry's suit, barring any surprises. In July 1529 the trial was adjourned on a technicality. A formal recall followed.

Although the fault was hardly his, Wolsey had not come through for his master. His fall was at hand. His unpopularity, both in the country and with his court rivals (especially those clinging to Anne Boleyn's skirts), made him an eligible scapegoat. So did the king's impatience with the long tutelage of a minister who in many ways outsized him. Wolsey was indicted under the Statutes of Praemunire and was convicted on his own confession. The legal case against Wolsey was trumped up as the means to his political fall. He may have been technically guilty of some of the charges. (The offense of Praemunire—roughly, so acting as to derogate from the king's jurisdiction, usually to the advantage of ecclesiastical jurisdiction—was vaguely defined. By not disputing the charges, Wolsey accepted the fact that his conviction was inevitable.) The forfeiture of his secular offices and private property was an automatic result of his conviction. Although forced to give up many of his ecclesiastical emoluments as well, he retained his Archbishopric of York. For a few months after his fall, he lived in his archdiocese and attended to its affairs. He died naturally while being escorted to London to face further charges, probably of treason, at the urging of his political rivals, who could not rest easy while so formidable a man was at large.

His divorce suit apparently lost, his great minister gone but not replaced, the king was at loose ends. He was by no means ready to give up the project of undoing his old marriage and contracting a new one, yet he had no firm strategy to make the Pope relent. In need of expedients, he summoned a Parliament. So assembled one of the most momentous Parliaments in English history, the Reformation Parliament, which was to last from 1529 to 1536.

Calling a Parliament turned out to be a useful step. The members were disposed to complain and legislate against the Church without heavy prompting from the king. The legislation was technical, and the complaints were reflective of familiar lay grievances, mainly undue monetary exactions by Church officials. The king and his advisers saw promise in a Parliament hostile to the Church, for legislation harmful to ecclesiastical interests might suggest to Rome the prudence of reconsidering the King's divorce. Should a mild threat fail, perhaps this Parliament would furnish stronger medicine.

The king also pursued his case out of court by collecting opinions in favor of his legal contentions from a great many theologians and canonists throughout Europe. But bribery and politics motivated more of these men than did conviction. It was naive to imagine that Rome would be overwhelmed by such a contrived display of consensus.

Without a sharper purgative, the obstructed path to Rome was apparently going to stay obstructed. In the later part of 1530, the king embarked on a more deliberate and drastic policy to increase pressure on Rome. Signs began to suggest that he was even ready to consider some sort of take-over of the ecclesiastical apparatus in England if pressure should fail. Henry started by legally molesting the English clergy. The flexible weapon of Praemunire was used again, first against a number of individual clergymen and then, by an imaginative if abusive stroke of the legal process, against the clergy as a whole. Collectively charged with offenses they were in no practical position to dispute, the clergy met in their convocation to settle with the king. They consented to purchase a pardon with a handsome grant of money, but the king was not content with that. He demanded that the clergy recognize him as their Supreme Head. The king's later assumption of Supreme Headship of the Church in England marks the accomplishment of the Henrician Reformation. In early 1531, when he demanded the title of the clergy, Henry was probably not ready to start exercising Supreme Headship, but he was interested in a manifestation of loyalty that would shock Rome and commit the English clergy to him if trouble should continue to deepen. The clergy balked at the king's demand. Finally a compromise formula was put through ("Singular protector, only and supreme lord, and as far as the law of Christ allows, even supreme head"). The king was apparently satisfied. The clergy was pardoned.

In 1532, the government advanced along the road that led from browbeating the Church to taking charge of it. Now prompted by the government, Parliament approved a long bill of complaint against the English ecclesiastical courts. Armed with this evidence of popular grievance, the king demanded that the clergy concede him extensive powers to supervise its future legislative activities and to preside over an investigation and revision of the current canon law. The clergy gave in. From seeking the title of Supreme Head, the king had proceeded to put himself in power in an important area of ecclesiastical affairs.

Then the government struck Rome's financial nerve. In 1532 Parliament enacted a bill forbidding the payment of "annates," a kind of succession tax due to Rome from new bishops. The theme of Henry's policy was still one of pressure, for the act included a clause suspending operation until the king proclaimed that the statute should be put into effect. But the days of pressure and retractable take-over were nearly past.

In the summer of 1532 the aged Archbishop Warham died. He was succeeded as Archbishop of Canterbury by Thomas Cranmer. A dark horse for the office at the time, Cranmer lived to become the founder of the Protestant Church of England. When appointed, he was a Christian humanist with only a sympathetic interest in Protestantism. He was thought of primarily as an enthusiastic supporter of the king's divorce (perhaps, too, as the modern type of clergyman, for whom strong measures and innovations might pose no problem). By choosing Cranmer, the king judged correctly that he had a man he could count on. The Pope did not object to the appointment. Even if he had any doubts about it, he did not want to exacerbate his quarrel with England by haggling over patronage. The favorite candidate for archbishop, whom Cranmer outran, was Stephen Gardiner, Bishop of Winchester, a major apologist for Henry's ecclesiastical revolution who later repented his role, a conservative canon lawyer and lifelong foe of Protestantism.

Sometime in 1532 Anne Boleyn's politic modesty broke down. She was pregnant with the future Queen Elizabeth when Cranmer married her to Henry in January 1533. A conclusive judgment that the king's first marriage was void now had to be produced. Rome or no Rome, his majesty was in peril of bigamy. Perhaps events were allowed to brew to this crisis because a "no Rome" decision had been virtually made. Perhaps that decision had become attractive. Parliament cooperated by passing, in March 1533, an act forbidding appeals to Rome in ecclesiastical cases. Archbishop Cranmer then held court and decided that the king was not living in bigamy. In English law, as just remodeled, there was no appeal from his sentence. Queen Anne, the king's first lawful wife, was soon crowned.

The Appeals Act was decisive beyond its immediate use for settling the king's marital state. Cutting off the Pope's appellate jurisdiction in ecclesiastical cases came close to creating a national, state-dominated Church. After the Appeals Act, the task of king and Parliament was to work out the details of such a Church—as it were, to "make it official." Theoretically, the Pope's court could have been eliminated without bringing down all other relations between England and Rome, but by now the king was deeply involved, and the Appeals Act was deliberately written to resound beyond its immediate purpose. The preamble spoke of England as an "Empire," exempt by the very nature of "Empires" from foreign jurisdiction. Such language caught echoes of ancient history and late-medieval antipapal theory; the effect was to suggest that God-given temporal authority was also spiritual authority—the right and responsibility of emperors to oversee the Church in their domains.

The year 1534 was the Reformation Parliament's most productive legislative season. The new order was worked out. Taxes formerly paid to Rome by the English clergy (so-called First Fruits and Tenths) were not abolished but were annexed to the king's revenue. The king's virtual power to appoint persons to positions in the ecclesiastical hierarchy was legally formalized. The decapitated appellate system for ecclesiastical cases was supplied with a new head: appeals to the king could be lodged in his chancery, the king being authorized to appoint commissioners to hear the appeals. The Pope's licensing and dispensing powers were vested in the Archbishop of Canterbury. The law of treason was rewritten so that public opposition to the new regime was subject to the severest penalties. An oath to test acquiescence was devised. Finally, the Supremacy Act made it official that the king was Supreme Head of the Church.

The Supremacy Act *recorded* that the king was Supreme Head; it did not purport to *make* him Supreme Head. In what does the office of a lay Supreme Head consist? Part of the pragmatic answer has already been given: the king was to be titular head of a juridical and administrative apparatus that, save for its connections with Rome, was to continue substantially as it had before. Clerical persons were to accept the king as the sole focus of ultimate loyalty, the lord of their order, just as temporal persons accepted him in their sphere. We have seen what the revised law expressly authorized the king to do to run the apparatus under him. The Supremacy Act indicated in general terms what further rights and duties the king should have: he was to "visit, repress, redress, reform, order, correct, restrain, and amend . . . errors, heresies, abuses, offences, contempts, and enormities." In other words, the king was seen as having supervisory and disciplinary powers over the Church broader than such definable jobs as appointing bishops and providing for the disposal of appeals. However, these broader powers had to stop somewhere. The Supreme Head, unlike the Pope, was not a priest or a bishop. For that reason alone, there were functions necessary to the traditional operation of the Church that no amount of supremacy would allow him to perform. As close to God as kings were thought to be, a lay Supreme Head could not pretend to capture the full aura of papal authority. The Pope's unique office at the head of Christendom made him a creative source of doctrine—ultimate interpreter of the tradition by which the body of Christian people renews its hold on a common truth. No king could presume to be quite that. If the Supreme Head was to extirpate heresy and see that his clerical subjects taught the truth, he could not stay away from doctrine. Yet he could not pronounce doctrine with a Pope's voice. The Henrician Reformation was tacitly committed to the proposition that Christian truth was settled, that it was more in need of vigilant enforcement than living growth. For the rest, we can consider what a Supreme Head is by looking at what a succession of them did.

Parliament did not make Henry Supreme Head, nor did it legislate that it would share in his supremacy. The king, not the king in Parliament, headed the Church. It was not the intention or effect of the Reformation acts to make any exercise of the supreme headship subject to parliamentary approval. Statutes were used to set up the new order, and later to operate it, from a mixture of legal good sense and political prudence. In some cases, legislation was necessary to strengthen the new arrangements with secular sanctions. In other cases, legislation was at least a great convenience. Maybe the king could have rearranged the Church's judicial and administrative system on his own authority, but it was useful for avoiding legal and extralegal disputes to have the rules in black and white on the statute book, and it was valuable, for the sake of notoriety, to have such vaguer constitutional "facts" as the supremacy itself recorded on the tables of the law.

Although Parliament's role was for the most part unavoidable, Henry VIII did take Parliament into his confidence willingly: he invited and secured its cooperation in reordering the Church. It was obviously wise to proceed to revolution with so easily assembled a phalanx of public support. The effect of "revolution by statute," however, was to leave some doubt hanging over the future—as to the Supreme Head's power to take certain measures for the Church *without* statute and as to Parliament's right to consider ecclesiastical questions without the monarch's permission.

Henry VIII did not go over the brink completely on his own. Nor, although Parliament and the country went along in a spirit ranging from enthusiasm to stunned acceptance, did he avoid impressive opposition. He found another great minister to help him at this crucial time: Thomas Cromwell. Cromwell had started his career in Wolsey's service and, after his master's fall, had transferred to the king's employ. Although he rose to something like Wolsey's viceregal role, he was a very different kind of minister. The churchman, diplomat, judge, and connoisseur of pomp was soon succeeded by the efficient man of business. Detailed administration and finance, Wolsey's weak departments, were Cromwell's strongest. Cromwell was better at delegating power yet shrewder at placing himself at pivotal positions throughout the government, whence he could control all its main operations. Like all great successes at court, he garnered titles and emoluments, but he was not a showy man like Wolsey; he was more interested in power than in credit, in work than in high society. For all his worldliness and ambition, Wolsey was a kind of idealist. Cromwell's horizons were bounded by the job at hand, and his satisfaction was confined to doing that job thoroughly. Yet he did not lack intellectual vision and commitment: he saw the ecclesiastical revolution as a whole more than other men did, and was more determined to push on with it. A government man through and through, Cromwell saw the narrow good of a concentrated, well-run national state as a true good. He believed that the English Church would flourish better under the wings of such a state than as a branch of an international corporation obstructive of the state's due sovereignty over all persons and institutions within its territorial bounds. He looked on Protestantism without prejudice, even with sympathy. Although his interest in religion was not intense, he was not a man to take fright at new ideas, nor was he a statesman afraid of strange waters. Yet the cautious instincts of a politician's politician also prevailed with him. Ruthless and innovative, he was also a defender of law and procedure. Much as he exalted the king's estate, the strong government he worked for was to be government in the English manner, one observant of the rights of Parliament and careful that administrative power would have lawyer-proof warrant.

By 1532 Cromwell was firmly situated in several offices and in the king's attention. His hegemony rose as the Church crisis climaxed, and it continued until his fall in 1540. It is difficult to estimate exactly how crucial Cromwell's influence on the king was, but it is unfair to Henry VIII's intelligence and ambition to suppose that he was led by the nose into revolution by a minister more able and more radical than he. But if Cromwell did not show the king where to go and spur him to move, he did show him how to reach the goal, and he boosted him over hurdles. Although Cromwell did not initiate the general idea of revolutionizing the Church, he was still responsible for many particular ideas and, above all, for getting things done. He was as assiduous at such jobs as drafting and redrafting legislation as he was in pure administration. Whatever difference Cromwell made to the outcome, the king was lucky not to be dependent only on himself and second-rate officials.

The fate of two men, St. Thomas More and St. John Fisher, marks the early opposition to Henry's break with Rome. When Wolsey was divested of office, More was promoted to lord chancellor, and his preferment launched the subsequent tradition of filling that office with a lay lawyer instead of a cleric. At the time of his promotion, More made it clear that he opposed the king's divorce. He consented to serve the government as a judge, but he refused the political role that would have been open to him if his conscience could have accepted the king's policy. He resigned as chancellor after the king forced the clergy to surrender its legislative independence. Having refused to take the oath by which men were asked to acknowledge the new dispensation, More was convicted of treason and beheaded in 1535. Fisher, Bishop of Rochester, was the brightest light of the English episcopate. A humanist of European reputation, he was also an accomplished technical divine. He had steadfastly opposed the divorce and had written learnedly against it. Like More, he perished for refusal to conform to the king's measures.

More and Fisher saw clearly what many others either failed to see or did not care to consider: that the king was in rebellion against the weight of usage, against the Church's accepted teaching as well as its recognized authority; that no amount of patriotism, or dissatisfaction with the Church as it was, or briefs in the king's favor drawn from history and assorted theoreticians, or legally incontrovertible acts of Parliament could disguise this fact; that the choice was between a church whose claim to authenticity depended on its standing above kings, "empires," and human law and a state that claimed competence to oversee the welfare of men's souls and to pronounce religious law. More and Fisher made their choice for the Church as men of informed conviction and courage. They were also men for whom death by martyrdom had meaning in a special Christian sense that made it more victorious than death for principle. Their executions shocked Europe. The world now understood that the King of England was determined to have his own way.

The Church of England Under Henry VIII

The Church of England now existed. Its Supreme Head was excommunicated. The declaration of independence had come out of the divorce crisis, but now independence was valued and justified for its own sake. From a good political son of the Church, Henry VIII had changed into a rebel. The Catholic powers must deplore him. Fortunately, they were so preoccupied with their own conflicts—with the struggle between France and the Hapsburg complex—and so accustomed to putting politics ahead of religion that at most times they posed no immediate threat. They could not wholly demote King Henry from his role as a potential ally. A half-century was to pass before piety and politics combined to mount a crusade against England.

Henry VIII had no use for Protestantism. His rebellion against an essential part of what the Catholic Church stood for did not shake the religious views he had held when he defended the seven sacraments. Even if his personal opinions had been less conservative, his position was not favorable for introducing major religious innovations. Henry had done one bold and shocking thing. Political prudence alone would recommend restraint on other fronts. People would be less likely to react against the government if the ministrations they received in church and the truth they were taught continued to meet customary expectations. Clerical cooperation was more likely if the status of clergymen was not undermined by a reinterpretation of the Church's nature and if their functions were not externally altered. The common consent of orthodox men was the safest basis for a national church, and there was no consensus for breaking with Catholic forms.

But Henry VIII could not stand still. The new legal and administrative arrangements, leaving what men believed and how they conducted their religious lives untouched, were not enough. Although the king himself was Catholic, there were others around the seats of power who would have chosen at least to borrow from the reformers to give the English Church a distinctive flavor. (When Protestantism was a new outburst of prophetic energy, lines were blurred. The exact degree in which the reformers were saying something incompatible with orthodoxy was hard to make out. One could be open to Protestantism without flatly embracing it.) In addition to internal pressure to move toward Protestantism, there was external political pressure. A bloc of Protestant states existed in Germany, and these were likely allies in a dangerous world. The more friendly to Protestantism England looked, the more attractive an ally she would be to Protestant princes.

Even apart from the Protestant movement, it was a time of religious dissatisfaction in England. Like any "new management," the Supreme Head was expected to do better than the old crowd. The Church's organization, ritual, and doctrine must remain Catholic, but that left plenty of room for reform. Christian humanism focused the dissatisfaction and showed the directions that reform might take. The Supreme Head was under pressure to make a record. He was advised by people with diverse backgrounds and motives whose ideas were often inchoate and eclectic. But he still had to move, to respond to the advice as best he could.

Bible-reading is a good example of the crosscurrents at play. The

Protestants favored wide distribution of vernacular Bibles. Christian humanists favored it, too. The most conservative Catholic need see nothing wrong in it. Mere officials could see it as a widely favored measure of Christian education, until they saw that too much Bible-reading seemed to be provoking independent thought and the official instinct for thought-control was aroused. Governmental policy on this subject followed an arc in the 1530s: first, the distribution of English Bibles was officially ordered; later, officialdom tried to restrict Bible-reading to the upper classes. Religious policy in general followed the same arc. At first doctrinal statements and instructions to the clergy contained mild concessions to reformist or semi-Protestant positions. There was no strong effort to repress thinking that was not rigidly orthodox. As 1540 approached, however, the government got tougher and more conservative. The reaction jelled in the Act of Six Articles in 1539, whereby the secular criminal law was enlisted to hold the Catholic line.

The explanation of the arc is complex. The more liberal phase came when a German Protestant alliance was being worked on. The ascendancy of particular politicians counted. So did official fear that "soft line" policies were promoting unorthodox and disloyal thought. After trial and error, moreover, a certain shaking down took place in the king's mind. As he got older, he grew more stubborn about having his own conservative way.

Save for his drastic stroke at the monasteries, Henry VIII did not in the end do much to change the Church within the framework of Catholicism to which it was committed. The main reformist achievement was a certain curtailment of the superstitious element in religious practice—excessive cultism, devotion to images, pilgrimages, and the like. Even codification and reform of the canon law, the project for which a measure of state control was originally to be used, came to little. On the whole, although Henry went a little way toward reforming the Church along the lines of Christian humanism, he fell far short of a thorough program. The Church of England acquired a really distinctive look among the mansions of Christendom only when it was turned over to Protestant architects under Henry's successor.

The verdict of failure in relation to such hopes as men had for a refurbished orthodoxy applies also to Henry's action against the monasteries. Between 1536 and 1540 monasticism was wiped out in England. The immense property of the monasteries was confiscated by the Crown and converted piecemeal into cash. The heart of the government's motivation was fiscal; only its pretense was reformist. But a convincing pretense has to be in tune with fact and with the drift of opinion.

Although it is misleading to speak of monasticism as a dying institution in the early sixteenth century (it certainly did not die in Catholic Europe), it was a sick institution. It needed encouragement, rethinking, and reform, such as it was to receive in the Catholic world. In England the doctor prescribed euthanasia and made off with the estate.

There were too many monasteries in England; the piety of founders and benefactors had been indiscriminate. As a result, many monasteries were small and isolated. Without the pressure of a sizable community devoted to a shared ideal and without the organization to attract able leadership, it would have taken saints to live monastic lives of high quality. Most monks and nuns were not saints. The larger and better-run monasteries must bear the brunt of a further indictment: English monasticism was overendowed in relation to its purpose. If the monasteries had been systematically engaged in social service, their wealth would not have been dead weight. While some monasteries did perform useful services, these were largely by-products. The chief end was contemplative. The worth of constant communal prayer and ascetic self-cultivation in the setting of a common life was the time-honored justification for the institution. At best, the monasteries did not need to be loaded with wealth. At worst, the cumbrance of riches dulled the edge of self-sacrifice associated with a monastic life.

These indictments do not mean that most monks were the lazy epicures of satire. The trouble was not deep corruption but routinization. A person should not choose the exceptional life of a monk without a serious vocation. The large number of monasteries and the relative ease of life that they offered attracted people who were not ideally suited to monasticism, and the environment often did not bring out the best in such indifferent material. However, the internal problems of a monastic establishment that was too much an Establishment were not new. The newer phenomenon was a more critical attitude toward monasticism. The institution was on trial from without. Inside problems as well as outside criticism made the monastic life less attractive to spiritual and intellectual talent than it had been in its heyday.

A government that cared about monasticism and considered it an indispensable feature of the Catholic way of life might have tried to save it. The most useful reforms would have been abolition or consolidation of the smaller houses and an attempt to reorient the monasteries in part toward service functions. Perhaps some of their property should have been removed from their control altogether and used to support other ecclesiastical and charitable activities. The nationalization of the Church would have facilitated such changes. But Henry VIII's government chose to turn the faults of the monasteries into a pretext for expropriation. Idealists who had given up on monasticism saw the possibility of providing a "moral equivalent" by rededicating the spoil to education and philanthropy, but the financial and political interests of the state drowned out their voices. The profits of expropriation went to the general expenses of government; thousands of acres once given to God went to the landowning class.

Henry VIII's strongest act of leadership as Supreme Head was to launch an investigation of the smaller monasteries in 1535. Thomas Crom-

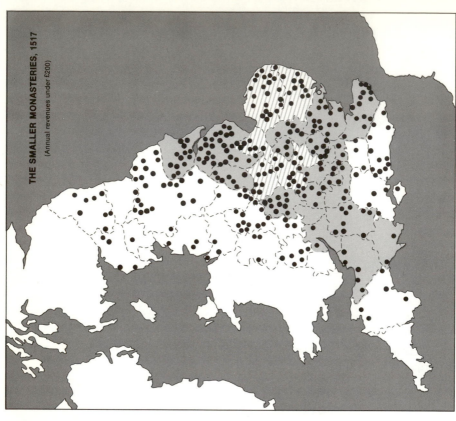

THE LARGER MONASTERIES, 1517
(Annual revenues over £200)

THE SMALLER MONASTERIES, 1517
(Annual revenues under £200)

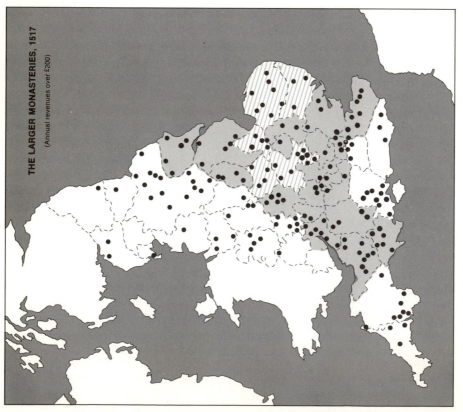

POPULATION DENSITY

 40 or more persons* per square mile

30—40 persons* per square mile

Map of population density and monasteries, 1517: The large number of monasteries, and the excessive number of small ones, corresponds rather closely to the historic distribution of population and wealth. Note, however, how many were in the thinly populated North, which responded to their dissolution with the Pilgrimage of Grace. (Adapted from Hughes, *The Reformation in England*, Hollis & Carter, London, 1951–54.)

well, who was behind the project, was put in charge of it as the king's vicar general (an ecclesiastical office, usually a sort of executive vice-president to a bishop). Cromwell's agents reported scandal upon scandal, much of it sexual. There is every reason to think that their findings were doctored. (Cromwell's reports can be checked against earlier routine investigations made by bishops, which revealed a good deal of imperfection but little serious scandal.) However, the government won acceptance of the brief it had prepared for a foregone conclusion. Shocking news from the monasteries was neither unexpected nor unwelcome. In 1536 Parliament dissolved the smaller monasteries and conveyed their property to the Crown.

The larger monasteries were next dissolved, by negotiation rather than outright abolition. Their ex-inmates were not mistreated. The ordained priests among them were mostly given positions as secular clergymen, and the rest were pensioned. When the technically voluntary process of surrender was completed, the abolition was confirmed by act of Parliament, a necessary measure to secure the title of the king and his grantees to the land. By 1540 monasticism was no more.

The economic and social consequences of the dissolution were not drastic. If the Crown had held on to the monastic lands indefinitely, its wealth and independence of tax income would have been much greater. But ready money meant more to the government. It did not sell off its windfall of new capital in a foolhardy way, but the process of liquidation was begun soon after the dissolution. Before many years, the land was substantially redistributed, and the money from the sales was spent. Confiscation and sale of monastic land did not upset the social structure. It did not create a new aristocracy of royal favorites who obtained vast estates dirt-cheap, although there were a few such cases. Nor did large numbers of landless rich leap into the aristocracy by buying land from a government greedy for cash. A huge block of land on the market did not make the price of land plummet, nor did it cause a heady spate of speculation and profiteering. On the whole, the government held out for and got fair value. On the whole, the land passed to families already established in the land-owning class. In many instances, the possessions of a particular monastery went to a neighboring aristocratic family, often a family that had patronized the abbey and leased the very land it now acquired.

The economic and social consequences of the dissolution were long-term and untidy. More land was in circulation over the long run than would have been if a large fraction of the country had stayed in the hands of perpetual institutions; that helped to hold land prices down. A larger amount of available land helped the number of substantial landowners to increase as the population increased (both the general population and that of the well-born, who had a better chance to survive to adulthood and to marry young and breed large families than other classes). A comparatively loose land market and a large landowning class made for mobility into and out of the gentry. The long-range as well as the immediate effects meant that the dissolution redounded mainly to the dominant class's benefit.

The political consequences of the dissolution were clearer-cut. It was a stroke of political genius, for it created a gigantic vested interest in the Reformation. Landowners, the political class, had no will to fight for the monasteries' rights nor for the religious values of monasticism. Gentlemen cast hungry eyes on the monastic lands. If a fiscally wise government would have been slower to liquidate its spoil, a politically wise one would satisfy that hunger, as Henry VIII's government did. Partnership between the king and other power-holders was cemented. By the normal course of exchange, that partnership was soon widened beyond the sphere of the original purchasers. This network of vested interests was extended even further by the diversion of a great deal of ecclesiastical patronage, together with the right to much of the income from clerical livings (which monasteries, as patrons, had been especially privileged to keep for themselves), from the monasteries to their lay successors.

However, since the dissolution was the strongest act of the new ecclesiastical regime and since it was so obviously an act of larceny by the powerful, it provoked sharper reactions than the government's earlier measures. The majority of monks took displacement in the same acquiescent spirit with which the secular clergy accepted state control. There were, however, a number of cases of resistance by the monks and of their trial and execution.

The abolition of the smaller monasteries precipitated the only episode of open revolt against Henry VIII, the so-called Pilgrimage of Grace of 1536. The Pilgrimage was partly a protest against the Reformation, with special emphasis on the wrong done to the monasteries. It was more a protest than a rebellion, more an ill-organized gathering to register grievances and create a threat of violence than a coordinated military effort. Indeed, the Pilgrimage consisted of a number of uprisings, each with its own local character. Although they were the essence of the revolt, ecclesiastical grievances were only part of a long list. In a sense, the Pilgrimage also expressed the alienation of Northern England (the disturbances centered in Yorkshire and Lincolnshire and extended to neighboring counties) from a predominantly southern government. The North was less populated and poorer than the South. The traditionalism of people who do not meet sophisticated ideas or mingle in the heavy traffic of wealth and power and who do not like what they hear of such thoroughfares was strong in the North. Conservative piety combined with resentment of high-handed destruction of familiar local institutions in the case of the monasteries.

The Pilgrimage of Grace lowered the king's batting average. But it did not spread or succeed. Its failure was not a triumph of superior force in an immediate confrontation with the weak. Internal fractionation and self-restraint on the part of rebel leaders and their gullibility in the face of deceptive promises by the government explain the collapse of the Pilgrimage. It was avenged in blood and mopped up by the king's noble military lieutenants. But no comparable threat was raised again. The momentum of this regional uprising did not pass to the larger community of the realm. The king held the substantial support of those who could command force.

Henry VIII's Last Years: How Stable Was the Henrician Church?

How did Henry VIII get away with it? Patriotism, self-interest, and dissatisfaction with the Church under its old management were stronger than Catholic principles and feeling for the sanctity of long-established ways—perhaps such a truistic summary is about as much as can be said. The government had no army, no police force, no right to figure its subjects as timid consumers of mass-produced enormities. The state shared power with noblemen whose ancestors had championed causes less appealing, one would think, than that of Holy Church. Ambition and traces of royal blood might have prompted some of them to oppose the Tudors, given so good a pretext. The fortuitous absence of an opposition leader with the personality and connections to carry other important men along with him may have been among Henry's hidden assets. But serious opposition from the class capable of discomfitting the king would have required vigorous stirring, and upper-class interests and convictions on the whole supported the king. Forty-odd years of largely popular and successful Tudor rule paid dividends, for the political class identified with the monarchy.

With slight variation, the same point holds for other classes. Although active resistance without a solid base in the ruling class would have been against all odds, the government could have been at least distressed and hampered by widespread signs of disapproval. After allowance is made for ignorance and the habit of obedience in accounting for popular acceptance of the Reformation, one must conclude that most people were not, in one sense, very good Catholics: they had not been inspired to think and feel in their way what a Thomas More thought and felt. Religion was personal and routine. The government did not interfere with such religion if it was outwardly orthodox. Catholicism had not been put across as a public commitment, a loyalty reaching beyond this world, apt always to be threatened by the powers of this world and demanding a choice between it and this world. The international Church was responsible for such lassitude. Bogged down in politics and legalism, taking itself for granted as a permanent wheel in the world's machinery, the Church had forgotten that Christianity of whatever theology is an evangelical faith. The Gospel must be preached, its demands explained, its emotional hold renewed. The English clergy was so far from full-blooded Catholicism that it found the king's measures hardly objectionable. People for whom more than routine religion was possible needed instruction and uplifting; they needed a cause. The Protestants were soon to be at their service. Although the Protestants preached a new theology and attacked many well-loved religious usages, they spoke with the voice of the evangelist.

How stable, we should next ask, was the Henrician Reformation? In fact, national Catholicism such as Henry VIII created did not last, nor did a rejuvenated national Catholicism come about. In Edward VI's reign, the national Church turned unmistakably to Protestantism; after a state-led return to Roman Catholicism under Queen Mary, England became Protestant for good under Elizabeth. Was this outcome chance or necessity? Both, no doubt, but necessity has the better case. The most important circumstance was that Protestantism existed. Protestantism had the evangelical offensive. It spoke to the dead at heart as a state religion could not do. The nationalization of the Church did not have to prevent a Catholic counteroffensive, but to recapture the offensive is harder than to man a receding defense. Compared to the Roman Church, which in many places did respond positively to the Protestant challenge, the English Church had two strikes against it.

Henry VIII had to portray the Roman Church in a way that could hardly be distinguished from that of the Protestants: government propaganda had to make the Pope a usurper and pretender; the divorce case required that the Pope be seen as scandalously indifferent to Scriptural law. It was hard to negate the papacy and yet affirm the orthodox tradition, hard to expose the monstrous pretenses of Rome and then say that the greater part of Roman teaching was after all true. To the Protestants, the Pope was anti-Christ. Might a loyal Englishman not take that designation as the strongly worded truth? If the Protestants had rightly interpreted the Roman Church, might they not also have correctly interpreted Christian doctrine? Why hold that the organization of the Church had been based on a "lying tradition," and yet cease to look for other lies repeated through the centuries when the Roman Church had been dominant? King, Parliament, and bishops pretended to discriminate the truth and falsehood in Catholic tradition. Did they deserve more attention than prophets who upheld the Gospel against all tradition?

Confusion was compounded by such measures as the dissolution of the monasteries. Monasticism in England had been found so hopelessly corrupt that there was no choice but to abolish it. To the Protestants, monasticism was the fruit of vicious doctrine and was bound to break out in visible corruption. Was the Protestant diagnosis not perhaps correct? Might other Catholic practices and opinions be traced to the same evil root?

Finally, Christian humanism was an ambiguous influence in the Henrician Reformation. Although it was the best hope for reform within the Catholic framework, it did not profoundly support Catholicism. It commanded talent, opposed the inadequacies of the status quo, and offered a vision of a newly Christianized national life. Yet it was perilously open to accommodation with Protestantism. It was to make that accommodation in England, for its influence was brought to bear on the national Protestant Church. While it softened the rigor of evangelical enthusiasm on behalf of common sense, it kept certain streams of Catholic tradition flowing in spirit of the strict Protestants' efforts to dam and drain them. Conservative Catholicism with the virtue of a living conservatism—that is, the capacity to restate old values in fresh terms in order to recapture their persuasiveness—was a real possibility in sixteenth-century Europe. It was capable of using Christian humanism without turning flat under its mild but seductive sway. In England, official Catholicism was dead conservatism—a stagnant expression of the legal and administrative mind. The state had unwittingly done its best to abort the potentiality of a Catholic resurgence merely by creating an anti-Roman national Church and using the opportunity to make such "reforms" as the dissolution. It unintentionally encouraged the sides of popular feeling and Christian humanism that pointed toward the Protestant way.

There was historical logic in England's drift to Protestantism, but historical accident cooperated. King Henry encouraged the drift despite his own religious views. His marital career makes a good starting point. Anne Boleyn, having given birth to Princess Elizabeth in 1533, went to the block in 1536. She and her confederates were charged with treason, but the root of their offense was adultery. Whatever had gone on, the king's disaffection was aroused by Anne's failure to produce a son. Catherine of Aragon had died in 1536, so Henry's third marriage was "free and clear." His third wife, Jane Seymour, a well-connected English girl, died shortly after the birth of Prince Edward in 1537. The fourth wife, Anne of Cleves, was a political pawn and a nominal spouse. The king's marriage to that dowdy German lady was promoted by Cromwell as part of his scheme for a German Protestant alliance. The king's dislike for Anne when he saw her in the flesh, plus the machinations of court rivals, brought about Cromwell's fall and ritual execution for treason in 1540. Henry's marriage to Anne of Cleves was annulled. The Howard family, who had promoted Cromwell's downfall, furnished the king's fifth wife: Catherine Howard's

Left to right: Catherine of Aragon, Anne Boleyn, Jane Seymour, Anne of Cleves, Catherine Howard, Catherine Parr. Henry VIII's six wives are landmarks for the political history of his reign. (*Left to right:* The National Portrait Gallery, London; Bettmann Archive; Kunsthistorisches Museum, Vienna; The Louvre, from Musées Nationeaux, Paris; Toledo, Ohio, Museum of Art; Terence Le Goubin, London.)

career was a replay of her cousin Anne Boleyn's. Another very young, but not very innocent, girl, she aroused the king's jaded sexual appetite. After a brief childless marriage, she was executed, 1541, for treasonous adultery. Henry's last wife, Catherine Parr, was the luckiest, for she survived Henry to enjoy some importance as dowager and to remarry. She was relatively sensible and mature, and her religious bent was Protestant.

Beneath this bare chronicle, we can find some of the themes of Henry VIII's last years. The king went the way of ex-athletes and bon vivants, to obesity and illness. He did not suffer a dissolution of personality or mental decline, but he grew less clear-headed, more ill-tempered, less confident, and more overbearing. After Cromwell's fall, he lacked reliable assistance and faced intense factional struggle. To one purpose the king held tight: the Tudor dynastic interest. He kept marrying and hoping for more offspring. Failing to produce more, he had to arrange the succession with the materials at hand. Jane Seymour had paid with her life for a male heir, but the worst problem was solved: Edward would succeed. But Edward was a child and Henry was a sick man. The perils of assuring a minor's succession and of seeing him through a regency without harm to the dynasty had to be faced. By English law, the king's elder daughter, Mary, was a bastard. She was an adult and a Romanist, loyal to her mother's memory. Elizabeth had been bastardized by statute following Anne Boleyn's fall. She was still young, a talented girl absorbing the high-pressure tutoring given a royal child. In 1544 the king decided to restore Mary and Elizabeth to the succession by statute—in that order, failing issue by Edward or further issue by himself. The succession plan shows mainly that Henry's first attachment was to his family. (Including Mary subjected

the royal supremacy to an off-chance risk, but the risk of attracting disaffection to her if she were excluded and of reducing the number of Tudors in line seemed worse.)

Henry let Edward and Elizabeth be educated by men too Protestant for his own taste. It is hard to know how consciously political a step that was. It would have been rational to think of insuring the royal supremacy by deepening the religious fracture, but one should not infer too much from Edward's early education. The prince was very young, although precocious, in his father's lifetime. Lines of doctrine were blurred, religious identities unclear. The essence of Edward's training was humanistic preparation for government.

Henry's arrangements for his son's minority influenced the subsequent move to Protestantism. But circumstance and accident may have had more to do with those arrangements than calculation. By his will, (which had been given public legal force by statute), Henry appointed a council of regency for his son. His choice of men to serve Edward reflects a desire to balance factions and religious points of view more than it does a decisive plan for the future. The political complexion of the moment, however, kept the council from being as heterogeneous as the king would have perhaps preferred. Because of an obscure conspiracy, the Howards fell into disgrace at the end of Henry's reign, so the strongest conservative faction among the nobility was out of the picture. Stephen Gardiner, the ablest conservative cleric, had fallen out of favor after a quarrel with the king, which may have concerned only a routine matter. The faction with which Edward's interests would be safest was that of his relatives, the Seymours. Although Henry preferred a balanced council to an individual regent, Edward Seymour, Edward's uncle and personal guardian, almost had to be *primus inter pares*. The new reign had scarcely begun before Seymour maneuvered his fellow politicians into making him lord protector, virtually a regent. Seymour and his adherents were pro-Protestant, perhaps more decisively so than Henry had anticipated. Among the clerics, especially with Gardiner eclipsed, Cranmer was the strong man. His religious views were known to be more radical than those of King Henry. Henry had both blocked Cranmer's religious aspirations and, out of personal attachment and gratitude, protected him against his enemies. Now his day as architect of the Church was at hand. King Henry may have died uncertain about the future of religion, perhaps muddled, perhaps wisely indifferent toward events he could not predict, but he died confident that he had provided for his son as best he could.

Evolving Anglicanism:
The Protestant Church and the Middle Way

The watchword of the Church of England has always been the *Via Media*, the "Middle Way." The phrase suggests splitting the difference between Catholic and Protestant. The Church that Henry VIII's divorce gave rise to has perhaps, over centuries, come to walk that narrow line. Historically, the middleness of the English Church has been a variable quality.

For all its conservatism, the Henrician Church was not wholly shut off from Protestant influence. It did not simply withdraw to its legal and administrative lines, forswearing every chance to see itself as mediator between Catholic tradition and the Gospel as Protestants declared it. But, at best, the Henrician Church was a middle way between hidebound orthodoxy and cautious Protestantism.

Luther's Protestantism was itself conservative in the external matters of liturgy and church government. As such, it could have furnished one kind of *Via Media*, for by the time the English break from Rome was accomplished other forms of Protestantism, in some ways to the left of Lutheranism, had emerged on the Continent. The greatest reformer after Luther was the Frenchman John Calvin, who settled in the Swiss city-state of Geneva. Partly because he had a more systematic and practical mind than Luther and partly because he had the opportunity to build a reformed church according to his own ideas and to make that church the dominant institution in the small society of Geneva, Calvin created a church whose visible worship and government contrasted sharply with Catholicism. Thereby Calvin provided a model for Englishmen and Scotsmen whose zeal came to be focused on clearing the Church of Catholic vestiges and undue subjection to the state. In theology, Calvin was basically at one with Luther, although his way of expressing the faith, his personality, and some of his detailed deductions from the common core differed. He was a moderate—on some points, between Lutheranism and the rival Swiss school deriving from the Zurich reformer Zwingli—and by no means dogmatic about imposing the liturgy and church government that he had worked out in Geneva on people in other situations. The clarity and comprehensiveness of Calvin's theology (stated and restated in the many editions of his *Institutes of the Christian Religion*) spoke to all orthodox Protestants, but zealous tempers took more sustenance from it than those who were looking for compromise or those who thought religious truth *should* be a little vague. Although more moderate than many Calvinists, Calvin was not a compromising mind, and vagueness was not his style of moderation.

The mainline Protestants substantially agreed on what they considered most important, but in the confined world of Protestant schools, to which England had to respond if she were to depart from Catholicism, there were differences that mattered. The sharpest debate in the middle decades of the sixteenth century was over the Mass, or Holy Communion, which, together with Baptism, the Protestants retained from the seven Catholic sacraments. All Protestants rejected the Catholic view that the Mass is, in a sense, Christ's sacrifice, repeated and renewed by his Church. They rejected the concomitant view that the bread and wine actually change, in "substance," into Christ's body and blood. Beyond this common ground, they differed on the nature and significance of the sacrament. Lutheranism insisted on Christ's bodily presence to communicants; Calvinism held that Christ's body and blood are meaningfully present, but in a spiritual rather than a corporeal way; the true "left," Zwinglianism, took the bread and wine as symbols, the sacrament as only a commemoration of Christ's death for man.

The English Church developed within the field of force defined by the continental Protestant groups, on the one hand, and Catholicism on the other. The poles operated on the field complexly. Religious changes in England—the moves toward Protestantism after Henry VIII's death as well as those during his lifetime—were acts of state. The faith by law established was always to some degree a "committee product"—an accommodation among different views, a reflection of the search for language offensive to no one. The government could not know the exact state of public opinion. It could assume that there was diversity, and especially that there were many Catholics in the population. Protestant leaders and mere politicians were hopeful that blurred or moderate language would be acceptable to Catholics. Such men were probably too hopeful with respect to clear-headed Catholics, but there were other Catholics, no doubt, whom a superficial traditionalism would satisfy. The private opinions of Cranmer, the most important religious leader in England, pointed in a clearly Protestant direction but nonetheless were vague and moderate. Cranmer had the virtue of openmindedness: he conscientiously tried to form his own views, was not always sure

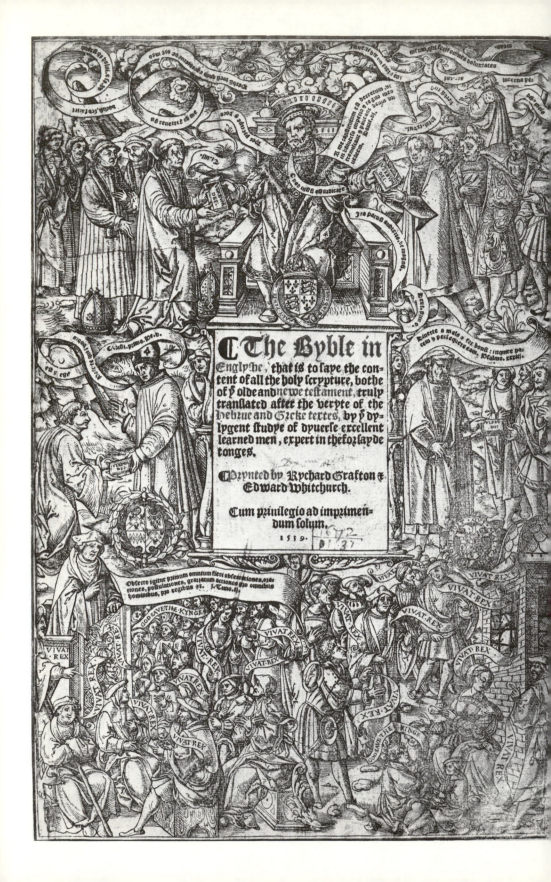

The Byble in
Englyshe, that is to saye the content of all the holy scrypture, bothe
of ý olde and newe testament, truly
translated after the veryte of the
hebrue and Grcke textes, by ý dy-
lygent studye of dyuerse excellent
learned men, expert in the forsayde
tonges.

Prynted by Rychard Grafton &
Edward Whitchurch.

Cum privilegio ad imprimen-
dum solum.
1539.

Frontispiece, Cranmer Bible, 1539: The vernacular Bible was a Christian humanist and a Protestant objective, which the Henrician Reformation first embraced and then drew back from. Several sixteenth-century translations led up to the authorized, or King James, version. (Courtesy of the British Museum.)

of them, changed his mind. He had a Christian humanist's distaste for dogmatism and an old government hand's respect for the political side of religion. With his flexibility, Cranmer was well suited to preside over religious decision-making by committee. On that process all the continental schools had influence—through correspondence among Protestant churchmen and through the personal presence of a number of distinguished reformers, who were received as refugees in England and welcomed as experts. No single continental strain was dominant, and a "right-to-left" spectrum is not a reliable clue to the schools' relative influence on the several English religious settlements.

The moving picture of evolving Anglicanism can best be stopped at four points:

1. By 1549 the first stage of reform had been accomplished. Visible changes from the Henrician model had been made, but Protestant doctrinal implications were held down. It is doubtful whether this settlement was intended to last. There was pressure for further change from the Protestant quarter, and officialdom was susceptible to that pressure. The architects of the first reform were probably not so much convinced that they had found the solution as that they had devised an acceptable one. Yet their solution *might* last; it might represent the limits of the politically feasible. It had features positively attractive to its designers. The main points of the settlement were as follows:

a. The liturgy was translated into English. In 1549 Cranmer published his first *Book of Common Prayer,* and its use was enjoined on all churches by an act of Parliament. A vernacular liturgy was part of the Protestant program, although it was in no way incompatible with Catholicism. The first *Book of Common Prayer* is a masterly piece of English prose. As such, it has its own feel and flavor. On the surface, however, it is close to a translation of the Mass in Latin. Catholics could not condemn the English service on doctrinal grounds. The only serious practical change was the allowance of "communion in both kinds"; that is, lay communicants were given the wine as well as the bread. For Protestants, communion in both kinds meant equality for all believers and the all-sufficiency of the faith they had in common. Setting the priest apart implied that the collective communion of the Church was distinct from the sum of individual communions and just as necessary. A Catholic must welcome the implication, but communion in both kinds as a liturgical custom is consistent with the Catholic theory of the Mass.

b. The first settlement was extraordinarily tolerant by sixteenth-century standards. Such instruments of thought-control as the Act of Six Articles were abolished. For the first time, it was legal to be a Protestant. By the same token, so long as one did not dispute the royal supremacy, there was no impediment to Catholic views. Attendance at churches using the new official service was not required by law. The main purpose of the new freedom was to allow Protestants to preach their truth. To the extent that the government gave help and direction to its clergy, doctrine with a Protestant slant was encouraged. If, however, the first settlement had held, something like true religious toleration might have come about. Catholics too conservative to accept the revised service and Protestants preferring a more thoroughly revised one could conceivably have been permitted to develop devotional bodies outside the established Church. Within it, individual congregations and ministers could have been allowed to take different directions with respect to doctrine and the details of liturgy.

c. The beginning of Edward VI's reign saw another raid on Church property comparable to the dissolution of the monasteries. This time, the government confiscated the property with which chantries and related religious foundations were endowed. It was a common practice for people to endow a priest whose main duty was to say Mass for the soul of the founder (or his kin or friends) in Purgatory. Such a foundation is called a "chantry." The government's motive in confiscating the chantries was again financial. And again it had the pretext of corruption, since the intentions of donors were often not fulfilled. Although priests supported by chantries often did useful things collaterally, such as keeping schools, a good case could be made that the wealth of chantries was inefficiently deployed for such uses. After chantries were abolished, the social services they had performed were as well taken care of by philanthropy, assisted by central and local government. The government also had a theological pretext for abolishing the chantries. To Protestants, the idea that Masses repeated on earth have any sort of relevance for the soul in its afterlife was anathema, as was the idea of Purgatory itself. Catholics were committed to those ideas, although liberal ones saw excessive preoccupation with mitigating the pains of Purgatory by such a mechanical rite as a superstitious emphasis in need of discouragement. Taken as part of the first Anglican settlement, the dissolution of the chantries was a gain for the Protestant side, but it was not incompatible with Catholicism of a humanistic stamp.

2. In 1552 the Church of England was resettled safely within the Protestant hemisphere. Its moderation was now derived from its technique of mixing Protestant elements, some less antithetical to Catholicism than others, and from its avoidance of extremes which all mainline Protestantism repudiated. The change is to be explained largely by the accumulation of Protestant pressure. Zealous and able Protestants were free to preach and politick. Official circles were more friendly to them than to conservatives.

Although popular religious opinion is hard to trace, it is probable that Protestant preaching was visibly "taking" with the laity, especially in such places as London, which the government could observe from day to day. The Protestant party wanted further reformation, and in many ways the path of least resistance was to give it to them. Meanwhile, Protector Somerset had fallen from power, for political rather than religious reasons. His successor, John Dudley, Duke of Northumberland, was a ruthless politician with little interest in religion, except as his power over the Church gave him opportunities for profit. Initially, conservative churchmen thought they might do better with him than with Somerset, who was more genuinely Protestant. But as it turned out, Northumberland was ready to take the path of least resistance toward further reform. Somerset might have felt a personal stake in the first settlement, especially its tolerant aspect, which was to some extent an expression of his humane temperament.

The chief document of the new settlement is Cranmer's second *Book of Common Prayer*. This time, the part relating to Holy Communion was considerably changed to imply a Protestant interpretation. The intra-Protestant contention over the sacrament was resolved ambiguously. By the time of the second settlement, some voices were demanding such changes in the service as the abolition of kneeling to receive communion. Apart from its association with the Catholic past, kneeling was thought to imply Christ's corporeal presence. Moderates could welcome that implication, or they could reply that a mere ceremonial gesture of respect implied nothing, or they could keep quiet, leaving their attitude in suspense. Cranmer favored keeping quiet, that is, requiring the communicant to kneel as accustomed but giving no hint in the text of the ritual to indicate what the kneeling meant. On this point, the extremists won a last-minute victory: after the prayer book had gone to the printer, a footnote was inserted in a "stop presses" way explaining that kneeling did not imply adoration of the sacrament as God's body. Cranmer neither much liked the addition nor disapproved it on principle. So it went with "religious settlement by committee"; such was the new Middle Way.

This time, the Act of Uniformity, by which Parliament required the new prayer book to be used, made attendance at parish churches compulsory. Catholics were now bound to take part in services which could be squared with their beliefs only by clutching at every ambiguity. Drawing up a frankly Protestant statement of official doctrine was the main unfinished task, to which Cranmer addressed himself.

3. When Elizabeth came to the throne in 1558, after Queen Mary's return to Rome, she had several options before her and several models already tried. She wanted to restore the royal supremacy and leave the religious character of the national Church unresolved for the time being. Although it is difficult to determine her personal predilection, it is possible that she would have preferred to stop at either Henrician Catholicism

Frontispiece, *Book of Common Prayer:* The first translation of the Latin liturgy into English was published by Thomas Cranmer in 1549. Its use was enjoined on all churches by an act of Parliament. (Courtesy of the British Museum.)

or the kind of Middle Way that the first Edwardian settlement represented. In any event, she preferred to wait and see, to avoid offending the Catholic elements in the country and the Catholic powers abroad. She had religious views of her own, but these did not add up to a systematic theological position; they did not outweigh her political prudence nor her disposition to tolerate a variety of opinions, as long as the royal supremacy was recognized and religious convictions were not allowed to justify civil nonconformity.

However, the queen did not get her way. A settlement was forced upon her when she wanted to postpone the question. She had no chance to work out a solution reflecting her own preferences and the leisurely fruits of experience. The Elizabethan settlement was a compromise arrived at on grounds the queen did not choose. On the other hand, her point of view was included in the compromise. Throughout her reign, she was determined to adhere to the settlement that she had not quite voluntarily accepted at the outset. She was loyal to it partly in the interest of peace and quiet—because the matter had been settled, and because good subjects, in the queen's opinion, should be content with what she and her Parliament had decided. Having compromised once, she was unwilling to compromise again. Yet the substance of the settlement was probably close to the queen's personal position. She would like to have handled things differently, but there is no reason to think she would have come to a very different conclusion.

Settlement was pressed on Elizabeth at the beginning of her reign because the distinct Protestants were in a strong position. A sizable group of influential Protestants had gone into exile during Mary's reign. They came home with the natural zeal of an opposition returned to office, confirmed in the Protestantism that had cost them the inconvenience of exile and eager to enact their program without tarrying. The exiles and their sympathizers were the loudest voices in Parliament, whence dissatisfaction with the government's cautious policy was unmistakably expressed. The ecclesiastical hierarchy was filled with Mary's Roman Catholic appointments and was, therefore, without influence. As soon as personnel could be reshuffled, the Church was bound to fall into the hands of Protestant bishops, several of whom had been exiles. By political standards, the government was wise to give in to the men who were happiest to see Elizabeth on the throne, although they were unwilling to be reined in by a cautious government. Giving in to their demand for an immediate Protestant settlement did not mean consenting to everything these Protestants preferred.

One of the effects of exile was that divisions among the Protestants opened up. Some wanted to depart from liturgical and doctrinal tradition more radically than the English Church had done in Edward VI's reign. Others either positively approved or had no trouble accepting the second Edwardian settlement. The more moderate position was the Protestant focus at the beginning of Elizabeth's reign. Some would have liked to go further, but the Protestant settlement that had already been tried made the best rallying point against a government that did not want to go so far.

To reach a settlement at all, the Protestants had to compromise. What extremists regarded as a minimum program had to be further attenuated. The second Edwardian prayer book was restored with a few changes. The principal change muddled the communion service so that its meaning became more ambiguous than before. Compulsory attendance at churches using the prescribed service was reenacted. An official statement of doctrine was subsequently worked out by the new Protestant hierarchy. Their work, which built on that of Cranmer, was promulgated in 1563 in the form of Thirty-Nine Articles of Religion. Although the Anglo-Catholics of a later day were to argue that the articles can be construed in a Catholic sense, the authors had no intention of obscuring the Protestant-Catholic line. Their intention was to make official doctrine clearly Protestant. The formulations tended toward Calvinism on crucial points.

Formally or legally, the Elizabethan settlement was final. The prayer book and articles remain the basis of the Anglican Church today. In its immediate context, the settlement represented a Middle Way in two senses.

(1) With respect to Holy Communion, and in its general tone, no commitment was made to any one form of continental Protestantism. The Church of England could claim to draw on all the major versions, to embrace and tolerate their varying emphases, or to offer the kind of amalgam that is rather a creative blend than a mere mixture of borrowings. (2) In common with the second Edwardian settlement, the Elizabethan one sought to dissociate the English Church from opinions typical of what is called the "radical reformation." Since Luther's original rebellion, some Protestants (sharp dissenters from Catholic teaching and subscribers to justification by faith) had developed opinions that the main Protestant groups regarded as shockingly unacceptable. Those opinions were not really influential in England until the seventeenth century. The makers of the Elizabethan settlement thought of themselves as moderates partly because they were at pains to reject what they saw as heterodox Protestant extremism. In this respect, they shared the middle of the road with Luther, Calvin, and other "respectable" Reformers.

4. Let us stop the camera once more, a couple of decades beyond the Elizabethan settlement. Officially, things stand as they stood at the settlement. Actually, time has made its alterations.

First, the country was solidly and conventionally Protestant. It is hard to know at what rate ordinary people had come to think of themselves as Protestant, to understand what Protestantism meant, and to live their religious lives in a Protestant spirit. But after a few decades under the Elizabethan settlement, a Protestant tone pervaded religious life and thought, and the great majority of Englishmen proudly identified themselves as Protestants. There were *Roman* Catholics in England, but they were a minority group, on the border between uneasy de facto toleration and active persecution. There was no longer an indeterminately large fund of popular Catholic feeling. No basis existed any longer for the political calculation that religious conservatism was the price of popular acceptance of the royal supremacy.

Second, numerous convinced and reflective Protestants were dissatisfied with the official Church. Much of this dissatisfaction came from participants in the official Church: its ministers and laymen who partook of its services as the law required. In different specific ways and with different degrees of intensity, such people advocated change in the official Church. The state Church seemed to them not monstrously anti-Christian, like Rome, but bureaucratic, set in its ways, unwilling to put real energy into improving the quality of religious life, uninterested in making England's Protestant commitment as clear-cut and meaningful as it should be. Let us call these critics by their historical name: Puritans.

In a sense, there had been Puritans earlier. In Edward VI's reign and at the beginning of Elizabeth's, there were those who wanted the liturgy, in particular, to break with the past more cleanly than moderate Protestants required or, in some cases, would accept. Passage of time had spread and radicalized such sentiment. To Puritans, the Elizabethan settlement was at best a good beginning for more reform. To the government, the settlement was final: continuing reformation failed to come about. The search for a purer, more intense, and more Protestant national religion was not renewed. Official opinion stood firm and, worse, obstructed the private initiative of Puritans. Those to whom continuing reformation and renewal were axiomatic goods had begun to believe that the state-controlled episcopal system was an immovable obstacle to God's program.

Finally, at our later Elizabethan stopping-point, we shall find some people positively devoted to the official Middle Way, as distinct from those merely content with it. The Edwardian and Elizabethan settlements were political products. Compromise had been the prevailing note. Contrary to the cliché, a compromise need not leave all its participants angry. There were those to whom the early settlements had intrinsic, as well as political, value. The passage of time multiplied the number of such people and changed the meaning of their commitment.

During Elizabeth's reign, men were bred up in the established Church. They grew attached by habit and taste to its dignified form of worship. Although the Elizabethan settlement was a politically conditioned blueprint, some people were better able to build their religious lives by following that blueprint than by moving into the prefabricated edifices of continental Protestantism or Catholicism. Meanwhile, Puritans attacked the national Church. Attack begot defense. The Puritans saw their opponents as dim-spirited bureaucrats, more interested in maintaining their authority and enforcing the rules than in the soul of a Protestant nation. The Puritans were largely right about the officials, including the queen. But the officials had acquired a constituency. Among those who cared for the established Church on religious grounds were to be some of the finest minds, imaginations, and moral personalities in the history of English Christianity.

The developments of Elizabeth's reign gave a new meaning to the Middle Way. Catholicism stood apart as always, and the national Church walked well away from that extreme. Puritanism had come to define the other side, claiming the true pedigree of Reformation Protestantism. The Anglicans in the middle disputed that pedigree, but to the Puritans these were half-baked Protestants. The Anglicans would not admit to that. But the subtle pressure that sometimes causes men to accept their critics' categories was at work. Might an Anglican not think of himself as neither Catholic nor Protestant, but simply Christian? Might the Church of England not be the Christian Church as it was in the beginning, before the body of the faithful had been torn apart? Might the Middle Way not lead to the center of Christ's meaning?

A Protestant Nation in the Making:
Edward VI and Queen Mary

National self-consciousness and patriotism were assets on the government's side throughout the Reformation. Officialdom pretended that the Pope was a foreign prince, who had usurped jurisdiction in England and thereby encroached on the king's imperial authority. That legalistic way of speaking rang a popular bell. Long experience as an independent, centralized nation with a distinctive system of government and law; xenophobia and self-satisfaction bred by experience of contact and rivalry with foreigners; a long medieval history of political bickering with Rome—such factors made the identification of religious revolution with national self-assertion convincing. The Protestant phase of the English Reformation both exploited and deepened the sense of nationality.

By the later Elizabethan period, conscious Protestantism and conscious Englishness had fused. England was not only *a* Protestant nation; in a sense, she was *the* Protestant nation. On the Continent, Protestantism was the exclusive or prevailing religion in a heterogeneous collection of city-states, regions, and territorial states formally subject to the Holy Roman Empire. The Scandinavian kingdoms and Scotland had become Protestant. But only the Queen of England presided over a major-league power that was both officially and actually Protestant. Within the reformed camp, England was the national state with great reserves of civic tradition and cultural identity. Civic tradition prepared the way for a state religion; England's cultural identity took new nourishment from Protestantism.

Enthusiastic spirits saw England as a chosen nation. To England alone among full-scale states had God made his Gospel manifest. Monarch and people were knit together in a unity transcending the organic bond of commonwealth and enriching its meaning. Together they stood, moral witness and physical defender of the truth which so many centuries of error had obscured. Duller souls only perceived the manifest destiny of Protestant England more dully: a right-thinking Englishman is a Protestant, a "very good thing." Pit an English Protestant against almost any number of the Pope's lackeys, and one would see what allies true faith and true manhood can be.

The successive religious settlements just discussed were the most important events of Edward VI's reign. The king's life was the more pathetic for being promising. Edward was a genuinely precocious child. The hothouse education to which he was subjected, combined with his natural educability, made him something of a "little old man." Had he survived to adulthood, he might have been an unusually serious and intelligent monarch. A certain lack of joyfulness need not have been an important defect. His father's gusto and charisma had been aspects of a knightly character on whose less attractive face there was a good deal of the bully and the slob. Edward had been trained for the role of a sober, learned, humanistic prince. If he had had the chance, he might have filled it well, but then history would have lacked the diversion of a great actress, Queen Elizabeth, adapting that high-minded part to her sex. As it turned out, Edward did not live beyond tutelage. His precocity was such that he understood the religious and political issues of his age and took something of a personal hand in public affairs. Basically, however, his minority reign was an open season for politicians, who, without an adult master for whose attention they could compete, scrambled for the privilege of manipulating a juvenile king. The tuberculosis that must have darkened King Edward's life and conditioned his character dispatched him at the age of seventeen.

The atmosphere of Edward VI's reign was feverish and creative: it was a time of low politics and high idealism. Economic trouble and political shambles brought out the worst and best in men: rapacity, rebellion, and repressiveness, pious fervor and social concern. The two leading political figures, Somerset and Northumberland, embody the reign's disparities. Somerset monopolized power skillfully, but he was not successful in retaining it. From the point of view of those whose support mattered, he mishandled the crises he was faced with. To a large extent, his good qualities explain his failure. He was maneuvered out of power and eventually to execution by Northumberland, his treacherous erstwhile confederate. The Machiavellian Northumberland was smart enough to win hegemony, but he was not smart enough to block Queen Mary's accession and put his family on the throne by manipulating the Protestant cause.

The first wave of religious reform provoked an uprising in the West of England. Like the Pilgrimage of Grace, the "Prayer Book Rebellion" was partly a conservative religious reaction and partly an expression of agrarian unrest and regional aggrievement. At about the same time, in the summer of 1549, there was a peasant revolt ("Kett's Rebellion") in the important county of Norfolk. The Norfolk rebellion was against oppressive landlords, but insofar as it had a religious element it was Protestant. The rebels, who were not unsophisticated, associated a square deal in the countryside with the high-sounding promise of a new deal in religion. Both rebellions were put down. The power-wielding upper orders knew their duty.

Overt disturbances are unlikely to improve the credit of incumbent governments, especially with a privileged political class whose fear of the populace has been aroused. Protector Somerset was damaged further by his liberal response to the disquiet. He was a serious believer in the social justice preached by the advocates of commonwealth. He favored relative leniency toward those whose grievances had led them into illegality, and

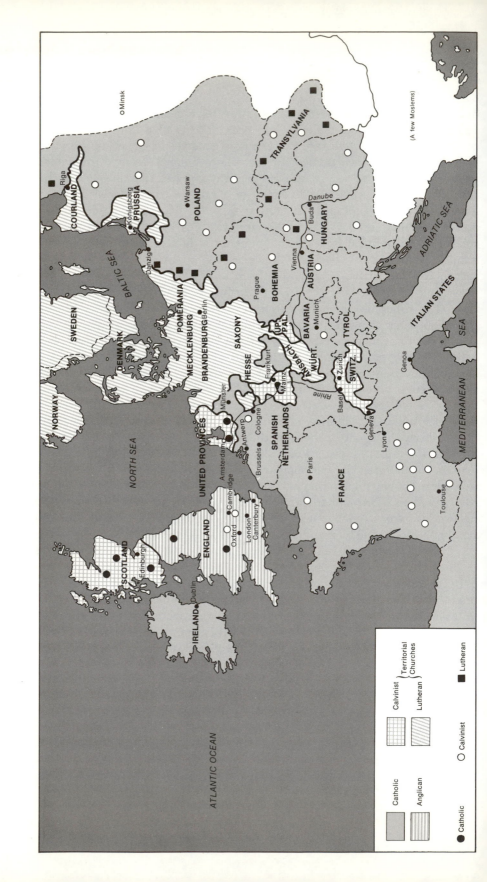

O Minsk

(A few Moslems)

ADRIATIC SEA

Riga
COURLAND
Königsberg
PRUSSIA
Danzig
Warsaw
POLAND
TRANSYLVANIA
Danube
Buda
HUNGARY
Vienna
AUSTRIA
Prague
BOHEMIA

BALTIC SEA

SWEDEN

NORWAY

DENMARK

POMERANIA
MECKLENBURG
BRANDENBURG Berlin
SAXONY
UP.
PAL.
BAVARIA
Munich
TYROL

NORTH SEA

HESSE
Frankfurt
Mainz
ANSBACH
WÜRT.
SWITZ.
Zurich
Basel
Rhine
Geneva
Lyon

ITALIAN STATES

Genoa

MEDITERRANEAN SEA

Münster
UNITED PROVINCES
Amsterdam
Antwerp
Cologne
SPANISH NETHERLANDS
Brussels
Paris
FRANCE
Toulouse

ENGLAND
Cambridge
Oxford London
Canterbury
SCOTLAND
Edinburgh
IRELAND
Dublin

ATLANTIC OCEAN

Catholic

Anglican

Calvinist } Territorial Churches
Lutheran }

Lutheran

Catholic

Calvinist

A religious map of Europe, *c.* 1600: England's position as a Protestant nation, in a Europe in which Protestantism often maintained itself in enclaves, can be seen from the map. The success of the Counter Reformation had considerably reduced Protestant territory by 1600.

he set out to remedy what he took to be the underlying ills by an anti-enclosure drive. The idealistic lord protector did not endear himself to realistic landlords.

The government was meanwhile beset with other problems. Once his takeover of the Church was accomplished, Henry VIII had resumed his favorite avocation and led the country back into war against France and Scotland. Now Somerset was saddled with expensive and unflourishing hostilities. The monastic haul was mostly spent on military follies that left nothing to show for them. The chantries were dissolved to meet the continuing emergency, but still the emergency went on. Monetary inflation, caused by the introduction of large supplies of precious metals from the New World into Europe when population and economic activity were growing fast, had begun to appear in England. Inflation was made worse when the government debased the coinage to help meet its bills, a practice introduced by Henry VIII and continued by Edward VI's administration. Such devaluation also stimulated the export boom and contributed, along with the more fundamental fact of an overexpanded single industry, both to the social dislocations of prosperity and to the collapse that came shortly after Somerset's fall.

How much Somerset's social policies and the generally troubled and chaotic state of public affairs had to do with the palace revolution that dislodged him is hard to say. Personal factors, including a scandal involving Somerset's brother, must be added to the disfavor caused by some of his measures and his failure to deal efficiently with day-to-day problems. Northumberland engineered the shake-up and put the pieces together for his own profit. He presided in a spirit of venality over a country in economic collapse and religious excitement. Against this background of low politics, Protestant England was born. Hugh Latimer, the greatest pulpit voice of early English Protestantism, preached justification by faith *and* social justice. Nicholas Ridley, almost as great a preacher and a greater practical churchman, worked hard in his diocese of London to make nominal Protestantism real. Thomas Cranmer applied his theological intelligence and literary genius to the creation of a new national Church. Economic distress called forth sane secular analyses of public problems. It was the worst of times at court and in the country; it was also a time of distinguished men and new thought.

As Edward VI's life ebbed, so did Northumberland's prospects. For genuine Protestants, too, Mary Tudor's succession was an evil prospect. It is not surprising that Northumberland should have tried a coup. He had everything to gain for himself, and he had reason to think that his fellow politicians and partisans of the new religion would back him. Northumberland had married his son, Guildford Dudley, to a cousin of the king, Lady Jane Grey. Lady Jane was hardly next in line after Mary, but she ranked high enough in the royal family to be a reasonable candidate. Although only a youthful pawn in Northumberland's hands, she had the personal qualities of an attractive candidate. Like Edward and Elizabeth, she was a polished product of humanistic education. Northumberland appealed to King Edward's Protestant feelings and persuaded him to make a will leaving the kingdom to Lady Jane. Of course, it was not in the king's power to bequeath the realm, but the will might be persuasive to waverers. Northumberland's political brethren lined up behind the scheme—at least, they seemed cooperative. Accordingly, when Edward died, Lady Jane was proclaimed queen. But the plot then collapsed. The first requisite of success would have been to capture Mary, but she was warned and escaped to the stronghold of friends. The surrounding noblemen took counsel. No one outside Northumberland's court circle had any relish for his scheme. The duke set forth to fight his foes, but he attracted no support and surrendered. As soon as he left London, his fellow conspirators at court came out for Mary. A known Catholic came to the throne all but unopposed, save for a desperate politician's gamble. Lady Jane soon lost her innocent head; a real martyr to politics and a pseudomartyr to the Protestant cause—for Protestantism was not ripe for rebellion against the monarch and the law.

Everything favored Mary's peaceful succession. A great deal favored her dream of reunion with Rome, if only because her right to be queen was acknowledged and her power to have her way would be formidable. She was Supreme Head in spite of herself. Thus, she had great power over the personnel of the ecclesiastical hierarchy and the day-to-day management of the Church. She would need the cooperation of Parliament to undo the Reformation, but she had on her side both the political leverage of the Crown and the vague understanding that the monarch's will was more entitled to respect in religious matters than in ordinary secular legislation.

On the legal surface, Queen Mary had her way, but she muffed her chance to rejoin England and Rome in true affection. If she had produced an heir, a succession of Catholic rulers might have effected a real reunion. Not having produced one, she failed to erect strong barriers against a return to Protestantism. Mary left English Protestantism less wedded to political submissiveness than she had found it. She had tried to dissipate an already strong association between religious independence and national dignity. She succeeded in reinforcing it.

It would be uncharitable to blame Queen Mary for failing to carry out a difficult assignment. She was the only grown-up Tudor for whom conviction was categorical. Because she put religion above the earthly instinct for political survival, she did not calculate the price of religious success. Besides their political sense, Henry VIII and Elizabeth had obtrusive egos, irrational sensitivities, and fixed ideas. Among the Tudors, only Henry VII had a hard, uncomplicated grip on reality. Mary falls at the opposite end of the spectrum—the neurotic. She came to the throne a middle-aged spinster. From adolescence, she had lived with her mother's disgrace; she was the conscious victim of personal injustice and her father's impiety. The toughest personality might react to such a life with redoubled loyalty to her despised faith and her Spanish kindred. Mary's zeal and rage worked outward to make her a determined and ambitious Catholic sovereign. The inward working of her emotions bent her toward fantasy and dependence.

Queen Mary's gravest mistake was her marriage to Philip II of Spain. Reunion with Rome should have been kept as separate as possible from dependence on any foreign state. Mary brought them together. The patriotism that favored ecclesiastical independence was reinforced by people's feeling that England had been made a Spanish satellite. Philip was interested in satellites and in the Catholic faith; he was not interested in Mary Tudor as a person. He was the most political of bridegrooms, with a busy man's excuse to avoid his wife's company. Mary fancied she was in love with a man. In reality, she was in love with an idea: England returned to her age-old obedience to the Holy See; and the queen married to the most Catholic of kings—a good Catholic woman fulfilling her womanhood in the comely estate of matrimony, breeding a race of "Defenders of the Faith," part English and part Spanish, like herself; the old Anglo-Spanish, anti-French alliance renewed; the Spanish royal house, once courted by little England, later rudely insulted, vindicated now by the union of two cousins, both of that noble line.

Queen Mary was in love with a royal wedding. That much she got. Her romanticism involved a real, if "sick," need for her man. In the end, she could not help discovering that she was unwanted for herself. Children were as essential to her success as a woman as they were to the long-run success of her religious policy. They did not come in reality. What came instead was a classic case of false pregnancy. We do not know from precisely what mix of physical illness and depression Queen Mary died in 1558.

There is no better context than this in which to observe that Queen Elizabeth married neither the widowed Philip II, who sought her hand, nor any other of several proposed matches. Whatever psychological twists and political turns explain it, Elizabeth's spinsterhood had one great advantage: an ego strong enough to enjoy power was not frustrated by the conventions of female dependency. Elizabeth preserved her femininity by fancy-dress vanity and by a flirtatious romanticism that remained grotesquely alive when the course of nature would have made her a grandmother. Mary had wrecked her long-awaited chance to rule by playing the woman too much in earnest. John Knox, the great Scottish Protestant of his generation and an influential figure among the English reformers, attempted to disqualify

Queen Mary by composing a *Blast of the Trumpet Against the Monstrous Regiment of Women*. Although she had to cooperate with him to some extent politically, Queen Elizabeth never forgave Knox his opinion of female sovereigns.

Mary paid the unavoidable price of Roman Catholic restoration: holders of monastic lands were guaranteed their titles both by papal assurance and act of Parliament. Care was taken to confirm by statute those acts of the Henrician and Edwardian churches that affected people's ordinary lives, such as marriages and court judgments. With those prices paid, Mary's Parliament repealed all the Reformation legislation. England's reconciliation with Rome was elaborately recorded on the statute book. The Pope sent as his legate to England Reginald, Cardinal Pole, a symbolically appropriate choice since he was the queen's cousin and an internationally distinguished intellectual. He had long lived in exile, protesting the proceedings of his Tudor kin. Pole was too out of touch with England and too wanting in hard-nosed political sense to be a constructive influence on the queen. He was a fit person, however, to pronounce the realm absolved from sin and restored to concord with the Church. Parliament was less tractable and unanimous under Mary than it had been under Henry and Edward. There was one dangerous Protestant uprising ("Wyatt's Rebellion" in 1554). But in the upshot, Parliament supported the queen's policy, and the rising failed. The mixture of loyalism and indifference that allowed Mary to assume the throne allowed her to have her way.

The price of genuine and lasting reconciliation with Rome was higher than respect for vested interests. The queen's marriage to a suspect foreigner and England's consequent reinvolvement in an expensive and unsuccessful war with France did the Catholic cause immeasurable harm. Apart from that, wisdom would surely have been on the side of gradualism. Instead, Mary was precipitously repentant toward Rome and disastrously repressive toward the Protestants. The Protestants who could afford to go into exile were allowed to go. Exile disciplined an elite of brains and rank. Convictions toughened, familiarity with the continental reformers grew. As soon as they returned to England, the exiles would figure as a party of important people.

On those who stayed home, whether because they had no choice or because risk was more acceptable to their consciences than retreat, Queen Mary loosed religious persecution. If Mary had lived longer or produced a Catholic successor, heresy trials and the burning of those who would not abjure might have come to a successful reign of terror. As it turned out, Mary gave the Protestant movement its martyr-saints. They were not to be heroes of a lost cause but the inspiration of a party soon to be in power. Under Elizabeth, Protestantism triumphed as a cause that had come through the fire. Like the primitive Church it pretended to be, the Protestant Church of England sprang from the blood of its martyrs. An implacable popular hatred of Catholicism, fed on the remembered smell of burning flesh, was to bring suffering to many innocent Catholics through centuries of English history.

Four bishops and Archbishop Cranmer died for Protestantism. These men were also the martyrs of orthodox Protestant political theory. The bishops—especially Latimer and Ridley, who were burned at Oxford on the same occasion—acted out their duty according to script. No man, they believed, may resist or evade the secular authority God has placed over him. However, no man may deny the truth in obedience to secular authority: he should disobey passively and take the punishment, witness to the truth by suffering, and hope that his testimony will contribute to its victory in the end. Latimer and Ridley died with straightforward bravery and abundant hope for the future.

Cranmer went to his cross by a more tortuous road. Psychologically more tender than the others, Cranmer was subjected to more agonizing pressure to recant. He broke down and wrote a repudiation of his heresy, but that did not save him from the flames. At the stake, Cranmer repented his treason to the faith and thrust the hand that had written his recantation into the fire before it reached his body. His heroism was the greater for the weakness it overcame—and also, perhaps, for the doubt. Cranmer had never stood still in perfect certitude. He was perhaps neither wholly sure in religion nor wholly convinced in political theory. The script said, "Never resist, yet never obey an ungodly order." To Cranmer, it may not have looked that simple: however willing to pay the price of disobedience with one's body, one resists the authority in his heart by refusing to accept its version of the truth. If the heart cannot help itself, the lips at least can. Why should one presume in favor of his own judgment? Could God who puts kings over men not be speaking through them even when it does not seem so?

The formula of "passive disobedience" will not work for everyone. This is as true of modern men concerned with secular issues as it was for the sixteenth-century Protestants. Some will decide that "resist and take the consequences" goes too far, that authority's judgment—whether that of the democratic state because it is democratic or that of the Queen of England because she was God's viceregent—must be preferred to private conscience. Some will decide that the formula does not go far enough: Why not resist actively if one is prepared to resist at all? Among the exiles in Mary's reign, that question began to be asked. It began to be suggested that martyrdom might not be the only acceptable service. There is no surer way to make men doubt the formula of passive disobedience than burning fellow men before their eyes.

Save for the illustrious few, the victims of Mary's persecution were little people. That was the worst of it. There was a romantic fatalism in the sixteenth-century attitude toward those who achieve greatness. The

Burning of Father Latimer and Bishop Ridley: Latimer and Ridley were "major martyrs" of the Protestant cause and Protestant political theory. Foxe's *Book of Martyrs*, with such illustrations as this, created the heroic legend of English Protestantism. (Courtesy of the British Museum.)

Wheel of Fortune was a common image: Dame Luck spins her wheel, some men rise to power and prominence. She gives it another spin, and down they go. The erstwhile winners were expected to be good losers. Politicians who ended their careers on the scaffold met death in style—with heart-warming (or blood-chilling) valor, with loyal eloquence on their lips. Holy men bore witness to God's Word with their bodies at the last as they had with their tongues before: it was their role. When humble people went to the stake, they were not following so predictable a path. When ordinary men saw other ordinary men put to death, they saw naked cruelty and injustice. It was too late in English history for people to discount the suffering of innocuous victims as the due fate of heretics. Secularization— if that is the name for the belief that a man's moral conduct and social usefulness are more important than his religious opinions before the authorities of this world—had proceeded too far.

   The Marian persecution was not a holocaust. Authority was not vindictive nor contemptuous of due process. Protestant tradition exaggerated the number of victims. But do statistics matter? Is mythology not more important than fact? On her assumptions, Queen Mary did in sorrow what must be done to save souls and to return the realm to its duty. On Protestant assumptions, her work was the devil's. Should God's people take trouble to be fair to Satan? Should they not rather publish the enormity of his designs and the grace in Israel's deliverance?

No historical record was ever set down more promptly or more consequentially than that of the persecution. Nor has history ever been more quickly and decisively interpreted. Interpretation and myth-making were indistinguishable—perhaps they always are. The task of compiling the record and expounding the myth fell to John Foxe, a prominent Protestant exile and one of the most influential of English historians. Foxe's *Acts and Monuments* (popularly known as the *Book of Martyrs*) was first published in English in 1563 and republished time after time. Next to the Bible, it became the staple fare of English Protestants. As "English Protestants" gradually became almost synonymous with Englishmen, the *Book of Martyrs* grew into the marrow of national consciousness. It reached the borders of literate culture, for it was a book that people read who did not read much else. It celebrated the heroic age of English Protestantism and gave explicit shape to the sense that England was a chosen nation.

CHAPTER THREE

One may think of Tudor-Stuart history as having two major nuclei. The first we have described by the title "Renaissance and Reformation"; that nucleus is centered around the middle of the sixteenth century. The second is centered in the middle decades of the seventeenth century; it may be called the Great Rebellion, the Civil War, or the Puritan Revolution, but by any name it was the most serious civil disruption in English history. The in-between period is not less important for being less nuclear. The monarchs whose reigns define this chapter and the next symbolize two aspects of the intermediate period: consolidation on the one hand and the emergence of problems on the other.

Elizabeth I was a net success. Perhaps she was not the political genius some of her admirers depict; her reign was not the Golden Age that it appeared to be in the troubled perspective of the seventeenth century or the romantic one of later times. But Elizabeth comes out ahead on the only balance sheet applicable to this world. She lived a long time and never lost her grip on her job. She built up a great fund of credit in her subjects' affections. Even those she exasperated respected her; she played up to those whom patriotism, chivalry, and imagination disposed to idolize her; she was a woman of unmistakable intelligence and commanding personal presence. Her decisions were no more uniformly rational in motive than

Elizabethan–Jacobean England I: Equilibrium

those of other people, but they were pervasively reasonable. The problems she could not solve were swept neatly under the rug.

James I was a net failure. Many of the problems he faced were not his fault, but he lacked both the judgment to make the best of things and the art of distracting people from the issues. Elizabeth was a hard act to follow; James put a disreputable comedy on a stage long dominated by a *grande dame*. A duller man might have been more overwhelmed by financial crisis and political dissatisfaction, or he might have been more successful at such humdrum things as saving money and keeping the reputation of the court respectable. James was not dull, just mixed up and miscast. He was a foreigner—long experienced as King of Scotland, but battered by that tough apprenticeship. He was plagued by such ills of the psyche as mild alcoholism and homosexual leanings, as well as by a more diffuse instability. Although defensive about his authority, he was unable to make it felt. He took the dignity and responsibility of kingship very seriously, but he could not restrain his passion for amusement. He thought well of himself but was also insecure; a need to be loved and admired made him prey to flatterers.

Even so, James I does not emerge as pathetic. Brains and zest for life, often cleverly expressed, lifted him above his troubles. Partly because his talent was that of an intellectual rather than a statesman, his gifts were little help toward surmounting political crises. Even so, he had the skill to survive. He was a fit king for a restless age that was gathering to breakdown. Elizabeth was suited to a careful, consolidating time.

Despite their differences, Elizabeth and James fall within the same political framework. Their conceptions of the monarchy were similar. The seventeenth-century revolution broke the framework within which they operated. It was never really reconstructed. Compared to what went before, the Elizabethan-Jacobean framework was not radically new, but the cultural and religious changes of the earlier sixteenth century partly caused and partly cooperated with a significant restructuring. At Elizabeth's accession, the Tudor system of government was still inchoate; by the time of James I's reign it was becoming clear that the Tudor system would not work. Let us begin our discussion of the bridge period by looking at the changes and continuities in constitutional history during the sixteenth century.

Elizabeth I: The Spanish Armada, depicted in the background of this portrait, gave the queen her finest hour, but beneath the glorious surface her reign was entering its declining days. (Arthur J. Anderson.)

The Assumptions Underlying
the Tudor Constitution and Its Inheritance

The Tudors inherited a distinctive political tradition. In the words of Sir John Fortescue, who wrote in the reigns of Henry VI and Edward IV, England was a *dominium politicum et regale*—that is, England was a monarchy both strengthened and limited by popular elements in the constitution. Most people in the sixteenth and early seventeenth centuries agreed. Let us take a synoptic view of the assumptions and institutions that Tudor Englishmen inherited and—subject to the changes we shall examine in due course—passed on to their heirs.

The king was no figurehead, but he was not entitled to rule entirely by discretion. He was not beholden only to God nor bound only by moral standards. Rather, he was to administer the realm in accordance with English law. If that law was to be changed, the subjects' consent must be obtained—in practice, the consent of Parliament, where everyone was presumed to be represented. If the king needed money beyond his own income, he was obliged to obtain it through Parliament. These limits on the king were not considered derogations from his majesty. On the contrary, just *because* his subjects were safe from arbitrary legislation and taxation, the king should enjoy the clearest moral, legal, and material preeminence.

Every subject owed first allegiance to the king—a personal allegiance such as a vassal owes a lord or, since one is born to it, such natural obedience as a son owes his father. The administration of the law belonged to the king. Within the legal system, he was always titular judge (performing his duties in practice through professionally learned judges). Sometimes the king was plaintiff; he was never defendant. "The king can do no wrong" meant that he could never be sued in his courts. If a subject had a complaint against the king, he must petition him for redress. The king was obliged to render right, but he was not liable to submit to judgment like other people. The king's preeminence was intrinsic to the constitution of the realm. Desuetude and usurpation of royal rights were not supposed to affect it, however long the encroachment continued. However, the king was not free simply to take his own: if he had a complaint against a subject, however just, he must proceed by law.

Prevailing political theory emphasized the satanic wickedness of rebellion under any conditions; sinners should bear oppressive kings as God's chastisement. The other persuasion to patience was trust in God's providence: God will bring tyrants down eventually and restore the state of equilibrium in which decent kings enjoy their privileges without abusing them, and obedient subjects are rewarded by the enjoyment of their legal and participatory rights. Faith in the English balance between *politician* and *regale,* and the Christian balance between long-suffering and divine justice, was reinforced by the classical idea that a mixture of elements is the key to stability. England's "mixed constitution," with a place for the elements of monarchy, aristocracy, and democracy, was much prized. The components were urged to be their best selves and to stay within bounds; the system was supposed to have the balance that naturally resists disintegration. These strands of thought—native, Christian, classical—were mixed to form a syncretism. The components strengthened each other, but the mixture concealed contradictions and evaded hard questions.

In practice, the king held the leading role in the political process. Parliament, the living embodiment of the *politicum,* could meet only when the king summoned it and could stay in session only as long as he chose. The king had an absolute legislative veto. He was free to confer titles of honor and thus the right to sit in the House of Lords. He was also free to invite any number of new boroughs to send members to the House of Commons.

Offices in the government were essentially in the king's gift. His ministers were not subject to parliamentary confirmation or removal. Although offices were often in the nature of property (that is, the holder could not always be removed at will) and although some agencies of the government were so built into the legal structure that they could not be abolished by royal fiat, the king still enjoyed great freedom to reorganize the administration. The "civil service" consisted of the king's servants. There was no heavy line between public office and positions in the king's household, nor between state affairs and the king's private business.

The law, both the common law and the statutory law, was above the king, but as its supreme administrator he had considerable freedom to control its applied force. For example, he could pardon criminals, and, within limits, he could dispense with statutes. He could confer jurisdiction to administer the law, and he could exempt from public duties. He could alter a subject's legal position in minor ways by proclamation. As presiding officer of the legal system, the king was conceded a certain power to implement or "fill out" the law—typically, to regulate the economy in ways presumed to be endorsed by the law—without consulting Parliament.

Finally, the king was the "fountain of justice," in the sense that the aggrieved were always entitled to apply to him directly for relief. Turning to the king instead of the regular courts was supposed to be specially justified, but the idea that the king is available to the injured was so strong that the justification was not always scrutinized very closely. Sometimes an ordinary remedy was only nominally obtainable because of corruption or intimidation in the courts; sometimes a man without a chance at law might find common justice on his side. The king's power to intervene in cases of the latter sort was conceived as power to "mitigate the rigor of the law,"

An English court at the time of Henry IV. *Top:* five judges of the Court of King's Bench; *at left:* the jury; *in front:* the prisoners. The medieval common law, shown in action here, was the past's greatest bequest to Tudor-Stuart England. It continued to develop, but most of its essential forms remained. (The Masters of the Bench of the Inner Temple, London.)

which was distinguished from changing the law. By the beginning of the Tudor period, the royal power to administer justice in individual cases had been pretty well divorced from the king's person. This power was embodied in the king's council and his chancellor. (The chancellor specialized in claims calling for justice against the letter of the common law, and under that head developed the branch of Anglo-American law known as "equity.") However, the closeness of these organs, especially the council, to the king and the idea that the royal "fountain of justice" could never be shut off meant that the King had considerable freedom to reorganize and expand the capacity of extracommon law justice without consulting Parliament. This provided an indirect way for the king to alter substantive rights and liabilities.

The king's most unbounded area of discretionary power was in foreign affairs. If he was able to finance the enterprise, he was free to make war. He was commander-in-chief during war and could enforce his control by martial law. He could conclude peace whenever and on whatever terms he liked, and he could make any treaty commitments he saw fit. Foreign and military affairs were within the king's "absolute prerogative," meaning his discretion uncontrolled by law. (The absolute prerogative was contrasted with the king's "ordinary prerogative," a series of specific royal privileges that were simply part of the law.)

The modern idea that states are essentially dependent on taxes was foreign to sixteenth-century England. Tax income was regarded as supplementary income to meet special need. It was expected to be required at intervals. Good subjects should be generous. They should trust the king in the areas left to his discretion, and should not deny him money too blatantly in order to control him. On the other hand, the king should not be too demanding. He should live on his own income from day to day and make a bona fide case for special need when he requested a tax.

The king's dignity and authority, as well as his freedom in the areas left to his discretion, depended on his having reasonable financial autonomy. He should be rich enough to exercise his prerogatives without asking for help (and therefore a sort of permission), although his freedom should have limits. His wealth and style of life should greatly exceed that of his closest competitors in the aristocracy, although there should be a rich and powerful aristocracy between the king and the common people. No competitor should be so "overmighty" as to threaten law and order. No subject should be great enough to force himself and his clients on the king, thereby corrupting the state by private interest and infringing the king's control over his administration. Yet great men were needed to keep order in the localities—to do part of the job of government and to save the king expenses. They deserved recognition and reward for their contributions. A balance was the ideal: keeping enough weight on the king's side was as important as maintaining the aristocracy's side.

The king's income came first of all from the large portfolio of land in his direct possession. His position as ultimate landlord of all England under the still prevailing feudal-tenurial system of land law was a second source. Customs revenue was also in effect the king's own income. (Although most customs were in principle parliamentary taxes, they were in practice automatically voted to the king for life.) The legal system brought in appreciable income because the property of major criminals was often forfeited to the Crown, and fines were attached to lesser offenses.

These sources of income could vary widely in value. If the king owned a relatively large amount of land (as the Tudors did even before the dissolution of the monasteries, due to such factors as the forfeiture of huge estates for political crimes), he was relatively well-off. But perpetuation of a favorable position was not guaranteed. There was no legal restraint on the king's power to alienate the Crown's capital and income, although there were minor checks in the form of special procedural hurdles. It was not easy to manage the royal estates for maximum profit; the property was too large to keep track of perfectly by sixteenth-century techniques of management. Also, the king was under constant pressure to divert parts of his revenue to aristocrats and courtiers whose services called for reward, whose social position called for subsidy, or whose political support came at a price. The feudal revenue was by nature a windfall income. Its value varied with the government's administrative zeal, the ability of its lawyers, and the political advisability of pressing upper-class families. The legal system yielded income in proportion to the strictness of law enforcement—and the political feasibility of strictness.

Beside his straightforward income, the king had some questionable resources. Occasionally, he levied a "benevolence"; occasionally, a "forced loan." Since somewhere in the storehouse of law and politics, the king was sure to have means of causing unpleasantness to noncontributors, a wise man would eagerly chip in as little as possible. Benevolences and forced loans were never frequent and never regarded as unobjectionable. Yet the king was entitled to maintain his income. Although taxes were in theory free gifts, subjects were not morally free to withhold them too stubbornly. A benevolence or loan might amount to a tax on those relatively able to pay—perhaps a more rational tax than parliamentary subsidies, which were assessed by a fixed and obsolete system and weighted against the poorer property holder. In moderation and in the interest of balance, the king could strain a point. Another resource was the king's control over the monetary system. The privilege of coining precious metals into money, thereby authenticating their genuineness and giving the coin nominal value, was a royal monopoly. Matters of coinage were within the king's absolute prerogative, which meant that he was free to manipulate the currency—for example, by minting new money with less precious metal per nominal unit—to the advantage of debtors, including himself. Semilegal taxation, plus such honest loans as a king was able to arrange, plus currency manipulation usually gave the king reasonable room for maneuver apart from savings out of regular income and taxation. Reasonable room, but not much more, was what the king was supposed to have.

In theory, the king had power to conscript men and supplies for war, but that did not come to much. The law was somewhat unsettled; in practice, the king could not use his foreign and military powers to conscript an army and navy for overseas war at much less than the market price, although powers of impressment and commandeering could be used to supplement an essentially mercenary system. But men were forced to serve the king for home defense and order-keeping. The aristocracy often took care of these matters without being formally compelled to do so. There was no standing army requiring a regular military budget, although strongholds and stockpiles of weapons had to be maintained. There was no police force, and much civil service was furnished for nothing. Some of the king's income was derived from the absence of what we would consider normal expenses of government; some of his "expenses" consisted of leakage of income to aristocrats, from whom, however, he obtained at least partial value in service.

When cash came to the king, it was his to save or spend. Taxes were not appropriated to particular purposes, and no income was earmarked for public expenditures. If the king spent too much on pleasure, ostentation, largesse, and adventure, Prudence might shake her head, but Law made no complaint. A king who neglected "public relations" on his side of the balance by failing to cut a magnificent figure and to build up a loyal and decorative aristocratic backing let monarchy down as much as one who impoverished the Crown. To maintain the regal side of *dominium politicum et regale* took luck. It also took careful mixing of the components of royal strength: wealth and expensive prestige, homely pacific virtue and the profit and glamor of war.

Tudor Innovations in Government

With the above picture of continuing assumptions and institutions in mind, we may examine the changes the Tudors made within the inherited framework.

The sixteenth century was a decisive period in the history of Parliament. The Tudors did not alter the basic rules: Parliament's right to consent to taxation and legislation, its dependence on the king. They did permit it to become a different kind of institution with an altered sense of itself. They helped Parliament become a stronger embodiment of the *politicum*, a more active counterforce to the *regale*. In a sense, the Tudors nurtured a son toward the fateful day when father and son must wrestle. But the process was not simple. It is useful to distinguish what Henry VIII's reign meant for Parliament from what Elizabeth's reign meant; the partially contradictory tendencies of the two reigns both contributed to Parliament's development.

How often should Parliament meet? How much legislation and taxation should there be? Is the ideal of a mixed political system better served by a fairly constant "parliamentary presence," or by regarding Parliaments as occasional assemblies? One answer is as follows: although legislation is necessary to correct abuses from time to time, the legal system is sanctified by long usage and universal acceptance. It can hardly need much legislative tinkering. Abuses are often correctable in other ways: by the monarch's power to implement the law in detail and mitigate its rigor, by the courts' duty to apply it intelligently. Something is wrong if taxes have to be imposed frequently. Why then should Parliament meet often? If it has to meet often, the reason must be "to give the monarch general advice, to keep him in touch with public opinion." Those sound like useful functions. In moderation, they are. But the monarch is trusted to rule within the law and his resources. A wise monarch will want advice, but need he invite it indiscriminately? Should he not be free if he chooses to rely mainly on his council? If Parliament has to be endured when it is not wanted, will it not tie the monarch's hands? For example, will the king be free to exercise independent judgment in foreign affairs and walk the intricate and secret paths of diplomacy if affairs of state are being publicly discussed by an ill-informed and perhaps divided assembly? Therefore, Parliament should not meet too often. It should not think of itself as entitled to give unlimited advice. Otherwise, the *regale* will suffer more than the *politicum* gains.

Such, in effect, was the opinion of Queen Elizabeth and James I. Henry VII would have had no quarrel with it. But the reign of Henry VIII came after Henry VII's and before Elizabeth's. Due to no theory or intention so much as to the exigencies of the Reformation and the ease of securing Parliament's cooperation, Henry VIII's reign and the ensuing brief reigns of Edward VI and Mary made the "parliamentary presence" a fact of life. But it was not a fact of long enough duration to gain the force of prescription. Elizabeth's return to more occasional Parliaments was not disapproved. However, Parliament's heavy activity and involvement with momentous issues during the Reformation decades had effects. The prestige of being a member of Parliament gained with the collective prestige of the institution. People could see that legislation need not be confined to patching up the venerable body of the law—that it can indeed reshape life. A stronger sense of the importance of Parliament, the experience that members gained by attending its sessions—the day-to-day tangles of a body in regular operation—led to institutionalization. Procedure became more formalized and the niceties of procedure became more interesting to members. Corporate pride was reflected in a touchier concern for "privilege"—the freedom of members to speak their minds with impunity, to avoid some forms of arrest during Parliament, and to determine such matters as challenged elections. (All of these were liberties whose exact bounds were disputable.) Experienced members came to identify themselves as "Parliament men" and to regard themselves as experts in "the law and custom of Parliament." These developments were not sudden, nor were they consolidated in the reigns of Henry VIII, Edward VI, and Mary. The conspicuous importance of Parliament in those reigns gave an impulse to the Elizabethan Parliaments. Although Parliament did not meet as often as before, continuity was not lost during Elizabeth's reign. The institutionalizing process continued through long, stable years and was abetted by new developments.

The Elizabethan phase of Parliament's development was nourished by conflict. The queen held a conservative view of Parliament's role in the face of an emergent counteropinion, which divisive religious issues stimulated. Although Elizabeth tried to avoid too many Parliaments, she fully recognized the wisdom of taking counsel with her subjects and of allowing members of Parliament to have their place in the sun. But when Elizabeth faced Parliaments, she faced troublemakers, which is close to saying that she faced Puritans. Those who wanted further reformation in the Church were represented in Parliament. Hard-line Puritans were a small minority, but their zeal made them persistent; their determined interest in their program made them act in a more partylike way than was quite respectable in sixteenth-century politics. The queen refused to consider the Puritan demands in substance, and, in addition, she took the position that religious affairs, being subject to the monarch as sole Supreme Head, should not be discussed in Parliament without invitation. In short, the queen made an issue. Perhaps it would have been wiser not to have done so, for where there was a constitutional issue opposition to the monarch's point of view would spread beyond those intent on revising the Church settlement.

Elizabeth's general theory was that Parliament should not discuss matters within the areas left to the royal prerogative. Unless invited to do so, they should not discuss those matters with a view toward legislating; much less should they discuss them merely to register dissent or to prod the monarch with unwanted advice. The queen's theory provoked an answer: Parliament's traditional freedom of speech means that members have a right to introduce legislation on any topic and to say what they think in connection with any proposed legislation. For that matter, freedom of speech includes the right to resolve, to address the monarch with expressions of solicitude for the nation, and simply to discuss. Surely the representatives of the country meet to let it be known what the country is worried about, to make the unity of monarch and people a reality based on communication.

Parliament men who were not Puritans were attracted to the theory that expressed the greater trust in Parliament's capacity for participation. Issues beyond the Church extended the conflict between the royal position and Parliament's corporate pride. Parliament men shared with other subjects the hope that the queen would marry, or at least that she would settle the succession. That hope was most intense among the staunchest Protestants, for whom the danger of a Catholic claimant was most terrifying, but one did not have to be a Puritan to dread the Pope and civil trouble. While Parliament publicly urged the queen to marry and to do something about the succession, Elizabeth maintained that those matters were outside its jurisdiction. She naturally felt her marriage to be a personal concern, and she may have had qualms about usurping the place of God in choosing her successor. The real strength of her position, however, was that negotiations for a royal marriage belonged to foreign policy. The question of succession also had diplomatic implications. Such matters had to be governed by considerations of "policy"—in Elizabethan usage, a word close to "strategy," requiring secrecy. The queen had excellent reasons for her attitude, but her theory of Parliament's role was hard for its members to accept.

Conflict carried the maturation of Parliament forward in Elizabeth's reign as the absence of conflict had fostered its growth before. Parliamentarians thought and cared more about their privileges as they were challenged. Parliament's earlier participation in religious affairs (and also its recognition of royal marriages and its settlement of the succession) put the queen in a reactionary light. The enhanced sense of national unity in a common Protestant faith made the queen's insistence on separating the spheres of monarch and people seem gratuitous. Meanwhile, other changes reinforced Parliament's accumulating self-confidence.

The royal power to create noblemen, and so add to the House of Lords, was used sparingly by the Tudors. At the beginning of the Tudor period, bishops and abbots, essentially royal appointees, were a majority of the House of Lords; the number of lay peers was low. The Reformation changed the picture by sweeping the abbots away. New growth by the ennoblement of laymen was slow. Elizabeth was reluctant to create noblemen with status beyond their resources, and she did not want to spend her own resources to endow new nobility. There were great advantages in having no more titled noblemen than one could take care of. A moderate number of peers could be provided with public employment and dignities; each could have his share of privilege, graft, and patronage without impoverishing the Crown or making slighted grandees restive. The Elizabethan nobility was small enough for most noblemen to have a role in the government and hope of serving their self-interest by court politics. Most new creations earned their titles and riches in the queen's service, and most noblemen identified with the government's policies and with its executive distaste for parliamentary meddling.

The story of the House of Commons is different. Conflict with Queen Elizabeth was concentrated there, for the lower house was emerging into unprecedented independence and standing. Elizabeth's reign was the chief period of the house's quantitative expansion, and qualitative changes accompanied it. Basically, the supply of borough seats was increased to meet demand. The demand did not come from people who lived by their trades in the towns, which were nominally represented, but rather from gentlemen who wanted seats for themselves and from noblemen who wanted seats for their clients, relatives, and factional confederates. Gentlemen were better educated and more aspiring to a public role. London and the court grew more sophisticated and exciting as gentlemen grew less content with country life from birth to death. The regular royal service could not accommodate all the well-born people who hankered for a wider stage than their manors and local societies furnished, nor all those whom noblemen and courtiers might wish to favor. Many of these born into the fast-breeding gentry managed to stay gentle, while others less well-born bought their way into land and gentility. There were large "county societies" of socially prestigious and wealthy people—"nests of gentlefolk"—competing with each other and forming factions. New ways to compete and new ways to score in the scramble for status, whether for oneself or for a noble patron, were needed. More seats in the Commons were a good way to satisfy these needs. They cost the Crown nothing in money.

A larger House of Commons, with more men of notable ability and men who enjoyed the confidence of class and local success, naturally took a more generous view of the house's privileges than the queen did. Even so, conflict stayed within bounds during Elizabeth's reign. Aggressive dissenters remained a minority. Many aristocratic M.P.s were uninterested in politics, uncertain of their opinions, and unwilling to offend the queen. They could often be swayed by oratory, but in the end they could usually be brought around by governmental pressure, including the queen's special blend of sweet talk and tantrum, and by the managerial arts of Parliament's most professional members, the queen's privy councillors. Basically, the government had a reliable majority without resort to the hard-nosed game of electioneering and party building by patronage that politicians of a later day would master. Queen Elizabeth would not have approved of that game, for her theory of Parliament came to a "separation of powers" position: Parliament and the monarchy should stay in their respective territories; each should be free in its sphere. The mutual trust required to make such a system work was basically present in Elizabeth's reign, although by insisting on her theory the queen helped Parliament develop counterattitudes that later subverted it.

In administration, the sovereign's control over government was exercised constructively and to the monarchy's advantage in the Tudor period. Up to the 1530s the method of government was flexible and personal. The king had a large official council, partly honorific and functional mainly as a judicial body. The royal servants who counted in daily decision making were those who unofficially had the king's confidence and who worked closely with him. A system that was not too heavy with bureaucracy made it possible to reorganize and tighten the conduct of business. The Exchequer was a slow-moving old lady. In the early sixteenth century, the larger part of the king's revenue bypassed the Exchequer and went straight into the king's chamber, nominally a treasury for the king's household and other immediate expenses. The chamber was more accessible to the king's personal supervision and to ad hoc reorganization, and it was easier to move money through it. Under Henry VII and the early Henry VIII there was a good deal of inventiveness aimed at dividing the chamber's revenue into still smaller and more manageable units—in effect, committees to keep tabs on particular kinds of income and to enforce collection. New permanent bureaus were avoided, but a kind of specialization was developing. Henry VII's financial success testifies in favor of both the informality and the organization of his system.

The Reformation and Thomas Cromwell's hegemony saw further movement—in a sense, in the same direction and, in a sense, in a contradictory one. The confiscation of First Fruits and Tenths and then of monastic land brought the Crown new classes of income and bundles of property. The wisdom of special agencies to handle limited types of revenue was increasingly appreciated. Bureaus were created by act of Parliament to administer the new riches. Here was a note of change: statutory agencies apparently meant to be permanent made the government less malleable in the king's hands. Reorganization was also legislated for older classes of revenue already regarded as ad hoc specialties. Cromwell's administrative style and circumstances explain the new approach. He understood the value of legal craftsmanship in the dangerous matters of religious revolution. It was a good idea to put the power to deal with expropriated property on the firmest legal basis. The new agencies were to have judicial powers, which of course should rest on an indisputable warrant. Cromwell also understood that a presiding administrator can be more effective if subordinate agencies have a guaranteed place and defined powers. Parliament perhaps appreciated having a hand in administrative reorganization as in so many other state affairs. Perhaps the creation of new offices for the indefinite future was welcome to the class that would aspire to fill them.

Yet, although there was a strain of counterpoint to the tradition of flexible royal government, a lasting new order hardly emerged. The advantages of fractionating revenue, accounting, and jurisdiction were appreciable but not overwhelming. In 1554, after substantial liquidation of the monastic haul, the new bureaus were abolished, save for the Court of Wards, which handled the feudal revenue. Their functions were reabsorbed by the Exchequer. Centralization won out, but so did bureaucracy, against the more maneuverable chamber system. The Court of Wards survived to the mid-seventeenth century—more a hotbed of corruption and private profiteering than a steady enforcer of the king's rights. On the whole, the strength of Tudor financial administration was its capacity for change and experiment in various directions.

The most striking governmental change—a basic reorganization of the king's council—was pioneered under Henry VIII and confirmed under Elizabeth. The council was greatly reduced in size and compartmentalized to perform two functions separately. It is conventional to speak of the shrunken body as the privy council. In its Elizabethan heyday, the privy council was small enough (a dozen plus) to function continuously as a unit. Its members—some leading officeholders, some professional royal servants whose main job was to serve on the council, some noblemen— were expected to work regularly at the two aspects of their assignment.

The privy council met frequently, almost daily much of the time, to perform the first of its functions, political and administrative duties. The same men also met at regular times (certain days of the week during the periods of the year when the ordinary law courts were in session) to perform the council's second function, the judicial. When serving as a court, it came to be called (after its meeting-place) the Court of Star Chamber.

As an organ of administration, the Elizabethan privy council was a distinctive institution. The monarch did not attend the council's regular meetings. It was not a standing committee to give the queen direct advice on the matters she had to decide. The tradition of informality still prevailed at the top. (One official, the secretary, grew in importance as the monarch's direct assistant.) Although the privy council discussed high affairs of state and many lower-level matters that reached it by one route or another, its formal role was chiefly to handle the stream of complaints that flowed to the Crown and to serve as an "internal security" board. Complaints that required judicial disposition were redirected to the regular courts (including the Star Chamber, for some misdemeanors and trespasses), but many private quarrels, official malfeasances, disputes over economic privileges, and the like that were brought before the council could be dealt with in a sub-judicial (although often nearly mandatory) way. In addition, much of the council's energy went into searching out and investigating reports of spies and conspirators—in other words, performing a police function in a police-less society, including the exaction of confessions by torture. Apart from its specific work, the reorganized privy council was an advantage for royal government, for it assumed some of the queen's burdens without threatening her control. By functioning regularly and collectively, it gave the government a sense of oneness and enlarged the aura of the state. A board of dignitaries with power presented a solemn symbol to those who came into its presence, whether a trembling subject or an honored ambassador.

To summarize, Parliament gained corporate strength in the sixteenth century, but its subordination to the Crown was never more insisted on than under Queen Elizabeth. The administration became more institutionalized, but thereby it enabled the monarch to govern an increasingly complicated society more effectively. Royal government rose to the challenge of a larger population than the kings of the past had had to keep in order. Internal peace and law-abidingness probably surpassed the medieval norm. Although conflict was more widespread than ever—there were more people jostling each other, in their native quarrelsome spirit, within a richer web of economic interests and social ambition—that conflict was increasingly channeled into litigation and political rivalry. The government was able to expand the facilities for peaceful contention and to crack down on lawless violence. The royal side of government—executive and legal—needed to be asserted; it was asserted in new ways without becoming less royal.

At the same time, the royal side of the constitutional balance was becoming economically lighter. The monarchy's sixteenth-century success story is a tale of impending material crisis. Henry VIII's youth robbed him of one fortune; in his old age he squandered another. The spoliation of the monasteries was an unprecedented and unrepeatable chance to endow the Crown. The political reasons for selling the spoil were excellent; the political reasons for wasting the proceeds—another pointless war against France—were nil. Henry VIII sold out his cherished heirs. From mid-century, the path could only go downhill, although Elizabeth did her best to slow the descent.

The serious monetary inflation from about 1540 greatly increased the Crown's expenses, as it did those of everyone else. On the income side, the Crown's problem of keeping up with inflation was special. Inflation was not bad for landowners, of which the Crown was the greatest. In fact, the inflation of the sixteenth century was good for them, since an increased quantity of money was accompanied by sharp population growth and no basic rise in agricultural productivity. Because people need food before anything else and because more people were pursuing an inelastic supply of food, agricultural prices rose more than prices of manufactured goods and labor. Landowners who looked after their interests could collect their share from agricultural prosperity by raising their rents and finding tenants who could farm profitably and pay higher rent. But it took good management to survive. Inflation separated the landowning sheep from the landowning goats. To maintain reasonable economic independence, the Crown needed to be a sheep; in fact, it was the worst of goats.

Large landowners as a group were slower to adjust than were more modest ones. It was harder for them to economize, to keep an eye on all parts of large portfolios, to avoid being ill-served by the employees they relied on. Yet in the end the larger private landowners came through successfully. To tide them over, they had access to credit, to supplementary income from public employment, and to profitable connections in the business world. Being a great man in the world of court and metropolis was expensive, but fashionableness and power in a political mechanism lubricated by influence were also keys to opportunity. The chance to marry money or to merge landed holdings by the conquest of heiresses was not the least advantage of being a distinguished match. The best legal advice and estate management were ultimately most available to the rich and sophisticated, but it took time for the techniques of lawyers and agents to catch up with the complexities of big, heterogeneous estates. On the whole, it took all of the sixteenth century and some of the seventeenth.

The Crown was the extreme example. The monarch was supposed to be a much bigger landowner than his nearest rivals. So he was, but he had a more miscellaneous collection of interests, each with its own legal and economic peculiarities. He had much temporary property, such as wards' land, neither as manageable nor as worth the price of managing as permanent holdings. He had a larger administration, and the administrators were political appointees, who felt the pressures of politics as well as the temptation to corrupt practices. And the top level of government was necessarily preoccupied with more urgent matters than economics. If it took large private landowners time to adjust, it would take the Crown longer. Although expedients and credit were more available to the Crown than to the greatest subject, the monarchy never got the needed crucial breathing space. By the time large private owners succeeded in overcoming their problems, the Crown's prospects had been ruined by erosion of its capital base.

Under Elizabeth, the fault was not extravagance. The queen managed to stay out of war for nearly thirty years. She paid the price of aristocratic political support, but in such a way as to get her money's worth, for she had to an almost neurotic degree the parsimonious instincts that her situation required. But in the end came the war against Spain and "colonial war" in Ireland which occupied the last fifteen years of Elizabeth's reign. The absolute price of war had risen considerably over the sixteenth century with increasing fire power and oceangoing ships. As popular as the war was and as heroic as the queen's victorious reputation was, there was no chance of financing war from taxation. The tax system was obsolete and stereotyped; it would not yield anything like the percentage of national wealth it was nominally supposed to yield. Although the Elizabethan economy was stable and moderately expansive, real national wealth had not grown fast, relative to population. The distribution of wealth had become more lopsided. Yet the rich felt poor in a time of inflation, rising standards of consumption, and estate building. However heartily they supported the government, the rich would not pay the bills. The monarch, who was responsible for defending the realm, had to pay a disproportionate share and to sell property for that purpose. By the end of Elizabeth's reign, the ideal of reasonable financial independence for the Crown was slipping into fantasy.

Elizabeth I:
Order Realized. Order in Peril

In Elizabeth's old age, English political society was assuming an unhealthy complexion. It was fittingly presided over by an old lady who could not kiss her girlhood goodbye—a skinny, wrinkled old lady dressed up in jewels and brocade. On the surface, glamor was never thicker. The tensions and dangers of the reign seemed dissolved. Some of the queen's subjects still had reasons, and new reasons, to criticize her, but in her triumph she stood forgiven—"a great old girl," we might say: to her contemporaries, she was "Gloriana, the Fairy Queen." Set in her ways and unrelenting in her prejudices she might be, but she was old—old but not weary, impressive as ever, and more formidable for the rich political experience and deserved success that set her off from all the world. She had passed many trials, and in her finest hour she had outfaced death. For in 1588, when the great Spanish Armada with an invading army behind it lay off the southern coast, she had stood at the head of her people, hammering resolution home with ringing eloquence. The *prima donna* had commanded the stage, had given English valor and Protestant zeal their cue. Her courage was convincing because it was real. Now, the crisis victoriously past, she stood at the head of a Protestant crusade and a thriving national enterprise. She summed up England in her mythic person. That, after all, was what monarchy was about—not Puritans and Parliament men, court factions and public finance. Among English monarchs, a capricious, flirtatious, secretive, cautious, temperamental, indecisive, bluestocking spinster was the last of the great captains, her father's daughter and the last of her line.

A skinny, wrinkled old lady dressed up in jewels and brocade: sadness underneath the glamor; worms gnawing at the flesh, moths wasting the vesture; the slow encroachment of economics and ideas; the space of free monarchy—moral and material space—closing in. The stage was more cramped, with less room for heroes and actresses. Let us look at the other side of the late-Elizabethan coin.

We have noted the deterioration of the Crown's material base. A poorer government with a war to pay for was all the more afflicted by the demands of aristocratic personal politics. Elizabeth had been artful at keeping the powerful happy. She had not overexpanded the titular aristocracy. She had apportioned favor and payoff among different factions, minimizing jealousy, promoting peaceful competition, keeping the grandees loyal to her. Toward the end of her reign, demand began to overtake supply: more gentlemen had aspirations to shares of a diminishing pie; winners and losers in the sweepstakes of court politics were more visibly distinct.

It is symptomatic that Elizabeth's last quarrel with Parliament was over monopolies granted by royal charter—a device for rewarding courtiers while making a little money (by charging something for the privilege), as well as a way of regulating the economy. The legality of monopolies was questionable, and they were offensive both to unlucky favor-seekers who failed to get them and to people injured in their trades. In the upshot, the queen was forced to cancel several monopolies in the face of Parliament's complaint and was defeated in a test case brought in hope of vindicating her prerogative to grant them.

Since 1570 England had been free from rebellion; in 1600 the specter reappeared. Let us sketch the intervening time. The first decade of Elizabeth's reign was a continuation of the unsettled mid-century period. It remained uncertain whether the queen's decision for Protestantism, and for a particular brand of it, would last. Her marriage was never so open a question as in her youth. The character of the reign would obviously vary according to the husband she was sooner or later expected to choose.

Court factions were not the same as religious parties, but in those days they had religious rallying points. Since the Henrician Reformation, there had been a conservative faction—Catholic in doctrine and taste, if not Roman Catholic. In the early Elizabethan years, conservatism was most identified with the old noble houses enjoying territorial hegemony in the North of England. On the other side, there were aristocratic families and rising royal servants with a clearer Protestant identity than that of the queen, among them exiles from Mary's reign. In 1569 a complex struggle over factional influence and religion eventuated in the major Elizabethan rebellion: a pro-Catholic, antigovernment rising led by the northern earls. It was successfully and savagely put down. The back of the old-fashioned superaristocracy, as well as the spirit of the North, was finally broken.

The Pope, who had so far kept a door to England open, excommunicated Elizabeth in 1570. Commitment to Protestantism was final. In the wake of rebellion, the evil of disloyalty was never more vigorously preached. In the wake of deliverance from popery and rebel noblemen, that preaching was largely to the converted. A spirit more authentically Elizabethan than the swashbuckling mood of the war at the end of the reign prevailed during its middle years. It expressed the queen's temper and that of her best servants. The 1570s and early 1580s were not without tensions, but they were the "plateau" years of the reign, a time of external peace, moderate prosperity, loyalism and royalism. By and large, people minded their business and respected a government that knew its business.

The queen was in her prime. So were the able men, her contemporaries, who served her. They served her well partly because they talked the same language. The most outstanding man was William Cecil, later Lord Burghley, Elizabeth's confidential adviser from her youth, for many years principal secretary and then lord treasurer. No single man was a first minister under Elizabeth in the way Wolsey and Thomas Cromwell had been under Henry VIII, but Cecil came close. He did not always agree with the queen, but he was wholly loyal to her and thoroughly compatible—painstaking, practical, cautious, given to a courtierly indirection and subtlety concordant with like qualities in his mistress. Although he made a fortune from public service and founded an aristocratic dynasty, he more than paid for it in hard work and disinterested counsel. Behind Cecil stood men of similar stamp, the ablest second echelon in the Tudor-Stuart period—courtiers all, as one had to be, but also sober, responsible officials—men like Sir Nicholas Bacon (father of the famous Sir Francis) at the chancery, or Sir Francis Walsingham, after Cecil the man who did most with the office of secretary. Over against Cecil and others like him stood the prime courtier and favorite, Robert Dudley, Earl of Leicester, son of the Edwardian minister Northumberland. Leicester had been a strong candidate for Elizabeth's hand; he was the one suitor she would probably have married for love had not a tangle of politics and scandal prevented it. (The scandal was the suspicious death of his first wife by apparent suicide when the tide of his fortune was rising.) But Leicester remained at the top of court society after his big chance had passed. He was a scheme-spinning courtier of great "interest" (connections and influence on the patronage side of government). Although what he used his interest for was often not to the queen's taste (he favored the Puritans in religious politics), she was comfortable with his type. Whatever more she saw in him, they were contemporaries bound by personal loyalty.

Elizabeth and the politicians closest to her were of a generation. They had grown up in a time of political insecurity and religious contention. They were in positions of responsibility during the last phase of the time of troubles, and they had come through. No wonder they were play-it-safe people. Stability and order were the things they valued most, having known their absence. Deviousness and double-talk suited them: avoid commitment, look at all sides, keep several balls in the air, watch your step.

One sixteenth-century response to politico-religious turbulence was the posture known in France as that of the *politiques*. A *politique* did not think any religious cause worth a high price in civil disquiet; he need not favor formal religious toleration, but he could consider it as an option; he was fairly tolerant at heart, for his heart was secular; he made the unideological moves of the political game and accepted its dissimulation and compromise in order to contain ideology within the bounds of peace. There was a good deal of the *politique* in Elizabeth and her servants; the middle-of-the-road religious settlement expressed *politique* values. Elizabeth was tolerant of private differences of religious opinion; she was even willing to blink at the legally penalized Catholics when they gave no sign of political disloyalty. She had no sympathy for Puritans whose commitment led them to disregard, flaunt, or agitate for changing the rules of the established Church. Quiet submission to law and authority was the test of civic virtue. As a group, the queen's chief advisers, even men as close to her as Cecil and Leicester, were more open than their mistress to the religious left. But the difference was not fundamental. The statesmen's duplicity sometimes concealed their partial disagreement with the queen, but it also expressed their own hesitation between the Protestant and the *politique*. The latter strain was the deeper one in a generation that believed above all in not rocking the boat.

The same mood prevailed in the country. The hard-core Elizabethan age was not exciting. Respectable conservatism, acceptance of a world that could be worse, national smugness, and the devoted pursuit of self-interest were the predominant attitudes. The fruits of the Renaissance and Reformation were gathered into barns. Protestantism worked itself into the bone as prejudice and stock response. The established Church gained firmer adherents as people became used to it and as it became a focus of patriotism in the face of attack. A period distinguished for its statesmen was relatively undistinguished for creative spirits. Yet the fruits of humanism were ripening in the consolidation and diffusion of educational improvement. Indeed, humanism was never more truly ascendant—not humanism at its most stimulating, but at its most authentic. Humanism belongs in a statesman's world. Civic spirit, moral decorum, moderation, and cultivated intelligence with a practical slant—such were its virtues. The hard-core Elizabethan age was blessed by outward security and blighted by an inward fear of disorder. It was blessed by high, if limited, standards. It was the breeding ground of perhaps the most creative generation in English history, the active generation of Elizabeth's old age and her successor's reign. She was not at home with that generation, although she were its "Fairy Queen."

Even so, the Elizabethan plateau had its tensions. Most of all, there was continuing fear of Catholic conspiracy. The internally reformed papacy was newly dedicated to fighting back against the heretics. Many of the Roman Catholics in England were simply loyal subjects, content to accept the semitoleration in the private practice of religion that the government preferred to accord them, which it did partly in the hope that their resistance to the state Church would eventually wither away. Others, affected by the new wave of zeal in the international Church, were wary of just such a withering-away. Their immediate object was to keep the Catholic faith alive. Neither in reality nor in the eyes of Protestants could that aim be separated from hope that the political wind might turn in favor of the Catholics. How long would Elizabeth last? What would happen afterward? Even to ask those questions looked subversive from the Protestant-patriotic vantage point. Some of those who asked them became involved in plots for hastening the day—ranging, as plots will do, from semifantasy to dangerous schemes. Rome and Catholic intellectuals had given countenance to the view that notoriously bad princes, especially heretics, may justly be killed or overthrown. Official Elizabethan doctrine was "nonresistance" with added force because alternative political theories were associated with popery. Popular prejudice assumed all Catholics to hold an immoral doctrine of political violence. That was unfair, but appearances and some reality supported the notion. In the 1570s and 1580s, a Catholic counteroffensive was manifestly going on. Young priests from the English Catholic community were trained abroad, some in the militant Jesuit order. They came home as missionaries dedicated to keeping the faith alive. Necessarily, they came as thieves in the night. Politics and religion would have had to be more separable than they were for the secret agents of Rome to be taken as anything but saboteurs. The missionary-priests were brave men. Many of them died victims of the stepped-up measures of repression adopted by Parliament and the government after 1570. Some priests were involved in plots, but more were caught in the nets of their situation—not really doing anything subversive but inevitably assumed to be; hoping for an eventual political change abhorrent to the majority; not "loyal" as flag-wavers mean it; uncertain about what opportunities to further the cause would come along; tempted to believe that active resistance was a right and perhaps a duty, but aware of the moral and practical pitfalls in the way. The priests and their harborers were hounded by law that did not discriminate between clear and present dangers and political witchcraft.

The Catholic cause had its focus in Mary Stuart, the deposed Queen of Scotland. Because she represented the senior line of descent from Henry VII, Mary was the rightful Queen of England on the Catholic premise that Henry VIII's second marriage was invalid. On neutral premises, she had the best claim to succeed if Elizabeth should die without issue. Since 1568 she had been in England—accessible to Catholics and political malcontents and also in Elizabeth's power.

From the later years of Henry VIII's reign, a struggle had been waged between France and England for control of Scotland. Shortly after Elizabeth's accession, England substantially won the contest by cooperating with the Scottish Protestants. Mary was a Catholic, firmly tied to the French interest. (She had been brought up in France and had first married the French King Francis II, who died in 1560.) In 1567, as an immediate result of her suspected complicity in the murder of her second husband, Henry Darnley, and as an indirect result of the Protestant party's power, Mary was forced to abdicate in favor of her infant son, James VI, the future James I of England. After an unsuccessful try at a comeback, she fled to England, where she was received as a refugee and held as a prisoner.

Mary was involved in the schemes of the 1569 rebels and later in several plots. For more than a decade and a half, she was regarded with mounting suspicion. Most politicians favored getting rid of her, but Elizabeth stubbornly protected her. Queen Elizabeth was a monarchist and a legitimist. The way the Scottish Protestants had treated Mary met with no favor in her eyes. In addition, Elizabeth acknowledged that Mary had the best title to the English throne after her own. In the end, Elizabeth worked quietly to insure that Mary's Protestant son would succeed to England. Yet Elizabeth was not finally able to save Mary Queen of Scots. In 1587, when Mary was caught unmistakably in a conspiracy and the showdown between England and Catholic Spain was approaching, Elizabeth gave her reluctant consent to Mary's execution.

By the mid-1580s, Elizabeth's noninterventionist foreign policy was breaking down. The war with Spain had approached by a long route. England's alignment had been basically anti-French up to the early years of Elizabeth's reign. Notwithstanding religion, Spain and the other Hapsburg states (the latter partitioned since Charles V) were the stars of the anti-French constellation, at the edges of which England shone with varying intensity. Starting in the 1560s, France was torn by religious wars and aristocratic factional feuding. She was substantially neutralized as a danger to England and Spain. Spain was liberated to become *the* Catholic power—

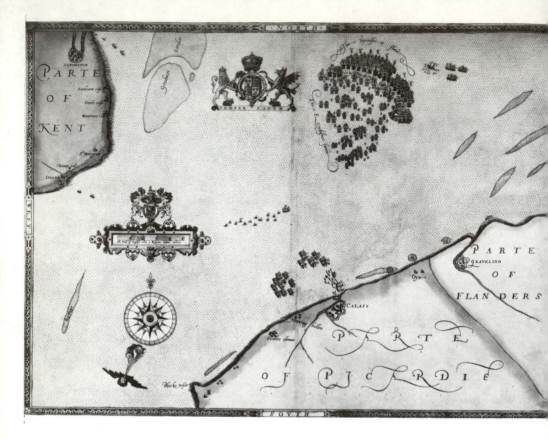

Map of the Armada by Ryther, from "A Genuine and Most Important Narration of the Glorious Victory": The Spaniards looked out to England from their base in the Netherlands, whence an invasion would have been launched if the Armada had succeeded. (Courtesy of the British Museum.)

whatever political meaning that might have. It turned out to have a great deal. Behind Philip II's ultimate decision to invade England lay a long history of hoping and planning by the papacy and the English Catholics under the leadership of their chief-in-exile, William, Cardinal Allen. Philip was susceptible to the crusading role, but the Armada was also the product of a deterioration of Anglo-Spanish political relations.

The decisive event was the drawn-out revolt of the Protestant Dutch against their Spanish masters, starting in the late 1560s. Elizabeth's non-interventionism was not neutralism. Both religion and England's political and economic interest in a friendly Netherlands put her on the side of the Dutch, and Elizabeth tried to use influence and pressure to persuade Philip to make peace with the Dutch on terms favorable to their aspirations. If estrangement from Spain was not inevitable for Protestant England, then Elizabeth's policy contributed to estrangement. If it was inevitable, then she helped the Dutch a little and let them fight her war.

Spain had become progressively exasperated with England. The famous seadogs Sir John Hawkins and Sir Francis Drake contributed to that.

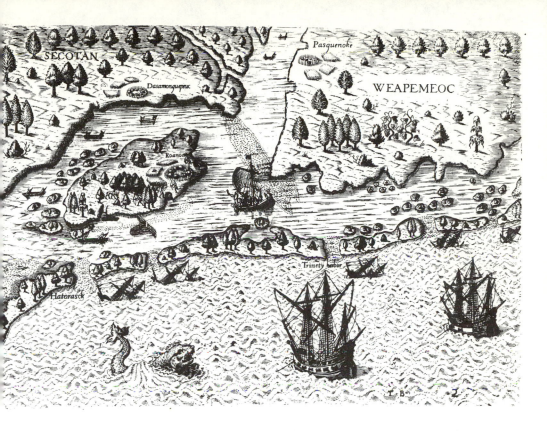

Landing at Roanoke, Virginia: England's imperial history lay decades ahead of the first tentative attempts to settle Virginia, but those beginnings are an important sign of the awakening of an oceanic power. (Courtesy of the British Museum.)

England under the Tudors was a tardy imperial power. Although the voyages of the Cabots put her in touch with North America before the turn of the sixteenth century, England had shown no significant interest in colonial expansion during the period when Spain and Portugal built their South American empires and achieved European greatness from the gold and silver of the Indies. Only in Elizabeth's reign did energies turn in the directions that ultimately made England mistress of the seas and colonizer of the globe—long-distance seamanship and exploration, attempts to open up remote markets (in Russia and the Near East, for example), and the extremely tentative beginnings of North American colonization in Virginia. Romance tends to envelop these activities, but economically they belong to a pattern of gradual diversification and expansion on the part of a country that had been basically old-fashioned in its mercantile habits. Men like Hawkins and Drake were glamorous pioneers of an opening-out of English enterprise that gathered momentum in the late Elizabethan and Jacobean years. By no means was all of this exploration glamorous, maritime, or warlike; by no means was all of it "rational" or profitable. After the middle of the seventeenth century England emerged as a new-style commercial power with a great deep-water shipping industry, an extensive trade in non-European products, colonies significantly settled by Englishmen and exploited for merchantable products and possible markets, and a state devoted to naval power and the promotion of commercial hegemony and empire. Behind these achievements lay nearly a century of experimental "diversification and expansion," rife with foreign and domestic projects. There were get-rich-quick schemes and dead ends as well as successful new lines of endeavor, in trade primarily, but also in manufacturing, mining, land reclamation, and urban real-estate development.

The English seadogs were flexible businessmen with strong ties to the state—a state interested both in its shrinking pocketbook and its international responsibilities. They were adventurers in the sense of "daredevils" *and* in the sense of "entrepreneurs." The queen encouraged them and invested money in their expeditions partly in the hope that they would discover something really valuable for England (preferably a gold mine), or, failing such luck, that they would fetch other profit home. Exploring the empty globe was a harmless quest; bringing home real treasure meant invading the South American trading sphere, claimed as a monopoly by Spain. Therein was the seadogs' political utility: they produced incidents. The queen could restrain their raids, as the Spanish knew. But she was only interested in doing so for a political price in the Netherlands. When the Spanish complained, she could disown responsibility for proceedings in which her own involvement was under the table. She could stall and argue, keeping the diplomatic front in the muddle of options and double-talk she throve on.

Much English opinion favored deeper involvement in the Netherlands than the queen could decide on or venture to pay for. Finally, after the assassination of their leader, William of Orange, in 1584, the situation of the Dutch became so perilous that Elizabeth could only pursue her policy by wading in farther. An expeditionary force under the Earl of Leicester was dispatched in 1585. The earl's commission was limited and his achievement more so, but now England and Spain were virtually at war. Philip was already working on his plan to take the heretic queen out of the game by a massive naval attack and an invasion from his base in the Low Countries. Spain had the excuse of provocation and the motive of religion. Philip also had a dynastic claim to England, the stronger after French-connected Mary Stuart had surrendered her headship of the Catholic party along with her head. After troubles and delays, the Armada was launched in 1588. Providence and the weather, maneuverable English ships and the seamanship of such sailors as Drake wrought its destruction.

The war continued through the rest of Elizabeth's reign. It was not so glamorous a war in reality as it was in symbolic color. Underfinanced and logistically and strategically ill-organized, it was rather a series of episodes than a concerted drive to a definable end. Piracy flourished under cover of war and under pressure from a needy state. Wild-goose chases and catastrophes counterbalanced dashing moments. England's safety, founded on the wreckage of the Armada, was maintained on a wide front, against the day when a tired war would give out and international affairs would move into new constellations.

On the Protestant religious front, differences intensified during the plateau years of Elizabeth's reign. The divisiveness of intra-Protestant dissension should not be exaggerated: people disagreed over how severely Catholics should be treated and over how much foreign crusading against popery England could risk, but without differing over premises. Even debate over Church matters, which did grow sharper, hardly destroyed men's sense of a common religious and national identity.

In the 1560s the Puritans were interested in simplifying Church ceremonies, mainly by eliminating the clerical vestments that survived from Catholicism. They also hoped that the clergy would be free to develop supplementary forms of religious life more congenial to Protestant spirituality than the bare prayer book service. They were disappointed on both scores. The queen's own predilection for uniformity and obedience was more decisive than the efforts of any adverse religious party. Frustration forced the issue of Church government. In the 1570s and 1580s many Puritans came to advocate replacing bishops with a Presbyterian system (a hierarchy of elected assemblies, partly clerical and partly lay). Some Puritans formed an underground Presbyterian organization as a model for the future.

More was involved in Presbyterianism than the mere form of Church government, however, and more than political frustration turned Puritans against the bishops. The deeper current was accumulating frustration with the quality of religious life and the growing belief that the established system was inherently unable to improve it. The Puritans argued that the discipline exercised by the Church was as important as the doctrine it preached. The bishops enforced morals and orthodoxy through their courts. The Puritans came increasingly to believe that sound discipline required escaping from that "temporal," legalistic way and putting spiritual instruments in its place: man-to-man admonition, community pressure (and ultimately exercise of the grave sanction of excommunication) by congregations that knew their sinners at first hand. The sinner should be thought of as a man to be saved by the threat of hell and the promise of grace, not as a criminal to be coerced into law-abidingness. Presbyterian government seemed to promise the optimum combination of "delegalized" localism and "federalized" central control over individual congregations.

Stronger feelings and debate over more momentous issues brought out still deeper tensions. On the surface, Presbyterians were not subversive of temporal authority. But the government began to question their citizenship —any opposition to the Establishment, not to mention attacking the legitimacy of its organization, was a political sin. Deep down, there was a valid issue, for Presbyterianism challenged the temporal community's right to religious self-determination. Supporters of the Anglican Establishment believed that the core of Christian truth is revealed by God. Beyond that core—touching ritual and ceremony, Church government and discipline—God has left human communities free to choose. In other words, he has left to governments, through which communities make their authoritative choices, the real power in religious affairs. The Presbyterians said the opposite: there are two realms, spiritual and temporal. In the temporal sphere, human communities and their governments may design the laws and institutions they think fit. But the spiritual sphere belongs to God. He has told men in the Scriptures how to organize that realm, as one would expect, for over the spirit God alone is Lord, insistent on his sovereignty and infinitely careful of his people's good. The Puritans would have given Queen Elizabeth all earthly honor. They would let her adorn the Presbyterian Church as Supreme Head. Their temporal homage was as good as gold, but they would have converted her ecclesiastical supremacy to a tinsel crown. The queen and her successors did not consider that a good exchange for what they had. They did not think that withdrawing religion from the scope of government would make government more respected and efficient. About that they may have been wrong. The seventeenth century would tell.

The Presbyterian movement of the 1570s and 1580s was largely academic and clerical, very much within the Church. It was not amenable to the most heavy-handed suppression, but the harassment of its leaders broke its hopes. In the later years of Elizabeth's reign, Puritanism lost something of its edge, although not its quiet influence. Public advocacy of ecclesiastical change declined as hope was foreclosed. The queen was old and incorrigible. With the help of her able anti-Puritan archbishop, John Whitgift, she was tougher than before in repressing overt nonconformity. Yet ministers who were Puritan at heart could carry on unmolested if they outwardly obeyed the rules and avoided controversial subjects. Their religious orientation was disseminated to growing numbers of laymen. Where that orientation was clear, antiepiscopacy did not lie very far beneath the surface. For the moment, in Elizabeth's late years, Protestant England was victorious. The most critical Protestant subjects could not complain about that.

In 1600, in a petty, ugly way, the spector of rebellion reappeared. Religious passions, where men had feared the specter lurked, were comparatively at rest. The old noble houses, where pride had for so many ages harbored the ghost, were not the threat they once had been. Faction, vaulting ambition, and the adventurism of a romantic war now cohabited with treason.

Beside Leicester (who died in 1588), the great Elizabethan favorite was the queen's winter flame, Robert Devereux, Earl of Essex. Essex combined beauty, courtly charm, and soldierly derring-do with the character of a juvenile delinquent. It would be grotesque to say the queen was in love with a nobleman more than thirty years her junior, much less he with her. But the conventions of courtiership were so close to flirtation that the queen could imagine she was spoiling Essex with something fiercer than the infatuation of a great aunt for an irresistible boy. Like most courtiers, Essex was after real power and riches, and he had a band of aspiring gentlemen in tow. The queen's gifted contemporaries had mostly died. Lord Burghley had bequeathed the tradition of responsible public service to his younger son, Robert Cecil, the queen's secretary. But the old Elizabethan equilibrium—faction balanced against faction, factionalism contained by public spirit—was gone. Essex, the new star, intrigued viciously against the Cecil faction. Noblemen and gentlemen on the tails of the leading figures competed for shares of a diminishing pie.

The upshot was too sordid to make a tragedy with Essex as hero. Elizabeth's last act was a low-key tragedy—of disappointment and betrayal, of life led out in dignity when one's friends are dead and one's values are old-fashioned. Essex parlayed a military reputation strong on swashbuckling style into a major command in Ireland. (Rome had for years encouraged the just discontent of the Catholic Irish against their English masters. The revolt of native chiefs that Essex, among other captains, was sent to quell was in effect a theater of the war against Spain.) After a capitulation compounded of disobedience to orders, bungling, and apparent cowardice, Essex came home in disgrace. Unable to repair his ruined fortunes otherwise, he put together a rout of disaffected gentlemen. A show of force was made in London with the purpose of capturing the queen and making her take Essex back, as it were, as total favorite. Treason with that intent was still treason. The coup was detected and foiled. Essex was beheaded.

CHAPTER FOUR

William Shakespeare

Bred up from the Elizabethan "plateau," William Shakespeare matured as
an artist in the late years of the old queen and flourished under King
James. England could afford Shakespeare because she had people and wealth
in the urban concentration to support a commercial theater. London gave
him economic success and challenged him to make art of crowded diversity.
The aristocratic London of court and the Inns of Court was accessible to a
poet with Shakespeare's facile talent; the more varied demands of public
theater helped him beyond copious fancy to the farthest reaches of imagination. His power to imitate in words the unutterable reality of all our
lives stretched also beyond his classical-Christian heritage. Humanism
affirmed man's hope to find his role in nature and live with dignity therein;
Christianity at its purest saw no fulfilling role for man, save as God's grace
intrudes and overcomes the world our lives are cast in. Rejecting neither
inheritance and doubting both, Shakespeare fused elements of each into a
new vision of man's lot.

Shakespeare's vision cannot be described in infinite words of prose.
But let us be foolhardy and suggest that it was something like this. As
nature's children, we must seek our roles within her cruel and crowded

Elizabethan–Jacobean England II: Disequilibrium

theater. We must invent values to give order to our lives, must try them in the fire and in conflict with other men. Our inventions fail, but the power to imagine and to choose enables us to live—not "naturally" as we ought, but as possible selves—until death finishes us. In the light of death, perhaps the sound and fury of man's self-creation will seem to signify nothing. Perhaps we depend on grace indeed for the sustaining energy to give an ill-comprehended meaning to emptiness, for occasional redemption in this life from hopeless choices, for the promise of "a new world's crown" beyond defeat. None of us is exempt from the assignment of seeking his humanity. If religious idealism holds out a further possibility, a dimension of freedom from the absurdity of being human, it is but another flawed scenario.

A useful focus on Shakespeare's relation to his age is his thinking about politics, a recurrent preoccupation and the theme of his English chronicle plays. Tudor England forged its historical myth, to which Shakespeare gave both a classic statement and a deep critique: fifteenth-century English history was the fruit of a political crime, the deposition and murder of a legitimate king, Richard II. The seed of rebellion sprouted in Henry IV's troubled reign. Although the model prince Henry V assuaged the commonwealth's disease, his achievement was undone under Henry VI, when France was lost and civil war broke out. Selfish noblemen tore the country

Left: Title page of First Folio, 1623; *right:* Swan Theater. Shakespeare, more than any other single phenomenon, is what Tudor history "has to say." London's capacity to support commercial theaters made his career possible. (*Left:* Folger Shakespeare Library, Washington, D.C.; *right:* University Library, Utrecht.)

apart, and the specter of popular rebellion sprang from undisciplined fields manured by blood. The sickness reached its crisis when the Yorkist victory threw up the unspeakable tyrant Richard III, but healing broke through; health quickened with the Tudor union of Lancaster and York. Providence had written a lesson in England's flesh: the crop of a king's spilt blood is radical evil. Break the bonds of sociability and subordination and man faces the senseless sinner in himself, as unloving and unloved as Richard III. We see that the force behind unbridled appetite is not of flesh and blood, rather of principalities and powers.

In retelling this story, Shakespeare turned a straight conservative vision into an ambiguous one, especially in his two-part historical masterpiece, *Henry IV*. In his Prince Hal (and the Henry V he becomes), Shakespeare created a symbol for the value of public order founded on good kingship *and* for all that is false in political rhetoric and cold-blooded in political ambition. Henry V can bind up a wounded commonwealth, but he cannot restore wholeness—cannot reach the "Jerusalem" that serves throughout the histories as the symbol of redemptive healing. The point is made in depth through one of Shakespeare's largest creations, Sir John

Falstaff. Falstaff embodies all that is wrong with England: lying, cowardice, ungoverned appetite, racketeering, and cynicism. He is also the vitality in the disorder, the physical truth that confronts the pretenses of politics, and the love in loveless England. In the end, Henry V justly rejects Falstaff. Henry is really a good king; he cannot escape the confines of the political virtues—the politician's manipulative arts, by which real public goods are attained and the deeper needs of communal life are left untouched.

Shakespeare's preoccupation with the political virtues and their limitations—the necessity of order imposed by Machiavellian technique and the denial of life exacted by impersonality, repression, and deceit—was responsive to his own age. In *Henry IV* "modern times" and "old times" are polarized, the latter focused on another ambiguous character, Harry Percy (Hotspur). The cerebral politicians Henry IV and Henry V represent a great gain compared to the old-fashioned blueblood, and a great loss in simple nobility. So Elizabethan sophistication contrasted to the memory of a sounder past, and that contrast crisscrosses and parallels the larger antithesis of politics and life. In his later plays, especially *Antony and Cleopatra*, Shakespeare's qualified faith in the political virtues is subjected to severer pressures. Yet the echo of a darker political voice in the late plays seems still to say what the histories began to say—that communities can hold together only if they are somehow in touch with "the mystery of things." As magic reaches beyond nature, political wisdom must stretch beyond the art of politics, for the grace that in the hour of death gives life.

Shakespeare spoke for the sons against the fathers (unconsciously, of course). Queen Elizabeth and her contemporaries had weathered peril and constructed a viable national order. A Protestant Providence smiled on the civic realism of sober men. Their political virtue was really virtue; their success was purchased at its just price. A younger generation, less disciplined by the struggle for stability, was more ready to see the shallowness of conventional wisdom and the precariousness of what passed for achievement. At the end of Elizabeth's reign, England was triumphant and sick. The high tide of patriotism floated the pirate ship Rebellion. Problems had been deflected by the queen's artistry, but the revels must soon be ended, the old magic must fail. A deeper political wisdom was needed to bind a more complex and sophisticated society in richer harmonies. Instead, the Stuarts brought a stubborn incapacity to live in the real world and a will to prolong the Elizabethan order without learning the already dated art of politics it depended on.

The Intellectual Spectrum

Although Shakespeare's insight was his alone, other intellectual leaders of his generation shared his stance of complex reaction against the styles and assumptions of the sixteenth century. Such "cultural radicals" (none of them political radicals) stand at one end of a brilliant age's spectrum; at the other end are those who fulfilled and elaborated the values of the fathers.

Next to Shakespeare, Francis Bacon is the grandest figure at the "radical" end. In their backgrounds and careers, as well as in their thinking, the two men could not have been more different. Shakespeare was a professional artist and a bourgeois success; Bacon, born a court insider, consumed his life in political ambition, and as a thinker he was first of all a "statesman of the intellect." His central achievement was to conceive and advocate a great collective redirection of man's intellectual energies. He was a royalist in the political controversies of his day, and a government man in the higher sense that he looked to state leadership for his schemes and deplored attitudes that stood in the way of strong, creative government. But at a deeper level he was something no other cultural radical of his generation was, a progressive. He believed that men thought and lived in cramped and stagnant ways. They could choose a new road to cultural release and practical amelioration.

Bacon's central idea, primarily documented by his *Advancement of Learning* and *Novum Organum*, was that detailed observations of nature could be built up to a new body of general knowledge, which in turn would yield technological applications. Existing learning was deficient because nature had not been approached directly and observantly. Instead, intellectuals had manipulated concepts constructed from partial observation and human biases. Natural philosophy ("science" in our vocabulary) was the least developed and most obstructed branch of learning, more locked into false approaches than the literary studies that had flourished in the age of humanism (and drowned that age with too much idle eloquence). Although he was not a serious practicing scientist; although he lacked appreciation for the most fruitful scientific work going on in his time; and although he misprophesied the philosophy and method of modern science, Bacon did foresee the ideal of a rigorously rewritten picture of the natural world. As a prophet of that ideal, he had immense influence on the science of the future. Bacon was ultimately in closer touch than most innovators of his generation with the "practical idealism" of sixteenth-century humanism, despite his awareness of its limitations. For Bacon as for the humanists, the still powerful scholastic mind was the chief enemy; like the humanists, he wanted men of thought to become involved in the real world—in nature as well as practical good works. He deplored the narrow religious controversies of his day and looked to the study of God's creation and the betterment of all mankind as a Christian's proper service. Although a royalist grandee, Bacon was something of a cultural democrat, for besides caring about the welfare of ordinary people he criticized the snobbism of contemporary culture and commended the craftsman's knowledge of how things work to intellectuals who failed to inquire.

Bacon's career in law and politics often pitted him against the most eminent lawyer in English history, Sir Edward Coke. There was also an intellectual issue between them. Although Coke's ideas lie buried in technical literature and in the implications of his judicial and political acts, he belongs on our spectrum and toward the radical end of it, for in his hands the law became a vehicle of social thought and part of the pattern of reaction against Tudor assumptions. A government lawyer and judge (until he quarreled with King James and was dismissed from the bench in 1616), Coke was a true believer in established political pieties, except that he believed in them in a new way. His "radicalism" was a new brand of conservatism; in his day, it was a subversive one.

For Bacon, custom was among the obstacles to progress; for Coke, it was the touchstone of legitimacy. The cumulative wisdom in tradition overshadows the wisest man, Coke believed, but the values in tradition are not self-evident. The eye must be trained to see them—and the training of an English lawyer was most apt for that end, the surest immunization against the vulgar rationalism that trusts its offhand conclusions and scorns what has stood the test of time. English institutions had passed that test, for they had survived through infinite ages, guarded and refined by lawyers equipped to understand them. On one side, Coke expressed the commonplace traditionalism and nativism that became many people's defense against unpopular Stuart government. On the other side, he transcended the commonplace and looked forward to the historically minded conservatism to which Edmund Burke gave classic expression in the eighteenth century. Coke drew on the extended knowledge of English history that lawyers and nonlawyers were acquiring toward the end of Elizabeth's reign. He was both a contributor to and a beneficiary of a new kind of historical interest—factual, documentary, and antiquarian, as opposed to humanistic historiography's interest in style and moral instruction. At the same time, Coke made ahistorical use of history, for demonstrating the antiquity and continuity of English institutions involved creating a mythic past. As the "new history" grew more scientific, it was capable of challenging Coke's social thought, although his values were ultimately strengthened by a more sophisticated sense of the interplay of change and continuity.

In the seventeenth century Coke's ideas furnished arms against the state. He was a legalist, not a liberal. The only rights that made sense to him were the positive rights of English law, warranted by usage—as much the powers of government as the immunities of subjects. But the first step to an appreciation of liberty is a firm conception of the rule of law. Coke gave a new meaning to Englishmen's attachment to their liberties in the old sense of "specific privileges rooted in legal tradition." In the course of the seventeenth century, the process of abstraction—from liberties to liberty—went forward.

When jealousy of liberties ran high, the humanistic ideal of statesmanship grew less convincing. Common lawyers competed with the ancient sages, native tradition with international culture. Elizabethan accents of policy sounded tinny against the solemn music of prescription. Results meant less, rights more. Trust in princes gave way before an apotheosis of the "ancient constitution." The English Revolution was basically in defense of that mythic image of a better order than the flesh-and-blood Stuarts were providing. Among the intellectual progenitors of the Revolution, the conservative Coke was perhaps the most important.

Toward the end of the sixteenth century, ideological gaps were opening, consensus was weakening. In religion, as Puritanism continued to develop its thought and style on already firm foundations, "High Church" Anglicanism took on new color. Institutionally, the mid-Elizabethan Church was the spiritual arm of humanist and *politique;* religiously, it rested in the fold of mainline Protestantism. As it was rethought by the late-Elizabethan generation, Anglicanism became harder for Puritans to dismiss as worldliness and vested interest; it became a truer rival to the self-appointed guardians of the Protestant way.

The greatest systematic writer in Anglican history, Richard Hooker, raised the basic attitudes of Elizabethan Anglicanism to a higher power. His *magnum opus, Of the Laws of Ecclesiastical Polity,* was written in response to Puritan criticism of the established Church. It transcends the genre of controversy and achieves a massive rhetorical victory over impatience and half-thought by painstakingness and tone—by fairness, courtesy, and respect for the discriminating use of language. The victory remains rhetorical, for Hooker was neither logically rigorous nor ultimately radical; he belongs closer to the "culturally conservative" end of our spectrum than the other figures we have discussed. But he found something the earlier Elizabethans had not discovered: a distinct religious voice for stating the basic Anglican arguments, arguments for the role of human communities and political authority in Church affairs. It was the voice of modesty and civility, of reasonableness against abstract rationalism. In arguing that God has left some discretion to man, that a spark of reason has been fanned alive in fallen man by the grace that overcomes his fall, he refrained from claiming too much for humanity. The Puritans, he would have said, claimed more, for while proclaiming man's nothingness and God's total sovereignty over his Church, they proceeded to read their predilections into God's Word. The "judicious Hooker" gave Anglicanism a voice it never lost; after Cranmer, he is its truest founder.

The new life in the Church of England had doctrinal, administrative, and literary aspects. In academic theology, the strict Protestantism that looked primarily to Calvin was challenged as it had not been since the Reformation. Debate was over shades of meaning, mainly the exact way in which the doctrine of predestination was to be understood. It was an intra-

Protestant debate, but it was significant because it gave differences over Church government and of religious temperament more of a doctrinal counterpart than they had previously had. In practical Church affairs, stepped-up repression of overt Puritan dissent under Archbishop Whitgift and his Jacobean successor, Richard Bancroft, reflected in part a shift in the hierarchy's conception of itself. Although unimpeachably loyal to the state, the bishops were more conscious of their independent dignity; the argument was heard that episcopacy is the divinely ordained government of the Church, as opposed to an option that communities are free to take. Greater seriousness about reforming the Church's deficiencies—not merely cracking down on Puritans—accompanied the clerical order's increased confidence. By proposing to do something about low clerical incomes and the partly consequential low quality of many ministers, the hierarchy stole some of the thunder of the Puritans, who pointed to such shortcomings as signs of an ungodly system and a feeble spirit. People with vested interests in abuses—and just old-fashioned people, unused to high-flying bishops and a little anticlerical at heart—gained a degree of paradoxical sympathy with the idealistic Puritans.

To Puritans, preaching was the core of the ministry, that is, the genuine preaching of men who were entitled by sound learning, prayerful study, and vocation to proclaim God's Word with the authority of his Church. The "canned" sermons given to Church of England ministers (partly to help clergymen who could not compose their own, partly to make sure that officially endorsed truth was preached by the rest) would not do. Practical considerations—undersupply of competent ministers and the patronage system's insurance that livings were often in incompetent hands—required the Elizabethan Establishment to play up the value of common prayer and the sacraments, even when they were not accompanied by a sermon. The new Anglicans around 1600 were less defensive about the Church of England's right to be itself and more ready to assert the "praying Church" against the "preaching." Nevertheless, the strongest testimony to fresh life in the established Church was in the spoken word, in sermons and religious poetry. The accomplished Puritan preachers of the early seventeenth century are forgotten toilers in the vineyard alongside two High Church homilists: Bishop Lancelot Andrewes and the great poet John Donne, who entered the ministry in middle age and became dean of St. Paul's. Differences in homiletic style accented the widening distance between high churchman and Puritan. The former tended toward wit in the seventeenth-century sense (not humor, but "intellectual ingenuity"), while Puritan preaching adopted a more straightforward expository manner. Yet both schools were learned and theologically demanding—equally far from either "camp-meeting" emotionalism or chatty topicality—and the differences between them are scarcely more important than those within. Andrewes employed the "witty" style in a formal, austere manner. For Donne, that style was the vehicle of a richer religiosity.

On our spectrum, Donne occupies a radical position of his own in religion, one next to Shakespeare's in literature. Although he perceived his ministry as a penitent break with the worldly love poet, the conflicting motifs of his life do hang together. The break his metaphysical poetry made with prevailing aesthetics is connected with his religious personality, his secular writing with his "divine" poems and sermons. Aside from the Puritan Milton, the most important religious verse in English was written in the ambience of seventeenth-century Anglicanism and in the style pioneered by Donne.

Decorum is the classical word for aesthetic and moral "belonging-ness." Humanistic sensibility rested on the conception of nature as an ordered arrangement of ideal qualities—graspable by the mind, visible to the senses, and imitable by art. Art creates sensible objects of heightened perfection, closer to the ideal world that is ultimately real than to the objects of everyday experience. But since empirical relationships are themselves reflections of the ideal, art should not basically violate ordinary expectations. It should put together what belongs together. The cultural radicalism of 1600 may be seen as a challenge to decorum on several fronts. In questioning the correspondence of "virtue" and "value," Shakespeare exemplifies the phenomenon, as do Coke and Hooker in perceiving a disjunction between "reasonable" and "rational," and as Bacon does in doubting whether man's logic is the clue to nature's order. Metaphysical poetry, with its discontinuities of feeling and imagery of unfamiliar associations, broke with aesthetic decorum; Donne's Christianity may also be seen as a departure from prevailing (and mutually antagonistic) standards of coherence.

Puritan sensibility was dualistic: Christian man lives "in the spirit," but also "in the flesh." In this life, man cannot escape the bondage of sin; all he can do is put on the whole armor of God and combat it. When he yields to the flesh, let him call a sin a sin; let him observe the decorum of keeping the adverse powers in his life—the Kingdom of Grace and the tyranny of this world—in their places. This idea lay behind Puritan insistence on keeping human considerations out of Church matters and Puritan resistance to luring souls Godward by such sensual baubles as liturgy and religious art. Christian humanism was more affirmative toward the flesh and more optimistic about transcending it: no gulf divides reason from revelation or natural goodness from Christian excellence. One road of self-discovery leads from flesh to spirit; all levels of value go together; one energy seeks the Good, whether it responds to physical beauty or presses on to God. Neither of these models fit Donne. His Christianity was deep, personal, and unclassifiable; in a sense, neither Catholic nor Protestant

(His family background was Catholic.) He was perhaps closer than any other Englishman to the saint most honored by both sides of the Reformation schism, Augustine. Donne, the poet of acute physical awareness and paradoxical wit, remained too much alive in the divine to experience the tensions of the Christian life so straightforwardly as the Puritans, but in the end that only says that he experienced them with greater dramatic intensity. Far from a Hooker's calm affirmation of Christian good sense, Donne shared Anglican resistance to dissociating flesh from spirit, human needing and valuing from Christian man's ultimate need to surrender to God. His complexity equipped him to grasp with peculiar force the central Christian paradox, the Word made Flesh, and there to find his tense resolution.

Donne's religion and the Anglican poetry in his tradition point to a dimension of depth in seventeenth-century Anglicanism that matters for history. Across the whole century, deep Christianity in Anglican form hardly spoke in voices numerous or comprehensible enough to challenge Puritanism on its own ground. Rather, the Church of England outlasted Puritanism on the strength of its low-key side—as the voice of reason, moderation, civil concord, and humanism. But the deeper note reached some ordinary people and helped recruit a new degree of loyalty to the Church. That loyalty was to claim its Cavalier martyrs in the Revolution (including King Charles I) and to bequeath a stubborn high churchmanship to the liberalized late seventeenth and eighteenth centuries. The "deeper note" was to survive in modern Anglo-Catholicism.

New ideas and sharper divisions of opinion in the community underlie the politicized conflicts of the Stuart period. Yet the Elizabethan synthesis of humanism, Protestantism, and national self-awareness survived into the seventeenth century. It was still most people's culture. It stayed alive by clothing the values of the Renaissance and Reformation in new and richer forms.

Although they were the dissenters *par excellence* and had the greatest potential for political radicalism, the Puritans were in some ways at the conservative end of the cultural spectrum. It was important politically that they shared ground with old-fashioned people who did not participate in religious dissent but were attached to the Elizabethan standards that the Stuarts seemed to offend. Although they made a point of keeping nature and grace apart, Puritans did not dispute the value of reason and secular culture in their sphere. As "natural men," they were earnest people, concerned for individual achievement worthy of their calling and for a society worthy of God's favor; "according to the flesh," they were practical idealists and respecters of decorum. They could be amenable to a Bacon's attack on the sacred cows of merely secular civilization and to a Coke's exaltation of timeless rights over trust in princes, but neither of those receptivities need take one far from the Elizabethan plateau. Although they objected to the kinds of literature they associated with frivolity and vice, including the drama, they were not antiliterary. They preferred literature that reflected common-sensical thinking, effective moral teaching, and the evident order of God's creation.

In the mid-seventeenth century, Milton fulfilled the possibility of synthesizing Puritanism with the humanistic literary heritage. Two Elizabethans, both a half-generation older than the figures we have discussed, were especially important for preserving and enriching that heritage. Sir Philip Sidney and Edmund Spenser were not Puritans, but spokesmen for the Elizabethan culture to which Puritans belonged despite their dissent. Sidney died young, while fighting in the Netherlands—a Protestant martyr as well as England's exemplar of the perfect courtier as Castiglione imagined one to be. His role as a culture hero almost equals his considerable contribution as a writer. In his important critical essay, *The Defense of Poesy*, Sidney gave the classic English statement of humanistic literary theory. He defended "poesy" against its rivals for the chief seat of edification, philosophy and history; that is, he defended imagination against sober-sided mid-century Protestant humanism by criteria it could accept. It was as if a release were called for—an uninhibited acceptance of fiction and romance, of delight in abundant language and artfully constructed scenes, of luxury that would still serve true piety and virtue. In Sidney himself, but more so in the major poet Spenser, that release was achieved. In his long allegorical romance, *The Faerie Queene*, Spenser created the masterpiece of Elizabethan civilization. On the political level of a many-leveled poem, he wrapped Elizabeth, the triumphant virgin and "fairy" queen, in the panoply of myth—in the Arthurian color of national fulfillment and the transcendental color of virtue victorious. On the moral and religious plane, Spenser traversed the tangled wood of poesy to say what saints and sober men were content to hear. Goodness is his final theme, the serious Christian goodness that is reachable only after knightly struggle, only after we have resisted chimeras that challenge our intelligence past its limits, until our dependence on grace is exposed. With the possible exception of Hooker, Protestant humanism nowhere spoke so deeply, and no poem so celebrates ideal nature in decorous art.

One final figure, entirely different from Sidney and Spenser, as essentially Jacobean as they were Elizabethan, stands at the conservative end of our spectrum: Ben Jonson. Jonson was the peer and antitype of Donne. Both were men of grainy intellect—salt against the sugar of poesy. Both looked beyond the native Renaissance fusion of aristocratic style and humanistic ideas that still defined the worlds of Sidney and Spenser—Donne to deep Christianity, Jonson to the classics. The children of the Renaissance, still awed by the ancients, parodied them where they were most schoolmasterly and imitated them best where they mixed classicism with native musicality and Christian knightliness. Jonson met the masters as a favored advanced student. He caught as no English predecessor had done the antique ideal of mature judgment. As a comic dramatist and lyricist, he stayed within decorum without being cramped by it. As a critic, he had a grip on taste and tradition that permitted him to criticize even Shakespeare intelligently and to honor merit different from his own. As Donne stands behind the "metaphysicals," Jonson stands behind much of the seventeenth-century verse written in more conventional modes. In longer perspective, he stands behind the Augustan mood of a century later, wherein the dreams of the Renaissance were somewhat ambiguously fulfilled.

The handful of leading figures we have discussed are signposts to the throughways, dead ends, and labyrinthine paths of cultural history. Along those ways, nonintellectual men moved and halted. That the body politic was coming apart we have read from the map of cultural history— unless it was growing to a new coherence.

James I: Constitutional Stress and Political Alienation

James I's reign is epilogue to Elizabeth's reign and prologue to the English Revolution. King James was fifteen years dead when England went over the brink. Political problems exposed in James's reign stood unsolved. But the breaking point that was to arrive in the 1640s had not yet been reached; no one had to cry "Intolerable!" We have sketched King James's character. His luck owes little to his human and political virtues. But, for all his disreputable qualities, James had intelligence—intelligence largely tangential to common sense but capable of surprising turns toward reality. The fifteen years of Charles I's reign made their own crucial contribution to breakdown; Charles I, a noble, unintelligent man, must not be denied his peculiar tragedy. Decisions were made, leaders preferred, impressions created that James might have avoided. Problems accumulate, breakdowns take time. But shifting qualities are as real in history as accumulating quantities. James I inherited an incipient mess, created a worse one, bequeathed to his son mostly wrong ways out. There was bound to be a catastrophe. Yes, but . . . A man may give up battering at a "No Exit," or he may walk through the wrong door to his death. By the same taken, those who took up arms against King Charles were substantially different men from those who took offense at King James. Was their threshold of pain perhaps lower, their readiness greater to cry "Intolerable!" and take power into their own hands? Perhaps. Yet the main explanation of the Revolution is that tensions piled up, as solutions failed to come and men aggrieved in different ways made alliances with each other.

The crux of the monarchy's trouble was money; its challenge was to live with the political discomfort of impecuniousness. It is glib to say that a king without meaningful independent income—adequate for liberal "ordinary" and patronage expenses, plus enough to insure a certain room for maneuver in foreign affairs—must be a slave to the policy preferences of Parliament. There were too many variables for that to be a simple truth. Could those in Parliament who really wanted something from the king before they would bail him out financially carry the normally loyal or indifferent majority with them? If the king was personally popular and moderate in his demands, could he count on a reasonable flow of tax revenues without strings attached? Could Parliamentarians disposed to use their bargaining power agree on what to use it for? *Dominium politicum et regale* thrived more on such uncertainties than on a material balance. The price tag on poverty was not necessarily prohibitive.

Peace was the largest item on the price tag. That part of the account James willingly paid: by making peace with Spain in 1604, he stopped adding to his inheritance of war debts. Peace made sense. The gain to Englishmen from peaceful trade with Spain and in the Mediterranean outweighed the booty, glory, and marginal power advantages they could have hoped for from continued war. To be sure, there was some political disutility in peace. It meant an end to heroics and to Protestant crusade, unfavorable comparison with Queen Elizabeth, and a public-relations loss to a monarch whose income and prestige depended on public relations. But peace had been the essential policy of the Elizabethan plateau. It had strained against adventurism and religious zeal in those days. Although he lost credit on one hand, James gained some on the other for an idealistic attachment to international peace.

King James plugged up the gaping hole of war, however, only to create or indulge a multitude of lesser leaks. The intemperance of his habits and ungainliness of his body carried over to his governance. He lived with an extravagance the respectable would have raised their eyebrows at if it had only been kingly magnificence. The king of poor Scotland thought magnificence his duty, and a little fun his right, in the land of milk and honey God had given him. But the style of life that Henry VIII had gotten away with—had even gotten credit for—James could neither afford nor bring off. An English Mars is one thing; a pedantic Scotsman is another. James overindulged high society's increased greed for position and favors, as well as for the entertainment his expensive, scandal-ridden, "swinging" court provided. Largesse and graft cost more than magnificence and fun. Patronage was badly managed at a time when competition for a diminishing loaf was more intense. Titles of honor were conferred much more lavishly than under Elizabeth. That brought in some cash—a new venality prevailed—but it also increased the ranks of those titularly eligible for other favors, for a return on their investment. Hungry Scots added to the demand on the king's bounty. James's first great favorite, Robert Carr (ennobled as Earl of Somerset), was both a hungry Scot and a pretty boy. Favors to foreigners only increased the claims of the English regulars, who were hungry too.

Governmental competence declined with the arts of patronage and public relations. Until 1612 a link was maintained with the Elizabethan tradition of public service in the person of Burghley's son, Robert Cecil (ennobled as Earl of Salisbury). But, in general, the forms of Elizabethan government tended to persist without the substance. The privy council continued in its pivotal role, but it grew larger, less well-coordinated, less professionally staffed. Privy councillors ceased to manage the House of Commons effectively. The king shared with Henry VIII laziness in business, as well as a taste for hunting and show. Henry's had been the laziness of a sleeping lion; James fancied all kings were lions, but he had no bite when he woke up.

King James did not make a consistent adaptation to the monarchy's financial situation. He was not a consistent man. Yet he was often a stubborn politician, partly because he had both rational and fixed ideas. His pet project at the beginning of his reign illustrates his aptness to persist and to go astray. His hope was to unite England and Scotland, at least to the extent that subjects of the two realms would have "reciprocal citizenship." The scheme was statesmanlike, a significant anticipation of the union effected a century later. In the face of xenophobia, conservatism, and the fear that too much of England would be given away to Scottish favorites, James could not get his proposals through Parliament. Having failed in the proper forum, he turned to an ill-advised alternative: the government went to the courts with a contrived case and got a nearly unanimous judgment that people born in Scotland after James's accession to the English throne could acquire real property in England. (Calvin's Case, or the Case of the Post-Nati, 1607. The incapacity of aliens to own real estate in England was their main legal disability. The decision held that someone born a subject of the man who was King of England could not be considered an alien with respect to the state of England.) The decision was not wrong (it bears the imprimatur of a famous opinion by Coke), but the strategy was wrong. The king showed too stubborn a will to have his way in spite of public opinion, to squeeze the result he wanted out of the law when the community would not grant it. Pyrrhic victories in the courtroom added weight to the Stuarts' doom.

James's quarrel with Coke (extending over most of Coke's time on the bench, 1606–16) illustrates the same misguided persistence. Compared with Calvin's Case, it also illustrates the king's inconsistency: when it suited him, he would stand on the law as the courts declared it; when it suited him otherwise, he would challenge the courts' competence to declare the law.

The feud was complex. Under the existing legal system, the common-law courts had the upper hand because they had the power to control the jurisdiction of other parts of the system, such as the ecclesiastical courts, the chancery, and the admiralty (which handled maritime and mercantile cases by the international standards of Roman law). Early in James's reign, the non-common-law components of the system complained about what they considered abuse of the common law's power. They claimed that authority of police jurisdiction was being used in ways that precedent and logic would not warrant—to deprive them of business and to control their substantive conduct. The loudest complaints came from the ecclesiastical system, led by Archbishop Bancroft. More than legalism was involved. The main bread-and-butter question was whether the ecclesiastical courts, which in principle had jurisdiction over tithes, would be allowed the freedom to enforce effective collection. Issues of prestige and theory overlay the material stakes. The hierarchy, close and loyal to the king, was newly sensitive to constraint by lay authorities. Vigilance lest the Church courts take a little too much was a dated attitude, according to the ecclesiastics. It had been suitable when the king and the subject needed protection against the Roman Church; it was inappropriate now that the common-law courts and the Church of England were coordinate agencies of one Supreme Head.

One ecclesiastical court, the high commission, was a particularly sharp focus of contention. It had been created at the beginning of Elizabeth's reign as a supplement to the ecclesiastical system (analogous to the Star Chamber vis-à-vis the common law). It was under direct control of the government and the top echelon of the hierarchy and armed with more procedural teeth than the ordinary ecclesiastical courts. When the common law regulated the high commission, the hierarchy and government felt it close to the bone. In the freedom and "teeth" of that court, the authorities saw their only means to crack down efficiently on Puritans and prominent people.

The legal rights and wrongs of the jurisdiction controversy are technical, but the king's handling of it is important for general history. The only real solution would have been legislative. The community simply needed to decide what rules of law it wanted in an area where the existing rules were tangled. Coke insisted in his repeated arguments with King James that he and the other judges would gladly follow any instructions Parliament chose to give. Until so directed, they would interpret and apply the existing rules with their best judgment, after hearing argument in particular cases. Deep down, King James probably knew the point was unanswerable, but he did not want to admit it. Of course, he would have accepted a legislative solution that pleased him, but it was clear that none would come. With respect to the Church, the king confronted what all high churchmen would have to face: vested interests, indifference, Elizabethanism, and, in some men, Puritanism. Parliament would do nothing for the hierarchy. More generally, most Parliamentarians did not doubt that the judges—successful members of their own class, authorized keepers of ancestral wisdom —knew the law better than bishops, Roman lawyers, and Scotch kings. If doubts on that score could have been stirred, the king's treatment of Coke and his brethren killed the possibility.

James's solution was plausible enough—"abstractly rational." He was titular head of the whole judicial system. His courts were quarreling among themselves over jurisdiction. He claimed no power to infringe the independence of the judges within their jurisdictions, but had he no authority, as a kind of umpire or administrator, to appease an internecine conflict? The king made his demand successfully, in the sense that hours of argument and reams of briefs could not be denied him. The judges were forced to justify their application of the law before the king and in the presence of their enemies. They encountered in the king, despite his arbitrational pretense, an advocate for the other side. The judges reasoned with the king under protest. The protest was loud and clear because Coke was the judges' leader. The idea that the judiciary must be rigorously isolated from politics was not yet commonplace. Judges did not have indefinite tenure *de iure*; they were expected to give the government legal advice on request; in actual cases and in the advisory capacity, they were supposed to be impartial, but a certain solicitude for the king's interests—a duty to make sure that he was properly represented and that he was not indirectly or inadvertently harmed—was incumbent on them. James's idea that the king was entitled to a marginal role in judicial policy-making had plausibility. Coke was creative in insisting that the plausibility was specious, that the rule of law requires faith in the training and commitment to fairness of those whose essential duty is to administer justice between party and party.

The other judges agreed with Coke but he alone had the guts and arrogance to stand up to the king. In essence, Coke won the jurisdiction controversy. The dragged-out proceedings petered out. The king did nothing that very much affected what happened in the courtroom when cases of the controverted sorts came up again. In the end, Coke's point was too good, the king's conception of his ubiquitous regality too vague. But James had his personal vengeance on the chief justice. Coke's dismissal from the bench in 1616 was the immediate result of a dispute technically different from the jurisdiction controversy but involving the same principle of judicial independence.

James's quarrel with Coke was possibly his most destructive contribution to the drift of history. By his stance in the fight, as well as by his general ideas, Coke showed the political public what it believed. The king appeared in opposition to the native legal traditionalism and indifferent justice that most Englishmen put their trust in. When he fired his chief justice, he drove the point home. The paper plausibility of James's case, even his basic acceptance of the rules of English government, as well as generally civilized standards of legality and reason, earned him little credit against the corrosive sense that this alien king and the people closest to him were aliens indeed—strangers to the values and assumptions that held the English community of the living and the dead together. As for Coke, he was only dismissible from office. He reemerged as a member of Parliament and lent the enormous weight of his prestige and learning to opposition politics. He was a worse thorn in King James's side in Parliament than on the bench. Sir Edward Coke in person and the antagonism between law and monarchy he had been made to stand for passed from James to Charles, a fateful legacy.

The jurisdiction controversy is also important for its alliance-making implications. The leading theme of early seventeenth-century history is the consolidation of Puritanism and secular traditionalism—in some ways a fragile marriage of political convenience, but ultimately more than that, a fusion and confusion of points of view, "forged" as opposed to "tacked together." The vocabulary that Puritanism furnished, a rhetoric and a conceptual framework, became convincing to men whose hearts did not really belong to the Kingdom of Grace—rather to the natural idols of self-interest, ancestral rights, and a secure legal order. In the jurisdiction controversy, we can see the seeds of marriage and misalliance.

The high commission makes a good focus for this point. By harrying extremist Puritans, it offended people who had some degree of religious fellow-feeling for them. Because of its methods, compassion spread beyond the borders of religious sentiment, for the high commission engaged in "fishing expeditions." In doing so, it was technically justified by the rules of ecclesiastical law, but its purpose was more systematically disciplinary than that of the ordinary ecclesiastical courts, and it threatened those whom it caught in its nets with severer punishment. Our privilege against self-incrimination comes largely out of the attempts of the common-law courts to curb the high commission's use of inquisitorial investigation. The technique offended a feeling one can have even about people one dislikes or takes no interest in—that men should not be asked to face unspecified charges or forced to betray themselves against the instinct of self-preservation. The feeling becomes stronger if the victims seem on the whole on the side of the angels—Protestants, after all. As victims, they move a little closer to the angels. The common law, already venerated for the mysterious wisdom locked in its technicalities, got added credit for espousing visible fairness. Because the high commission brought a number of upper-class people to the bar of ecclesiastical justice for moral and marital offenses, sinners were brought into the coalition. According to the Puritans, discipline was just what such types needed—only not before the high commission! As for the regular ecclesiastical courts, sinners, saints, and lawyers walked in step—tithe-evaders, bishop-haters, chief justices. When these strange allies looked across the field, they saw a seemingly alien state supporting the churchmen and supported by them. They saw in the king and important men around him (Bacon, for example) a theory dimly opposed to the Cokean theory that served their own material and ideological interests. It seemed to put equity over law. (Coke quarreled with the chancery and other courts of equity, while James supported them, with assistance from the future Lord Chancellor Bacon.) The countertheory seemed to elevate the general welfare of the community within a framework of general law over the specific law men knew to guarantee them in their property and personalities. The countertheory had its merits, its moderation, its affinity with the necessary loose ends of *dominium politicum et regale*. In one aspect, it was damned by association with churchmen and inquisitorial procedure.

Let us turn now from the issue-making, alliance-making periphery to the main arena of Stuart history: the king's confrontation with Parliament. James's relationship with the House of Commons was rocky from the start. A technical debate over parliamentary privilege at the beginning of the reign (the Case of the Bucks Election, 1604) set a tone more important than the matter of the controversy. The corporate pride of the house had fed on a diet of frustration. Faced by an untried foreign king, it pushed its claims, in this case to jurisdiction over disputed elections. In resisting, James was neither legally unjustified nor politically foolhardy. His mistake was typical: he argued too freely, picked too ideological a quarrel. By contending that the privileges of Parliament had no legal basis but depended on the king's grace, he gave a gratuitously theoretical impression that he neither understood nor accepted the English tradition of mixed government. In practice, his view of Parliament's place in the sun was Elizabethan. As he stated it, it sounded alien.

A more serious dispute with Parliament arose from a money-raising experiment. Early in James's reign, the government set out to increase its customs revenue by raising some rates without Parliament's consent. A merchant named Bate refused to pay the new surcharge on currants. He was sued for the tax in the judicial branch of the Exchequer (1606–7). The court held against Bate that the surcharge had been lawfully imposed, although it had not been granted by Parliament. Bate's Case was the first of three really serious Pyrrhic victories in the courts—in retrospect, three stepping stones to revolution. Each time the judges affirmed the king's position. The judicially declared law of the constitution was in each case unacceptable to a substantial section of the community. Each time, in one way or another, Parliament undid the courts' work.

It is unfair to blame the judges for partiality, much less corruption. In the case of "impositions" (extraparliamentary additions to the customs), the precedents were ambiguous. The general reasons on the king's side were at once cogent and portentous. The government won Bate's Case because the court assimilated the taxation of trade to the king's foreign policy pre- rogative. The argument is as follows: if the king's exclusive authority to regulate relations between England and foreign states is to be meaningful, it must include the power to control trade with such states. Suppose Eng- land is trying to exact diplomatic concessions from Venice. Suppose the king, who could make war on Venice without anyone's consent, tries to avoid war by forbidding his subjects to trade with Venetians. If the ends of foreign policy and the sanction of force are wholly in the king's hands, surely he must have the power to pursue those ends with the lesser sanc- tions of economics. If he could utterly prohibit Englishmen from trading with Venice, surely he can discourage such trade by subjecting the importa- tion of such Venetian products as currants to a tax over and above the regular customs. Taxation for revenue, including the taxation of trade, ordi- narily requires parliamentary consent. The king, therefore, must have a bona fide foreign-policy reason for using his power to tax trade. The courts, however, have no competence to examine the king's good faith and reasons of policy. The very conception of the absolute prerogative means that the king is not answerable in the areas left to his discretion. He must simply be trusted to limit his powers to their proper purposes.

Like all legal arguments, this one lacks the force of logical necessity. As a legal argument, however—a reasoned and coherent interpretation of a society's presumed understandings—it has real strength. Alas! the more thoughtfully and explicitly the courts formulated their understanding of the mixed constitution, the clearer it became that English society was divided over its fundamental law. The mixture involved such overlapping and conflicting components as Parliament's absolute right to tax and the king's absolute right to govern foreign affairs. As the courts interpreted the practical needs of government and the moral assumptions underlying the existing system, the parts could only be made to fit by presuming that the king would police himself beyond the point where judicial competence to define the boundaries of the mixture ceased. To many members of Parliament and the community, this interpretation rang false. The dissatis- faction was vague and groping, more emotional than rational, although certainly not unreasonable. It was hard to deny that trust in the king was both a subject's duty and an imperative of the constitutional order. But de facto, the king was not trustworthy. The real purpose of imposing additional customs was merely fiscal, and everyone knew it. (So each Stuart judicial victory was won by excellent arguments unrelated to the reality of the situation, a reality of bankruptcy and shyster schemes to wring money from the legal system.) But suppose we could dispel the bad taste of one-way legalism: once set down as a doctrine, was the conception of unexaminable and irrevocable trusteeship in the king a viable one? Perhaps the mixed constitution was a convincing model only so long as the conflicts inherent in it were not consciously faced.

Parliament responded to the unpopular decision in Bate's Case by proposing to reargue the issues. King James tried to forbid the Commons from taking up the case. He thereby raised a "freedom of speech" issue formally analogous to those raised by Elizabeth. But James's position was shakier. Elizabeth had taken her stand on the theory that Parliament should not embarrass the monarch by discussing such matters of policy as she alone had power to decide. James tried to keep Parliament from speaking its mind on a legal issue because, well, a competent court had decided the case and the subject was the prerogative. To say that a legislative body (the highest court in the land, as Parliament was still nominally considered) should not investigate the law was not very plausible. Surely Parliament had the power to reverse Bate's Case or to make a statute against impositions for the future (needless to say, with the royal assent). That could be doubted only on the basis of a royalism so extreme that even James I did not seriously entertain it, although in fantasy he would have liked to—that is, on the premise that statutes cannot define the prerogative. In the event, the Commons waved the banner of free speech in a good cause, petitioned the king for their rights, and got permission to have their debate. Parliament adjourned before any formal resolution of the issue of customs surcharges was worked out, but the opposition scared the government out of further use of that financial expedient.

The problems we have discussed so far appeared during the first half of James's reign; serious as tension already was, it grew much worse in the reign's last decade. Coke's dismissal in 1616 stands on the watershed. Thereafter, the suspicion that the bench was a servile agent of the government cast its deepening shadow. A divorce took place in people's minds between LAW as it really was and law as living courts declared it. In other ways as well, confidence in the government's integrity was increasingly attenuated.

Waste, favoritism, jealousy, and bad management prevailed at King James's court from the start. Salisbury's death in 1612 broke the link with Elizabethan competence. An episode in 1616 brought the shadow of public scandal over the court. James's favorite Somerset fell in love with the wife of the Earl of Essex (son of the Elizabethan traitor), a daughter of the Howard clan. The king, who took a prurient interest in court amours, promoted the lady's divorce and remarriage to Somerset. (Her first marriage was annulled on grounds of Essex's impotence. The tribunal of distinguished clerics that approved the divorce did the reputation of the hierarchy no good. In the long run, Essex avenged his humiliation by commanding the parliamentary army against Charles I.) Shortly after, Sir Thomas Overbury, a minor courtier and man of letters, was found murdered. The finger pointed to the new Countess of Somerset, who apparently had Overbury poisoned because he had tried to dissuade Somerset from his marital project. The immediate upshot was that the earl and countess, together with several accessories, were brought to trial. Although the principals were finally spared, the old favorite had fallen.

Like Coke's dismissal, this royal scandal stands on the watershed of James I's reign. Tension between "court" and "country"—between the nobles and gentlemen of the inner circle and those whom luck or taste confined to their local societies—was bound to grow with mere numbers of people and diversity of lifestyles. At best, James did nothing to maintain appearances, so that the insiders would more or less seem to deserve their favored position. The Somerset-Overbury affair raised a bad smell to the stink of corruption. Righteous prosecution of the offenders could not undo the damage. The court-country dichotomy grew sharper, owing, of course, to much besides a single *cause célèbre*. As LAW slipped away from the judges who administered the law, so the fleshly figure of socio-political hierarchy was drained of inner meaning. The outsiders, who dominated and represented the local "countries" of England, increasingly saw themselves as dispossessed holders of the right to rule, as possessors of the national fund of responsibility, merit, and noblesse. The courtiers who actually occupied the top of the ladder seemed increasingly a strange and separate breed, seducers of the king and caterpillars of the commonwealth.

Somerset's fall opened the way for a new favorite, George Villiers, ultimately Duke of Buckingham. For a decade and a half, Buckingham was to bask in unexampled favor. He was a young Englishman of genteel origin and dazzlingly handsome looks. Beauty was a weak title to the political influence he would wield. His gift for courtiership, devotion to the advancement of his relatives, and powers of ingratiation (equally effective on James's dotage and Charles's youth) offset a negligible talent for public business. He combined incompetence as a statesman with facility in the courtly milieu that his masters occupied.

James's later Parliaments, alienated from the government for the reasons we have discussed and by new foreign and religious grievances, struck at the courtiers with heightened hostility. Political passion abetted by antiquarianism rediscovered the medieval procedure of parliamentary impeachment. (In an impeachment, the House of Commons, having voted to accuse someone of a crime, prosecutes the case before the Lords, who serve as judge and jury, subject to no appeal. In practice, the procedure was used to bring down political figures.) A couple of courtiers were impeached, essentially because they were unpopular examples of their type, obnoxious mainly as monopolists. (The complaints and judicial decision against monopolies at the end of Elizabeth's reign had not done away with that species of court profiteer.) Two major figures fell, neither representative of the abusive venality against which impeachment was a legitimate weapon, both men whose real offense was able service on the wrong side of a widening political gulf. One was Lord Chancellor Bacon. The other was Lionel Cranfield, Earl of Middlesex. Cranfield made his career as a London "big businessman." In 1618, after holding lesser offices, he was made lord treasurer, a wise and unusual appointment. After long neglect, King James woke up to the need for financial retrenchment and reform. Despite the herculean size of the job, Cranfield applied his business ability and experience to good effect. His ruin (1624) resulted from the tangle of jealousies inside and outside the court. The bright moment in Stuart finance passed.

In 1618 the hostilities that became the Thirty Years War broke out in Germany. This was perhaps the largest event on the watershed of James I's reign. For a decade and a half, peace had made too much sense to evoke deep opposition. Now religious war had returned to the Continent. The interventionist strain in English politics reawoke, strongest as always where Protestant conviction was most militant. This time the interventionists had a plea of honor, for King James had married his daughter Elizabeth to Frederick, Elector of the Palatinate. The precipitating cause of the war was the effort of the Protestant interest in Bohemia to make Frederick king of their country. The Protestant revolt in Bohemia was promptly crushed by the Hapsburg forces, and the Catholics then overran Frederick's small state along the Rhine, driving the elector and his family into exile in the Netherlands. King James loved peace and had no money. The difficulties of rallying his chaotic government to a war effort and dealing with an unfriendly Parliament were formidable. The king deplored the situation and talked about doing something for his daughter and son-in-law, but he was lukewarm. Some English volunteers went to Germany with government assistance, but basically England stayed out of the conflict.

England's interests as a piece on the international checkerboard were perhaps best served by James's insusceptibility to the prick of honor and the spur of zeal. Spain and France were soon involved, Catholic monarchy against Catholic monarchy, the French maneuvering and ultimately fighting on the Protestant side. But, domestically, James's reluctance further alienated him from a vocal part of the community. To make things worse, early in the 1620s he set out to negotiate a marriage between Prince Charles and a princess of the Spanish royal house. Despite the international religious conflict, it was not in every respect diplomatically insane to seek consolidation of peaceful relations with Spain. A handsome dowry was expected—James can hardly be blamed for thinking of money! But the political cost of the proposed match was crushing. To blind one's eyes to that was extreme folly. The project betrayed how alien the king, the prince, and the court insiders were from the mind of the community; it made them seem even more alien than they were.

In the 1620s gloom with an admixture of paranoia overtook many English spirits. The fortunes of the German Protestants turned perilous indeed. And what was England up to? She was courting the arch-Catholic power, the enemy, whose humiliation by English arms was associated with a happier day in living, fading, and secondhand memories. The prince, accompanied by Buckingham, went to Spain in 1623 to pay his court and prosecute the negotiations. It was bad enough even to broach such a marriage, worse to send the heir apparent into the very den of Jesuits and inquisitors. Bad enough to deal with Spain at all, worse when Protestant states were at war against Spain's troops, allies, and financial power. Worse still that marriage was the object. A Catholic queen would be imported into England to spread such poison as she might beyond the harm already done by the assurances of free religious practice which would be given to secure the alliance—assurances to the lady and her attendants. And the Spaniards would want to discuss the English Catholics, too. At the beginning of James I's reign, the Gunpowder Plot of Guy Fawkes fame had capped the Elizabethan series of Catholic conspiracies. That last dramatic episode of its kind sealed for the new reign the spirit of fear and intolerance already so ingrained in Protestants. Nevertheless, partly because of his policy of peace with Catholic states, James I had been lenient with the overwhelmingly harmless native Catholics. The marriage negotiations looked like a new step on the perverse path of toleration.

Gloom descended. The wrath of God seemed to lie heavy on his people. Manichaean wars of religion raged again, and the Children of Light were getting the worst of it. Thoughtful men turned to the prophecies and computations of the apocalypse. Was the deepest pitch of darkness—the exhausting reign of anti-Christ ere the last trumpet and the saving dawn—perhaps at hand? Englishmen thought of their country as the champion of Light—a happy warrior in the past, now, should the worst be true, called to keep the faith and wait upon the Lord. England's leaders seemed deaf to that calling—as if willfully deaf, as if possessed by the enemy. Political paranoia was aroused. To the secular eye, it is obvious that Stuart government was the captive of complicated problems and bad judgment, of legitimate intentions somewhat misplaced and somewhat compounded with folly, of low-grade leadership on the inside and intractable opposition without. But does the secular eye have a monopoly of vision?

Major foreign issues seen through religious spectacles revived the old contention over Parliament's role in policy matters legally within the royal prerogative. King James stood on solid Elizabethan ground when he insisted that parliamentary criticism of the Spanish marriage and of his conduct toward Germany was out of place. In principle, the argument was as good (or bad) as ever; in reality, it had gone hollow. Feeling about the issues was more intense and widespread than in Elizabeth's day; respect for the government's basic integrity was thinner; the House of Commons' sense of its rights had fed on insult and misunderstanding; its members were hardened to criticizing the government, and they were practiced in opposition partly because the government had neglected the politicking, compromise, and quiet domination of parliamentary business that might have muted antagonism.

The heat in Parliament and the country was high enough now to forge the alliance between Puritan and secular conservative in earnest. An apocalyptic reading of the situation of the 1620s was most accessible to Puritans, but it was communicable to others as well. When (we may ask with modern analogies in mind) does the liberal begin to lose his sense of distance from the radical, to accept a vocabulary more absolute in its contrasts, more colored with dread and hope, than his own natural accent? Presumably, when trust in normal channels wears out, when resistance by those in power to dialog and change comes to seem perverse and irremediable. In seventeenth-century England, the equivalent of liberal sentiment was to most intents conservative. Partly correctly and partly mythologically, it saw Stuart government as innovative—in contrast with Elizabeth's reign and simultaneously in contrast with an idealized past rather less monarchist and rather more unambiguously Protestant than Elizabethan reality. Puritanism had a way to go from the 1620s before it acquired a dimension of genuine political radicalism. Puritans by religion participated in the secular idealization of the immediate and remoter past. In the terms of religion itself, they had a special capacity to think extremes, if not necessarily to advocate them here and now. It took time for even Puritans to conclude that the present structure of the Church of England must be torn down and rebuilt, much less that loyalty to the king and to the past was expendable for true religion's sake. But the struggle between darkness and light had a concreteness for Puritans that it did not normally have for more conventional Protestants. Puritans did not underestimate the enemy. They saw the pattern of his wiles where other men would normally see more commonplace malfeasance. In the twenties and beyond, conventional people lost confidence in their normal vision—in the "secular eye"—and gained respect for those whose focus on secular events was ardently religious. The Puritans' ecclesiastical antipathies assumed a heightened political relevance. The Anglican hierarchy was strongly identified with the government. Might it not be involved in the stratagems of Satan, even his advance guard?

It is ironic that politics started to be permeated by the outlook of

Puritanism in James I's reign, for in straightforward ecclesiastical policy the new Anglicanism was hardly triumphant, and respectable Puritans on the whole lived quietly enough. At the beginning of the reign, the Puritans had hopes—the typical hopes of "outs" who might do better with a new management. James himself had been raised in Scottish Presbyterianism. He was interested in Church affairs. At the level of theology, he was known to be in the Calvinist fold (where he remained). Might he not see the limitations of the Church of England as Elizabeth, whose personal prestige was tied with it, had not? But the Puritans' hopes were frustrated. Strong-minded churchmen in Scotland had given James trouble that he was glad to avoid in England by separating theology from Church polity and espousing the loyal, state-controlled Anglican bishops. The way in which James repudiated the Puritans' bid for consideration was typically well-intentioned and typically unfortunate. He recognized the settlement of the Church as an open question and held a conference (at Hampton Court in 1604), where the hierarchy and its critics were supposed to debate and inform their learned and impartial stranger king. At the conference, James, warmed up by the pleasure of debating, leaned too visibly to the Anglican side and made some insulting remarks to the Puritans. However, the breach was not drastic. The positive result of the conference was the translation project that produced the King James Bible, a Puritan proposal that the king accepted and a cooperative venture, in intention and reality "above party."

James's first appointee as archbishop, Richard Bancroft, was a zealous new Anglican of the administrative type. In the tradition of Whitgift, he was tough on nonconformity. But no amount of toughness could stop the discrete entertainment of Puritan opinions. Nor could it stop teaching and practice in Puritan religious style by clergymen with such legal tenure and protection by prominent laymen that only open misbehavior could dislodge. When Bancroft died in 1610, the line of strict enforcement of conformity was broken. For largely personal reasons, James appointed to Canterbury George Abbot, a mild, old-fashioned professor and theological Calvinist. Although conventionally Establishment, the Abbot administration was more of a frustration to zealous new Anglicans than to Puritans. James's reign was not an especially uncomfortable time to be a Puritan. At least on the surface, radicalizing pressure came more from politics interpreted through religion than from the persecution of the saints.

For all the menace of his final decade, King James shuffled to his grave on an upbeat. For the Spanish marriage fell through. Spanish intentions had never been serious. The prince came home deeply offended by the humiliating runaround he had been subjected to in Spain. Buckingham, erstwhile despised as promoter of the evil scheme, came home ranting against the perfidious Spaniard like a true-born Englishman. For a moment he was a hero. The Parliament of 1624 was a honeymoon of reunion. The king got ment in exchange for settlement of their bill for military assistance. In the middle of the year, he was seized by a detachment of soldiers and transferred to the army's custody. Toward the end of the year, he "escaped" to the Isle of Wight (where, since his enemies controlled the island, he remained a captive, though a less constrained one). As he was shunted about, he was wheeling and dealing with the factions among his conquerors, as well as plotting with his friends. At the beginning of 1647, the Presbyterians were well-situated to negotiate the kind of peace they wanted, save for the king's unwillingness to negotiate seriously. But they soon succeeded in so underestimating and mishandling the army that a settlement on their terms was no longer a possibility. Parliament wanted to demobilize much of the army without first satisfying the large outstanding arrears of soldiers' pay. A bread-and-butter issue prompted "trade union"-style organization in many units of the army, and the framework that was created lent itself to political organization under Leveller influence. If they hoped to keep control of their army, the commanders and their civilian allies had to cast their lot with it. Cromwell decided to do so in the summer of 1647. (One should remember that he belonged to both worlds, the Parliamentary and the military.) A large force proceeded to occupy the outskirts of London and so control the city. Although another year was to pass before Parliament was purged, and although the Presbyterians enjoyed a certain revival when the army was busy fighting the second civil war, government at military sufferance had become the fact it remained until the Restoration.

At the beginning of 1647, Independency as an approach to politics was inchoate. In the course of the year, it took shape from the Cromwellians' decision to break with legitimacy and act for Providence, and also from their encounters with the Levellers. For a while the army "grandees" (as, with a touch of mockery, Cromwell and his associates were called) needed to cooperate with the grass-roots movement in the regiments. The Christian enthusiasm and openness to options that made them Independents kept that cooperation from being entirely grudging. In the summer of 1647, a council of the army was formed, comprising electees of the privates and lower officers in addition to the commanders. For the moment, a degree of democracy was institutionalized in the army, although in the long run democracy was no more acceptable to the generals as generals than it was to them as politicians. In the fall of the same year the council held a conference at the church of Putney, just west of London. In a spirit of Christian brotherhood that was half unction poured over festering differences and half cement that enabled irreconcilable men to talk to each other, the political leadership of the army sat down to debate principles. There was already bad blood on both sides; on Cromwell's, there was determination to say "No" to the Leveller program. Yet, like the Athenians and the Melians debating before the inevitable axe of conquest fell, they contended as if battles were won by persuasion. The Independents emerged from the debates confirmed in attachment to class privilege and in awareness that their way of responding to Providence was not the same as that of the radicals. The conference itself ended inconclusively. In the aftermath, authority, more than force, finished off the popular movement's hopes. Late in 1647, one regiment mutinied at radical instigation. By intervening dramatically and dishing out rough punishment, Cromwell restored discipline. The private soldiers' representatives were quietly dropped from the council of the army, and the conventional ethos of military subordination was reasserted. In general politics, the Levellers remained a force for upwards of a year and a nuisance thereafter, but their moment was past.

By now, a new war was brewing. Cromwell's army was soon to sweep to the first of a series of new successes in the field. For some time to come, it was to be an employed and victorious army again. The second civil war was fatal for the king and for the conservatives who still hoped to deal with him, scrupled at killing him, or clung to as much of legitimate and traditional government as could be salvaged. Cromwell defeated the Scottish force that represented the king's best hope; the domestic royalists could not get off the ground in the face of a competent army. Before the military issue was resolved, the generals had decided that King Charles must pay for his incorrigible and bloody resistance to Providence. Accordingly, the House of Commons was purged of its Presbyterians by force; the purified body took all sovereignty to itself, to the Lords' derogation, and erected a so-called high court to try the king. Charles took every rhetorical advantage of the court's manifest lack of lawful jurisdiction; he met his foreordained beheading on January 30, 1649, with dignity and courage.

For a little more than four years, the Rump ruled England—not wisely, but not badly, perhaps one should conclude. Its folly was to do nothing about the future, to sit there as the embodiment of the commonwealth for no better reason than that it was the remnant of the last precommonwealth Parliament. It did not move to replace itself by a new general election, much less frame a republican constitution to last. In effect, the government was an oligarchy of politicians acceptable to the generals—well-worn politicians ruling directly as a modest-sized unicameral legislature, with executive help from a council of state. Its moral position was not strong when idealism and yearning for a fresh start remained in the air; it grew increasingly unpopular, both with the generals on whom its life depended (and who were not strangers to idealism) and with the community that paid its taxes and witnessed the personal corruption of some of its members. Cumulative disgust and small irritations, rather than some gross failure or well-drawn issue of principle, explain Cromwell's rather impulsive decision, in the spring of 1653, to expel the Rump and try something else.

In practice, the Rump period hardly proves that a headless, unplanned parliamentary government could not work. The civilian apparatus managed to keep the everyday engines of public life running without serious disruption or heavy human costs; without being very creative, the Rump managed

England

After the Restoration

enormous scientific, philosophic, and aesthetic accomplishment. The outward environment was still continuous with the past, and men still acknowledged an unstrained allegiance to the classical, Christian, and hierarchic values of tradition. At the same time, they broke through to modes of thinking more genuinely new than were those of the Renaissance and Reformation in relation to the Christian civilization of the Middle Ages.

The center of intellectual change was the scientific revolution. Natural science was not invented in the seventeenth century, but physical science was revolutionized. Greek and scholastic physics—the old conceptual vocabulary, the models into which the observation and interpretation of visible reality were fitted—were overturned by the work that culminated in the Englishman Isaac Newton's mathematical synthesis of terrestrial and celestial mechanics. A genuinely new way of doing something was discovered. The moderns had in one field outdone the ancients, had seen the law and order of the physical world, which the ancients had only sensed in dream and scattered insight. In one area, bounds were crossed which the traditionalistic culture of the preceding centuries would have thought it impiety to approach. The exhilarations of science were bound to spread beyond it.

It is no accident that the triumphant time of the scientific revolution was the period of neoclassicism in the arts and in the cultivated sense of life where art is rooted. As the moderns came to stand more on their own feet, they gained a kind of equal footing with the ancients. Partly because the moderns had made their way beyond some of the perspectives of the ancients, they felt surer of their ability to live up to the standards of rationality and decorum which antiquity still supplied. A cult of rules and regularity bespoke the age's confidence that it could "wrap up" the principles of sound judgment and apt expression as it reduced heaven and earth to elegant laws. Both the Maker of heaven and earth and the classical makers of civilization were robbed of some of their immeasurableness.

In an important sense, humanism was fulfilled in the last preindustrial century; that is, humanism conceived as an aspiration to the moral seriousness, as well as the formal polish, of the high civilization which antiquity stood for. The new science cooperated with mature humanism to produce a new standard of philosophic discourse. The peaks of postmedieval philosophy came in the seventeenth and eighteenth centuries, including the English tetrad of Hobbes, Locke, Berkeley, and Hume. Science forced a new concern with the theory of knowledge and a new rigor of method on philosophers; their continuing occupation with the humanistic subjects—ethics, politics, history—was reinvigorated by the scientific influence. In an altered intellectual setting, the terms of Christianity's alliance with secular culture and rationality were readjusted. Though infidelity appeared in the eighteenth century, most scientists and philosophers in the seventeenth labored under the continuing compulsion of Christian concerns. Yet, as compared with earlier Christian humanism, the tension between religion and "nature" slackened. Reason, duty, taste, and order seemed to be thriving in the world; the side of Christianity that denies the world was less prominent. Both the development of Puritanism during the Revolution and the reaction against it played a part in the much larger revision of outlooks that was going on in England and Europe while the Stuarts lived out the remainder of their history.

The Last Stuarts: Two Scenes

Following the contours of politics, we may divide the Stuarts' last act, the years 1660 to 1714, into two scenes. In 1688, King James II, younger son of Charles I and successor (1685) to the childless Charles II, was driven off the throne. James was a Roman Catholic and had strained the prerogative in order to improve the lot of his co-religionists. The beneficiary of the community's almost unanimous desire to be rid of James was William, Prince of Orange, the Dutch head-of-state. Long interested in English affairs, possibly ambitious for the crown for its own sake, and necessarily drawn to the prospect of enlisting the resources of England for his country's desperate struggle against France, William intervened militarily at the critical moment (and James's forces in England caved in). William's involvement had a family basis, for he himself was Charles I's grandson and his wife, Mary, was James II's elder daughter. Given a choice, most politicians preferred to depose the king in as legitimist a spirit as possible, for which reason some of them—among those who did not favor a still more conservative solution—would have liked to make Mary queen and leave William officially out of it. However, William, who held the cards, denied them the choice. He and Mary were made co-monarchs for their joint lives, William III to reign by himself if he turned out to be the survivor (as he did). Subsequently, the Crown was settled by statute on the Protestant heirs of the Stuart line. The male descendants of James II by his second marriage being excluded, the throne passed from William to James's Protestant younger daughter by his first marriage, Anne, and then to the collateral German House of Hanover.

The year 1688 marked a shift in political assumptions, as well as the removal of a king and reemphasis of England's commitment to Protestantism. The king was not demoted from his commanding place in the system of government, but tacit understandings and detailed arrangements were shifted and settled by the 1688 revolution. It was agreed that the king was no longer outside the purview of ordinary law and legislative control. The high royalism that had been woven into practical politics in the sixteenth and seventeenth centuries—without really subverting the tradition of limited monarchy—was relegated, with its Stuart champions, to the realm of political romance. The attitudes of English constitutionalism were reaccented and respecified into the light of fresh experiences. From 1660 to 1688 was a time of uncertain beliefs and standards, in cultural as well as political senses; it was a time of one generation's dying and another's growing up under the shadow of a civic trauma. After 1688, the country was beginning to settle into its identity, its style, and its consensus.

Internationally, 1660–88 was a period of peace, 1688–1714 a period of war. The exceptions to the first statement are two further naval wars against Holland (1665–67 and 1672–74), differing from each other in diplomatic circumstances but both pursuant to the commercial competitiveness that had already once broken the Protestant Anglo-Dutch alliance. The last Dutch War came out of an extraordinary tangle, in which the essential themes of Charles II's reign are reflected: England became involved—in a side-show operation—as the client of Louis XIV of France, whose central objective in the 1670s was the subjugation of Holland. Louis XIV succeeded to the French throne as a child in 1643 and died in 1715, so that the period of his adulthood and personal direction of affairs corresponds almost exactly to the bounds of this chapter. He was presented with a succession of dynastic opportunities to expand his hegemony; much of his career was devoted to pursuit of them.

"Containment" of France was the natural thrust of policy for most other continental states. Holland, a small, precariously situated state backed up by great wealth and an overseas empire, was near the center of the various configurations which opposed French designs. In 1668, when the first of Louis XIV's major adventures (against Spain, for contested territories in present-day Belgium) had put the French threat prominently on the map, England publicly committed herself to an alliance with Holland and Sweden, a maneuver that induced Louis to make peace for the time being. Two years later, King Charles made a treaty with France, which, by virtue of secret provisions, amounted to a clientage arrangement: Louis agreed to pay Charles a handsome annuity in exchange for support in the further military operations he was planning. Charles also agreed, for himself and his brother James, to profess Catholicism publicly at the earliest convenient moment, a moment that never arrived for Charles but that James seized at once. If (unlike the vast majority of seventeenth-century Englishmen) one is not shocked by Catholicism, and if one is less than convinced that an actively anti-French policy was in England's interest, then the deal was not so bad. The king got some income for little more than neutrality; the last Dutch War, in partial fulfillment of the commitment to France, brought England a little advantage in her maritime rivalry with Holland and was concluded by a separate peace.

The Glorious Revolution of 1688 brought England into Europe on an unprecedented scale. Save for four years (1697–1701), she was engaged in "world war" throughout the final subperiod—in two major alliances of most of the European states opposing two major French enterprises. The first war, known as the War of the League of Augsburg, came to a defensive victory for William III. He lost most of his battles, but hung on with the backing of English resources. When it was over, he had fought the French to a draw and in the process won their acknowledgment of his acquisition of England. Earlier in the process, he had consolidated that acquisition by defeating the Irish and Scottish partisans of James II in what may be regarded as outlying theaters of the larger conflict. (In the case of Scotland, the way was paved for the political union with England achieved in 1707.) The second war, in Queen Anne's reign, gained England more benefits, including the intangibles of national prestige. It was brought on by the extinction of the Spanish royal line, hence, the War of the Spanish Succession, and a complicated squabble over how a vast bundle of possessions should be divided up so as to satisfy several powerful dynastic claimants and also to preserve a balance of power acceptable to chip-holders without a direct interest in the spoils, notably England and Holland. In the event, Louis XIV claimed the whole inheritance for his grandson; the other major states, including England, went to war in support of the Austrian (Hapsburg) claim to a share and in the interest of "containment." Glory was garnered on the battlefields where the greatest of English generals, John Churchill, Duke of Marlborough, won his tri-

frame of mind. Hardly anyone alive after 1660 could so sincerely recall the sweetness of life before the storm, for as a young gentleman-lawyer he had belonged to its most intelligent circle, from whose atmosphere his moderate royalism and rational Anglicanism drew their nourishment. No one else stood so well for what ought to be restored and could not be, no one was so apt a counselor to the king-come-home-to-all-that, nor so naturally the chief of a government of old-timers.

Among other things, Clarendon fell victim to the "generation gap." In 1667, he was impeached for treason by the House of Commons; although never convicted, he accepted his political ruin and went into exile, where he devoted the rest of his life to writing. Something can be said for impeachment as a means of forcing the king and his ministers to pay attention to parliamentary opinion. Its utility had been discovered before the war, and not until the early eighteenth century did that hyperbolic technique become unacceptable. But it is too simple to suggest that impeachment was the only accessible, hence necessary, approach to ministerial responsibility. In a sense it was that, but it is also true that late seventeenth-century politics fed on rumor and suspicion, on unscrupulous ambition abetted by sincere panic and easy credulity, on exaggerated rhetoric legitimized by recent decades of extremism. The charges against Clarendon were a tissue of gossip, political objections to some of his public acts, and technical offenses which he may possibly have committed. It is unjust to two considerable men to put Clarendon's case in a class with Strafford's. Strafford was judicially murdered, but he had asked for it in the heroic vein—by taking major responsibility for extremely unpopular policies, staking his head on their success. Clarendon was made the scapegoat for misfortunes that were mostly not his fault and that, in any event, involved no crisis of the constitution. Strafford was thrown to the wolves by a king whose desperate straits had not wholly extinguished his sense of honor. Clarendon was sacrificed by a cagier king, who recognized the usefulness of a scapegoat and was not disinclined to make room for the younger courtiers waiting in the wings and raising dust. The connection between the two cases is that what had been done to Strafford and others was easier to do again; what had been done by a rebel Puritan Parliament was imitable by a Parliament that professed to abhor its predecessor's principles; what had been done to a proud "big loser" could be done to an old gentleman whose unhappy administration hardly wiped out his claim on his country's gratitude. Strafford lost his head, while there was no serious chance of Clarendon's losing his. But the antique pedigree of exile does not make it a humane remedy, and the politics of proscription bespeak a fevered commonwealth.

At the Restoration, from many people's point of view, happy days were here again. But the mid-sixties were a wretched time. In 1665 a terrible epidemic of bubonic plague killed thousands upon thousands. In 1666 the greater part of the City of London burned down. In 1667 the Dutch

Broadsheet, "A Looking-glasse for City and Country," 1665: Metropolitan life, always deplored in comparison with the pastoral, became more central for the political and intellectual élite after the Restoration. (Thames and Hudson, Ltd.)

fleet made a successful raid up the Thames estuary and destroyed some English ships at home base. The first two signs of apocalypse provoked their unsurprising share of neurasthenia. The third spelt disgrace and stood for all that had not gone well in the war against Holland. Across the board, the war had not gone so very badly, and the peace that concluded it immediately after the shameful Dutch incursion was an adjustment of interests signifying a draw. However, real inefficiency in financing and managing the war could be laid to Clarendon's administration, while malaise in the country craved a victim and a new start. There was no solid ground for a statesman out of the past to stand on—neither the king's loyalty nor any substantial segment of current public opinion.

No first minister succeeded Clarendon. The group of politicians who came into predominance upon his ruin is always identified as the Cabal, but that name is a mere joke (the first letters of their names spell "cabal"). They were in fact not a close-knit junta but five disparate characters loosely cooperating while each played his own game. Only one of the A's, Anthony Ashley-Cooper, later Earl of Shaftesbury, really deserves individual note. His was a great future, as prime mover of the effort to exclude James II from the throne and organizer of the well-organized later opposition to Charles II. He deserves the fame of founding the Whig party and credit as a master of fancy political footwork. His moral springs are hard to find; perhaps it is fair to say that the opportunist and the liberal were at one in him, that he was an ambitious man who was free of political superstition and clear-sighted enough about the country's interest to pursue it fairly consistently. Another Cabalist, Buckingham, the son of Charles I's disastrous favorite, played his own eccentric game throughout his career. The terminal L, Lauderdale, was in effect the king's viceroy for Scotland. The other two were the king's boys, the Catholic Clifford and the courtier's courtier Arlington. They were the only ministers who were in on the secret treaty with France of 1670.

That treaty, the last war against Holland, and the Declaration of Indulgence were the climactic events of the Cabal period. The foreign policy

London Fire, 1666: The Great Fire, which destroyed the old London and permitted a new one to be built, is an apt symbol for the troubles of the Restoration period and for its innovating thrust. (Thames and Hudson, Ltd.)

as such did not offend united public sentiment. Ashley-Cooper, for example, supported an anti-Dutch policy, a position reflective of ties with the mercantile community which were a constant element in his political base. An anti-Dutch policy necessarily involved making common cause with France, although not the king's cozy private relationship and pro-Catholic intentions. Reaction against the .attempt to impose toleration, however, got mixed up with fading enthusiasm for the war, an enterprise unlikely to command durable support among the Protestant, isolationist-leaning landowners in Parliament, even though they did not know the extent of the king's commitment. The king responded to vigorous criticism by retreating from both Indulgence and (a little later) the war, and the government was reconstituted.

The second prime-ministerial figure of the reign emerged from the reversal in the person of Thomas Osborne, Earl of Danby. On a different level than Clarendon's, Danby was a first-class man—an excellent practical politician. He was caught up in contradictory, in the end pathological, circumstances; his predominance lasted only five years and terminated in impeachment; but with allowance for the unstable times, he probably comes out as the best minister's minister of the seventeenth century—in a class with Thomas Cromwell and Burghley in the sixteenth century or Walpole and the younger Pitt in the eighteenth. He had both "inside" and "outside" strength. On the one hand, he served the king, although that meant, as it had frequently before, working with a master whose ideas of policy were not his own. He maintained his position at court without being a mere courtier: in cultivating a progovernment bloc in Parliament by practical husbandry, he became the first leading minister to be so centrally a parliamentary manager. On the other hand, he had a base outside the court, for he was a genuine representative of the segment of interest and opinion that counted for most in country politics. He was a staunch gentry-Anglican, indifferently prejudiced against popery and dissent and devoted to the privileges of the Church. His predilections in foreign affairs ran to the blend of Protestant sentiment, national pride, and caution toward adventurous interventionism that most squires tended to most of the time—a moderate pro-Dutch, anti-French position. Those were not his master's predilections.

Danby's fall came at the end of 1678, after the country had taken leave of its senses. In the fall of that year, one Titus Oates, a shady character of the type in whom "big lies" breed, revealed a Catholic plot to murder the king. Further revelations followed, from Oates himself and the other fantasizers and crazy opportunists who inevitably rush to such a bandwagon. Such skepticism as there was toward the imaginary plot was virtually extinguished by a lucky bit of evidence and a decisive dose of mystery. A minor figure in the Duke of York's (the future James II's) entourage was convicted for complicity in the plot on the basis of reckless utterances such as the small band of Catholic hopefuls were bound to make among themselves, and a magistrate before whom Oates had made affidavit of his fateful information was found dead in a ditch. (Whodunit nobody knows, but of course the murder, which may have been suicide, proved beyond doubt that the papists meant business!)

The more interesting mystery is the psychology behind fits of public credulity and the historical psychology behind this one. Readiness to believe in sinister Catholic designs was simply there; the Popish Plot was not the last occasion on which the suspicion surfaced, and back of it lay a century of real and constructive machinations—the real part miles removed from anything Rome and the Catholic powers any longer had the least interest in, but channels of paranoia, once dug, are perdurable. In a more obvious way than at any time since Elizabeth's accession, popery *was* inside the door, for it appeared that Charles II would produce no legitimate children, and his brother and heir was an avowed Catholic. A sense of danger that is not unrealistic can perhaps encourage belief in larger imaginary perils and make the least likely line of reasoning seem most convincing—here, that the Catholics would want to hasten their capture of the realm before it somehow escaped them. If there is a deeper explanation for the success of the Popish Plot, it lies in the unhealed quality of a postrevolutionary society. Suspicion and overreactiveness survived beyond the years when one's countryman was really one's enemy, when the government, whether royal or revolutionary, was sinister in the eyes of its antagonists, and when both sincere fanaticism and the rhetoric of precarious causes kept those emotions inflated. Displacement of such feelings onto the Catholics, the chronic scapegoats, was all too easy.

How necessary the Popish Plot was as political fuel is hard to say. The two main events that followed it, the destruction of Danby and the movement to exclude James II, might have worked out as they did without an overdose of the irrational. The former was the direct result of an independent revelation, the latter likely enough so long as a Catholic heir apparent existed and playing politics with an easily dramatized peril was a clear and present temptation. The plot, in any case, furnished ready-made melodrama.

The precipitating cause of Danby's impeachment was a disappointed diplomat's disclosure that the chief minister had dealt with the French and taken their money. He had done so, but far from treasonably in any respectable sense, for his dealings were by way of cultivating the relationship which the king continued to favor both for its own sake and for the *quid pro quo*. That policy was not Danby's preference; it was the king's privilege, under the supposed constitution, to pursue it. Having regard to real expectations and prejudices, the latter inflamed by the Popish Plot, it was disastrous for the truth to peep out. The king's interest was in keeping it from protruding all the way, which meant that Danby must take the rap and go. His impeachment was never carried through, but he was put in prison pending settlement of the charges against him and kept there for the rest of the reign.

The crisis over James's succession, from early 1679 to the summer of 1683, was the king's inning—a victory for Charles II's strategic position, tactical skill, and continuing claim on the majority loyalty of a repolarized community. It set up the rout of Stuart monarchy five years later by assuring that James would come in with a free hand and by catalyzing a reclarification of political attitudes. The Restoration had not overcome the schism of 1641–42—that "moment of truth" when a choice between trusting the king and pushing him beyond endurable limits was unavoidable—but it had softened and suppressed the fissure. The exclusion crisis called again for taking stands; in a new generation, a new and vulgarized atmosphere of political competition, it disclosed that the attitudes underlying the old parliamentary rebellion were alive. On the king's side, however, the crisis of 1641–42 brought forth the Cavaliers, to fight and suffer for the king and triumph in his restoration; the exclusion crisis produced the Tories, to help Charles II through his hour upon the stage, to prefer the awkwardness of a Catholic king to the scandal of scorning God's election and hereditary right, to swallow scandal sooner than endure a Catholic king who meant business, and to grudge at overdoing his deposition. The Whigs and the Tories, the two "parties" that contested English history from the late seventeenth century until the middle of the nineteenth, were conceived at the parting of the ways in 1641–42 and born in the exclusion crisis.

The quotation marks around parties above are a warning against anachronism. Political parties as we know them—institutions with a heavy superstructure of national and local organization—were not invented until well into the nineteenth century, after the Whigs had faded into the Liberals and the more durable Tories had euphemized their name into Conservatives. On the other hand, reasonably persistent polarities of opinion, and concerted action by politicians who agreed or who could forward each other's fortunes, were older than the Whigs and Tories. Those parties, however, came to represent rival identities in an age when one's political label and at least nominal principles had become more important sources of identity for upper-class people, relative to religious positions, local loyalties, and attachments to stars of the aristocratic firmament. Rather persistent and well-organized concerted action, correlated with the Whig and Tory labels, gave the parties a push in the late seventeenth and early eighteenth centuries. This early push in the direction of modern political parties was important, because for much of the eighteenth century the resemblance to later structures evaporated. But it evaporated without causing the labels, and some memory of the principles they stood for, and the notion that English politics are by nature a contest between two formidable PARTIES called Whigs and Tories, to vanish entirely. The momentum that survived assisted the emergence of coherent groupings in the early nineteenth century and their later elaboration into the bureaucratic political concerns of modern times. In the shorter run, the Whigs won hands down after the Hanoverian succession and thenceforth proceeded to quarrel among themselves over the spoils and the issues. The politics of natural and contrived "connection"—the interplay of government "machine," organized outside challengers, and semi-inert independent gentry—dominated the eighteenth-century plateau; the memory of party competition had little to do with day-to-day trade in power, policy, and payoff, although it survived in identities and could be turned to rhetorical use.

Charles II, Danby, and Shaftesbury were the patriarchs of the two tribes, the monarch and his ablest minister of the Tories, the chameleonic ex-Cabalist of the Whigs. By taking pains to organize a progovernment bloc and by cultivating a following among the pro-Church gentry, Danby created a prototype of the Tory party. He had nothing like the personal strength to save himself from impeachment; the prototype was short-lived. In 1688, however, Danby took a leading role in inviting William of Orange to intervene and was instrumental in bringing the sort of royalist-leaning, High Church opinion he represented behind the revolution. In that sense, he was a founder of the enduring Tory party—the fraternity of those who supported the revolution in fact and hoped to keep it as unrevolutionary as possible in theory and consequences; who accepted William III on the terms he would settle for and became the friends of his prerogative, yet were doubters of the expensive foreign policy he imported; who translated a good deal of their unsatisfied conservatism into protectiveness toward the Church. As for Whiggery, it was germinating during the Danby administration, when Shaftesbury, out of office, furnished rather more leadership than was par for Charles II's protracted first Parliament to the vaguely dissident, ex-Puritan, liberal elements who saw themselves in contrast to the government bloc and Danby's natural sympathizers. The Popish Plot and the exposure of Danby's machinations were the big opening for Shaftesbury and the people who looked to him; the impeachment was in a sense the first Whig cause (together with contemporary anti-Catholic measures). However, the king retreated, getting rid of both Danby and his hoary Parliament and putting together a new government of a mixed and moderate stamp, including Shaftesbury. With a new Parliament, the break-up of that brief togetherness, the emergence of exclusion as *the* issue and the king and Shaftesbury at loggerheads, the prototypical Whigs were ready to become Whigs in earnest.

To make a party, sentiment needs to be reinforced by organization. So it was on the Whig side, both inside and outside Parliament. After no general elections for eighteen years, there were three from 1679 to 1681. An unprecedented degree of collective activity to oppose the king's wishes took place. The old-fashioned standards by which such activity was not legitimate, the old discrimination between the subject's right to speak his mind as an individual and his duty not to "conspire" against the king by overorganizing his self-expression, were by no means dead, but their effectual moral force was diminished, and the king was smart enough not to rely on it. He fought exclusion with his prerogative, by dissolving and proroguing Parliament and taking advantage of his financial independence, but also by working at electoral politics on his side and cultivating the sentiment and interests that would make a party against Shaftesbury. By taking a determined stand against exclusion and employing the prerogative, Charles II stimulated a body of opinion that went into the Tory heritage— a preferential devotion to legitimism and to the monarch's freedom within the area that the traditional constitution left to his discretion, an attitude compatible with the sad duty of sloughing the monarch whose exclusion without trial was unthinkable. By promoting a "court interest" representing the Tory point of view within a narrower circle, Charles contributed to the acceptability of party politics and to the Tory self-identification as the "king's friends," an identification which persisted even when, in later circumstances, Tories were constrained to oppose his government and friendliness toward his personal objectives was rather more characteristic of the Whigs in possession.

In the upshot, the Whigs were successful enough finally to get an

Exclusion Bill through the Commons, but not through the Lords. The king's greater success was not ultimately owing to Tory strength in a party sense. He simply held the two cards that mattered. He had the constitutional power to stop exclusion, not only by saying "No" in the end, but by manipulating Parliament in such a way that it could never compel him to gainsay the national will directly; he was rich enough to use his powers without falling into the morass of questionably legal schemes and intelligent enough to avoid "repression." In the end, there was no way to frustrate him but force, or at least revolutionary bluff. Against the possibility of coercing the king, one should count his possession of a modest standing army (assuming it would obey him, as it probably would. Charles I to all intents lacked such an asset; James II's army went over to William of Orange rather than fight him). But the stronger counterweight to extreme measures—the king's other high card—was mere public opinion. There was a hothead vein of Whig opinion. After the last of Charles II's Parliaments, two murky plots were woven, and upon their disclosure a couple of martyrs were added to the calendar of Whig saints—not ignoble witnesses to the political faith in which the Good Old Cause survived, to the patriot's ahistorical conviction that the great case of the Tyrant versus the People was reopened. But cooler Whig heads realized that going outside the rules of the political game was neither feasible nor desirable. On the king's side there was a lump of in-between opinion, which grew as the panic of the Popish Plot wore off (Titus Oates was exposed as the fabricator he was). A similar kind of friendly inertia was working for Charles I after the first phase of the Long Parliament, only to be dissipated by the king's conduct, luck, and the success of politicians with a guaranteed parliamentary forum in keeping the pot boiling. Charles II did nothing to arouse the uncommitted against him, and Parliament was evaded. After all, he had only managed to insure the succession which his brother was entitled to, and what would actually happen under a Roman Catholic monarch was any man's guess, James being a fifty-year-old monarch who had so far produced no offspring by his second Roman Catholic wife and who had been through enough, one would have thought, to have learned discretion.

We should be humble before the mystery of how James II managed to spoil it all. Across the board, the Stuarts' mistakes were appropriate to the best idea they stood for: that the monarch is assigned by God to represent the long run, not to accommodate himself to what his prejudiced, enthusiastic, self-interested constituency will subscribe to here and now. James II's blunders seem to hit a lower pitch, to show an egregious knack for "blowing" his assets in pursuit of an ill-defined objective. And yet imagine a Roman Catholic monarch who was everything responsible Catholics, from the Pope on down, would have wished King James to be: holy (James's personal morals left little to choose as compared with Charles II's), sage, so zealous for the faith that he would truly study how to advance it in a hostile climate. Would such a man have had a chance to accomplish anything for his religion? Would he have been permitted anything more than to live out his life on polite terms with his subjects and pass the crown to his Protestant daughter, the Princess of Orange?

James II started out with a friendly Parliament, owing substantially to spadework done in the last years of Charles II: challenging borough charters legally, voiding them, and granting new ones designed to insure royal control over local politics. The general reaction against exclusionism worked in his favor. It was reinforced when the far-out Whigs staged an abortive invasion by the Duke of Monmouth, the illegitimate son of Charles II who was the leading proposed beneficiary of exclusion. (However, James lost some of the sympathy that "Monmouth's rebellion" won him by letting participants be punished severely and with insufficient show of judicial propriety.) The new king started off with an inherited group of Tory and middle-of-the-road ministers ready to serve him—a court backed up by a "king's party" in the country ruling class. Under these circumstances, perhaps the kind of anti-James we have imagined could have made some gains for Catholic interests—limited toleration without reliance on the dispensing power; acceptance of a few Catholics in public positions; a gradual dissipation of prejudice purchased by the king's scrupulous good behavior and trusting cooperation with Protestants. Perhaps enough good will could have been generated in even the short time available, a little more than three years, to make the birth of the king's son in June of 1688 a tolerable catastrophe. But would the prospect of a Catholic line extending forever have been accepted in any event? Serious overtures were made to William of Orange by Danby and other magnates within weeks after James's male heir was born.

Perhaps a man can be in so hopeless a situation that he might as well play the fool. Perhaps the folly of James II turns into the only kind of wisdom available to him, given his ambition to serve his faith, not simply to die in his bed like his brother. He died in exile, and so did his male progeny, but he may have taken the one wild shot he had at a Catholic Stuart future. A bid for dissenter and tolerationist support; as a means to that and other ends, a bet on the dispensing power and the unrisky proposition that the bench would sustain it; an attempt to use the established Church as the medium for selling an attack on its own privileges; getting the king's own creatures (Catholics largely, but also others whose creatureliness was dependable) into positions of authority, especially in the army—such were the elements of the "wild shot." It came to girding for a showdown and hoping to avoid the most dangerous kind—to writing off the ruling-class support which a well-behaved Catholic king could count on at the possible price of impotence, and gambling that miscellaneous support and an obedient army would deter or suppress a domestic rebellion; to figuring that the family connection, which James continued to cultivate, and diplomatic considerations would keep William of Orange out of English affairs. Yet to state a strategy is no doubt to overstate its deliberateness, and perhaps another set of calculations would indeed have been more promising. Isolation from the realities of public sentiment, undue confidence in his personal authority, overeagerness to fulfill in the span of his life the vision God had trusted him with—these false perspectives to which kings were prey were doubly distorted in James II's unclear brain and unstable soul. In one sense, he was the exposed bottom layer of a society that over a century had lost the gift for believing in its essential harmoniousness, its familial gift for trust in the face of conflict. Tudor society had been strong in that form of benign self-deception; so was England after 1688.

Handed a well-disposed Parliament, James II allowed it to sit for only a short time at the beginning of his reign, thereby raising the familiar specter of nonparliamentary government. Of the alarming implications of government by dispensation and the delusiveness of banking on the dissenters we have already spoken. Almost all politicians of substance were driven away as the central administration was made over to Catholics and cronies; the power structure was offended in its honor, prejudices, and material interests when the king's creatures were inserted into local government and the autonomy of semiprivate institutions, notably the universities, was tampered with. The faithful royalism of the Church was put to a test it was bound to fail, for the king insisted that his Declaration of Indulgence be read from pulpits and created a ghost of the high commission to strengthen his control over the hierarchy. (Seven bishops refused to obey and were prosecuted for sedition because they petitioned against the declaration. They split the judges on the legal issues and won acquittal by a jury on the facts in one of the final scenes before the curtain fell in 1688.) In every way, James set up his downfall. It took William of Orange time to make up his mind. Luck favored him when he did, for the weather allowed him to land his forces in November 1688 without the naval opposition he would otherwise have faced—the famous "Protestant wind," which permitted some of the conservative collaborators in deposition to argue that God had on this occasion changed his method of electing kings to the providential, a procedure formerly most in favor with Puritans and apologists for revolution. Then James tried to run away, instead of sitting tight and creating awkwardness by his personal presence. He was caught and brought back, then more or less allowed to escape for good, William being content to avoid awkwardness. By fleeing the realm of his own will (and sending his baby heir ahead), he handed his enemies the specious argument that he had abdicated the throne—specious, but comforting to those who liked the outcome better than they liked the proceedings. With a little bit of luck, King James just might have got away with an unpalatable regime capable of holding the throne for a Catholic Stuart line. But the bass note of folly sounds longest. Providence had prepared a decent future, including a generous measure of de facto toleration for Roman Catholics; it was time for the Stuarts to abdicate this world's crown and take up the scepter of romance.

Constitutional Change and Political Adjustment: 1688 and After

The mechanism of safe revolution was an unlawful assembly dressed up like a Parliament: William being in military possession, his peer-backers took political possession. They caused an election for the Commons to be held and a quasi-Parliament assembled, observing the usual forms except that the summons was not by any king's mandate. Like the transitional body that performed the quite different office of acknowledging the king by hereditary right in 1660, this body is referred to as a "Convention." It proceeded to squabble over the further forms to be observed and finally to get together on the best deal that could be worked out with William. The Convention passed a measure known as the Declaration of Rights: partly a bill of indictment setting forth alleged illegalities of James II's government, partly a statement of legal propositions to be taken as fundamental rules for the English polity; for the rest, a declaration that, the throne being vacant by James's abdication, William and Mary were joint monarchs. William and Mary then formally accepted the monarchy. Subsequently, the Convention was turned into a regular Parliament by its own vote and the assent of the new joint tenants of the Crown, and the Declaration of Rights was turned into a regularly approved statute or *Bill* of Rights.

One is well-advised not to worry about all the legal and logical loose ends of these proceedings. By setting down a list of important legal rights, making the claim that they had been violated, and recording that William and Mary were confidently expected to vindicate those rights, the Convention created the appearance of offering the crown with conditions and reserving the right to take it away again should they be broken. But that only amounts to saying that a Whiggish political theory can be projected from one aspect of a muddy compromise. There was no duty to generalize from an anomalous historical episode, and most people were reluctant to. The behavior of future kings is to be explained on grounds both more complex and less fancy than an implication of "contractual monarchy" in the form of the revolution.

The English Bill of Rights, unlike the American, is legally only a statute, and the limits it sets on the king are vaguely expressed. The hard constitutional effects of 1688 came in the aftermath. Whereas the Bill of Rights declared in general terms that Parliament should meet frequently and that a standing army should not be maintained without parliamentary assent, teeth were put in those provisions by the Mutiny Act passed shortly after William and Mary assumed the throne. That measure gave the monarch legal power to enforce military discipline and was therefore essential if a standing army was to exist. By restricting the act to one year, it was assured that Parliament would *meet* regularly; only in 1694 was a new Triennial Act, guaranteeing frequent *elections*, put through. Only in 1701 were the judges formally taken out of politics by the enactment of *de jure* indefinite tenure. In practice, Parliament's involvement in the country's day-to-day business took a new quantitative and qualitative jump. The most important aspect of that was a new responsibility for public finance. Although anticipated by a few precedents, appropriation of funds for particular purposes became commonplace only after 1688, when the voracious necessities of war were added to the constant presence of Parliament. With appropriating went supervisory investigation of the ways tax money was spent. Involvement in business at a new political level, and a new economic level in volume and sophistication, made Parliament more of a forum for conflicting economic interests than it had been in the old days.

William III was king by extraordinary fate; he was also a wise man—a rather sour and uncharismatic one, but clearheaded. He knew what kind of monarchism he was hailed for delivering England from, and how invaluable England was for his international purposes. He was not one to squander what he had. All the same, he thought like a king. He wanted to hold onto as much of his legal prerogative as remained and to stay out of the clutches of political factions. It was therefore with reluctance that he gave in to pressure for the Triennial Act of 1694, whereby he surrendered the king's power to keep a satisfactory Parliament in existence and any Parliament guessing as to its lease on life. By the time of the Triennial Act, William III had also surrendered some of his independence of partisan politicians. He preferred the practical counterpart of his unchallenged legal authority to appoint whomever he chose to state offices: a mixed bag of ministers, selected for their personal competence and readiness to follow his own lead, not overrepresenting any single confederacy or ideology. Having come in with almost everyone's support, he was initially able to keep his government nonpartisan or bipartisan, but by 1693 he was beginning to face the awkward reality of party. Specifically, that meant choosing between his own preference for the Tories and the Whigs' superior willingness to back his foreign policy and the requisite financial measures. The king had to accommodate himself to Whig opinions which he disapproved of, and a preponderance of Whig influence on the patronage side of government, in order to maximize parliamentary cooperation with his preeminently important war effort. (In altered circumstances, his successor, Queen Anne, faced the same dilemma. A High Church Anglican before all else, she was a preferential Tory, but for the first part of her reign it was necessary to rely on the Whigs to keep the war against France going.)

The Triennial Act was part of the price for accommodation with the Whigs. They were the beneficiaries of the first election after its passage, and the so-called junta of Whig magnates who dominated the government for the next few years prophesied the later norm for British politics: ministerial rule by the leaders of one party, in power because they have won at the polls and can deliver the vote in Parliament. There was still no conventional duty on the king's part to let successful party politicians manage his government; nonpartisan "king's men" still played a role; party organization and discipline remained loose. In broad perspective, however, the monarch was never again to escape from one form or another of dependence on party captains and commanders of parliamentary power bases. In 1710, the Tories rode war-tiredness and the queen's favor into power and concluded peace; the succession of George I both returned the Whigs and ended the distinct era of political competition that followed the Triennial Act and was in part caused by it. In 1716, the length of time between required elections was increased from three years to seven. The change is a marker between eras, because frequent electioneering promoted the cultivation of party identities and rhetoric by politicians and voters, whereas more durable Parliaments removed that catalyst and made it easier for ministers to build progovernment machines from a stable group of M.P.s. But the more important stimulus to party competition under William and Anne came from divisive issues which later fell away, real issues and symbolic ones.

The great wars against France represented a new kind of experience for an insular country. There were different degrees of interventionism and isolationism, different opinions as to how much expense the wars were worth, conflicting interests as to where the burden of financing them should fall. The Whigs and Tories already had enough tradition behind them, and typical enough constituencies, to assume predictable positions on these issues. The Whigs' inheritance prepared them to stand for an aggressive Protestant foreign policy; the Revolution of 1688 was not solely their baby, but they were its unabashed enthusiasts and ready as such to champion the House of Orange abroad as well as at home; their foothold in the generally prowar mercantile community turned them in favor of the financier's notion of how a grand-scale international role should be paid for. As for the Tories, their conservative ideas were primarily attractive to the country gentlemen who doubted whether English interests were fully equivalent to those of the international coalitions against France, whether the most expensive manner of fighting the wars (a large investment in land warfare) was necessarily the best advised, and whether the agricultural interest was not overcharged for enterprises from which the mercantile had more to gain.

Closer to the symbolic level, although passions on these matters were perfectly real, were the differences of attitude toward the Church and dissent which we have already sketched. Whig governments unsurprisingly used the king's ecclesiastical patronage to promote sympathetic churchmen —liberals in both political and theological sense. To much conservative sentiment (in both senses), the favored clerics seemed unrepresentative of the bulk of opinion among serious Christians and the workaday clergy (somewhat as the Arminians had seemed, from a very different perspective, in their day). "The Church in danger!" became an identity-giving Tory slogan, the attempt to ban occasional conformity its main translation into a plank. (The campaign succeeded, temporarily, when the Tories captured the government late in Queen Anne's reign.)

Constitutional issues, again both real and symbolic, also remained between the parties. Tories swallowed 1688 as a special case without abandoning their legitimism. They were not required to commit themselves to anything more than William and Mary and the provision for the succession immediately enacted (lineal heirs of William and Mary, and for default thereof Anne and her lineal heirs). In other words, nothing was provided for the contingency that came to pass: that there would be no heirs of the specified sorts, so that a choice had to be made between the collateral Protestant representatives of the Stuart line (Hanover, descended from James I's daughter Elizabeth) and James II and his heirs (domiciled in France and supported by Louis XIV). The Whigs were for insuring a Protestant succession forever by act of Parliament; the Tories opposed that in principle, but in the end they had no choice but to incur schism—some stomaching Hanover-by-act-of-Parliament as the only alternative to another round with a Catholic king, others holding out, come what might. The Princess Anne had a large number of children, none of whom survived. The death of the last hope among her offspring made it necessary, in 1701, to settle the throne on Hanover and exclude Catholics for the future. The statute enjoyed substantial Tory support; it was sweetened by provisions intended to prevent a new foreign sovereign from using England to promote his continental interests. But since more than a decade was to pass before the Hanoverians' title accrued by Queen Anne's death, there was ample opportunity for Tories to have second thoughts, to nurse their schism, and to see their suspected lack of commitment to the settlement exploited by the Whigs. When Queen Anne did die, most Tories accepted George I; some held out in earnest and became Jacobites, that is, outright partisans of the Catholic Stuart pretenders; others flirted with the Stuarts-in-exile, half from lingering conviction, half because an unquestioned Hanoverian future looked much brighter for the Whigs than for the Tories, whose devotion to it was bound to be doubted. In the event, the tinge of Jacobism hurt even the Tories who tried to stay away from it. The Whigs made a good thing of the accession of their candidate.

Against the grain of party politics ran the surviving currents of an older political order. "Courtier" begins to seem a dated word in the post-1688 world, but a politician who was really interested in power still had to "make it" at court as well as at the polls and in Parliament. Those who did so or were working at it—those who knew political life at the center, who came from or rubbed shoulders with the upper aristocracy which tended to be at the center, who experienced responsibility for high policy and the trade in office and patronage—were divided to a degree against country amateur politicians. That old tension cut across party lines and tangled them. Whigs shared an outlook, but it was not quite the same outlook in a magnate running the government as in a country gentleman or urban "citizen" who looked to the Good Old Cause. The latter—the "Country Whig"—had potential as a radical, a capacity to keep the spirit of the Great Rebellion, the commonwealth, and the exclusion crisis alive that Whig participants in privilege and officialdom could hardly be expected to have. At the same time, he had some affinities with his Tory opposite. For the Tory point of view was intrinsically more "country" than the Whig—more the property of mere gentry, more disposed to question the public spirit and expense accounts of *any* gang of successful inside operators. On the other hand, politicians trying to make careers at the center as Tories developed court ideas of what was practical and legitimate, the more so when they succeeded and got power. The upshot is that some issues tended to pull country politicians together in spite of Whig and Tory divisions. The typical country measure was the Place Bill, an attempt, without lasting success, to exclude officeholders from Parliament. The hankering for such legislation reveals the sense in which Whigs and Tories unhampered by official responsibility were alike: with differences of emphasis, the country branches of both parties cherished the mixed constitution in its old-fashioned, separation-of-powers form. The executive under the Crown was one component in the mixture, Parliament another. Given a Whig slant, the good old orthodoxy held that Parliament should be a free representative of the PEOPLE, not "owned" by ministerial politicians and the Crown. Given a Tory slant (with which Queen Elizabeth would have had no quarrel), the constitution called for a Parliament that was free to offer the government its spontaneous loyal advice but by the same token left the monarch free in his sphere, free from the undue influence of ministers whose officeholder dependents sat in Parliament. The two slants tended to coalesce, and both to oppose the interinvolvement of ministerial and parliamentary power to which the future of British politics belonged.

Party politics were mitigated by the court-country crosscurrent; by the considerable number of M.P.s who were scarcely removable from their seats by partisan rivalry; by the numerous M.P.s—strange in our world but normal in an aristocratic one—who were not really interested in politics and took their duties casually; by the ties of kinship and patronage which caused Parliament to fall into little factions over and above party—an aid to party leaders who could count on such private followings, but also a source of conflicting loyalty; by the continuing role of the nonpartisan operator. However, party politics were sustained by more than the issues we have reviewed and the electoral fever of the Triennial Act period. Human beings do not take politics equally seriously at all times, or seriously in the same way. In the most important senses, England was a much less deeply divided society, a much stabler one, after 1688. High partisan passion was a symptom of healing and of the incompleteness of that process. As in the period from 1660 to 1688, rivalry fed on cynical ambition and on sincere conviction shading into sincere mistrust. A game lately played with weapons, lives, and bloody righteousness was played rough in Restoration England; it was often played without the moral fervor which renders political blood profuse and keeps it from going cold. In Restoration England, the antagonisms of the revolution were still alive, though suppressed on the surface.

After 1688 the political game was still rough. Impeachment, for example, was still employed. But it was closer to a rough game with rules, the playing field better marked off in the form of constant parliamentary activity and frequent elections, the teams better defined as parties. A generation's time did not obliterate the underlying passions, but it altered them. On the one hand, antagonism was more open. Whigs and Tories were free, as incompatible supporters of a common restoration settlement were not, to admit that they differed on the fundamental principles of government. But the condition for that very openness was a diminution of real fear. The sound and fury of party rivalry was a step ahead of its significance in our period's last generation, yet for that to be true a generous measure of continuing significance was required—a reality to support the rhetoric, a reality comprising more than power-seeking and interest-conflict. The reigns of William and Anne were a classic age for political rhetoric; ahead lay the richer umbrageousness and deeper peace of a classic age of political management.

Intellectual Light: Politics, Philosophy, and Science

Political conflict in seventeenth-century England had an upper story of political thought. Indeed, it is testimony to a politicized age that thinking about politics could be an entry to thinking about other subjects. That is especially true of the greatest English political philosopher, Thomas Hobbes. His work was stimulated by, although abstracted from, his country's immediate troubles. The mid-century Revolution was the centerpiece of Hobbes's long life, which extended from the year of the Armada to the eve of the exclusion crisis. The Revolution, anticipated and come to pass, posed to Hobbes the central problem of his intellectual career—the challenge of cutting his way through thickets of prejudice and half-thought to a philosophic theory of man's relation to the state. That concern dominated his search for a philosophic theory of everything else, autonomous as his interest in the other branches of philosophy was. It would not be absurd to argue that Hobbes's thought is the most important legacy to mankind of the English civil war. The point is tenable partly because it transcends Hobbes himself and the doctrinal content of his writings. For a tradition followed from Hobbes, a tradition of "moral science," or the application of rigorous analysis to questions of value. The tradition was to go beyond the theory of political obligation that was central for Hobbes into modern ethics and some aspects of classical economics. In seventeenth-century England, it was represented by Hobbes's one philosophic peer, John Locke, better known than Hobbes as an epistemologist and, in politics, a Whig apologist who wrote at the pitch of philosophy. The English civil war, together with the contentions of the later part of the century, catalyzed a new level of political discourse that embraced diverse doctrines. At the same time, European intellectual currents—the new science and the new philosophy, Hobbes a major participant in the latter, an enthusiast for the former—were demanding that level of discourse in all fields.

Hobbes is a difficult thinker, on whose meaning there will never be agreement. We believe it catches the essence of his political teaching to say that he explored the foundations of any possible future royalist-Anglican position. In intent and doctrine, he was a great conservative; his reasons were radical, and therefore as unacceptable to his political friends as to his enemies Hobbes's controlling idea was the dependence of moral order on political order. Only when man creates the "artifice" of the state—only when he takes himself out of mere nature and allows his natural personality and freedom to be subsumed under the artificial *persona* of a sovereign state—is he able to live the humane, civilized, moral life that (paradoxically) is his "natural" end. In other words, man has ethical potentialities that differentiate him from the rest of nature (which Hobbes conceived as a system of mechanistically interacting atoms); only he might as well *not* have those potentialities—they will never come to anything—unless he creates the context in which they can be realized. The context is the state, to which we must commit ourselves, forswearing all claim to resist its law and authority in the name of higher moral principles. For when we invoke rights or claim a righteousness beyond civil law and constituted authority, we undermine the conditions under which there can be any meaningful, or operative, right and wrong.

In Hobbes's view, failure to grasp these truths caused the civil war. He blamed the war particularly on lawyers' exaltation of a disembodied LAW and on the Puritans' tendency to trim the state by separating a spiritual sphere in which conscience and the Church should be supreme. Worked out and applied to England, Hobbes's theory came to identifying the king as ultimate sovereign, and hence to support for the royalist position in the practical controversies of the seventeenth century. It came also to an extreme version of the Anglican fusion of temporal and ecclesiastical supremacy. In another direction, Hobbes's analysis of the relationship between moral man and political man led into his general philosophy, both suggesting ideas in other areas and drawing reinforcement from them.

His fundamental distinction was between nature as it must be conceived if it is to be understood (and as the new science was beginning to understand it) and reason, by which man does not read nature as it is, but creates the terms in which it can be made intelligible. (In the same way, reason does not enable us to live in peace and do justice, but to create a framework that is not given in nature, wherein peace and justice become possible.)

Even if he had not been largely misunderstood, Hobbes would have told contemporary conservatives, let alone liberals, what they did not want to hear. His theory of political obligation was consensual: we undertake our duty to the state by understanding that the moral imperatives we acknowledge will make sense only if we do so. By contrast, the seventeenth-century far right regarded political subordination as natural in itself. That position was classically represented by Sir Robert Filmer, a mid-century theorist whose influence was greatest posthumously, around the time of the exclusion crisis. An explicit critic of Hobbes and the main target of Locke's major political writings, Filmer derived subordination to monarchy from subordination to paternal authority, into which every man since Adam has been born. There was another sore point: for Filmer, monarchy alone was "in the nature of things"; Hobbes taught sovereignty, not monarchy, although he thought that sovereignty was more likely to be effectual under monarchy than under other forms of government. There again Hobbes rubbed the wrong way: effectuality mattered. He was suspected (with reason, although his point should not be understood too crudely) of de facto-ism, of saying (to be realistic), "If Cromwell is providing government, and the king who was previously entitled to obedience is not, then, rather than remain in warring anarchy, obey Cromwell." Conservatives of Filmer's stamp were legitimists: the title to be obeyed comes by indefeasible hereditary right, in principle from Adam.

As for liberals, they had nothing against consensualism, except that they valued it for purposes diametrically opposed to those of Hobbes: as a basis for saying that the human makers of states reserve the right to impose conditions on their creatures and to judge them. Whether liberal or conservative on practical issues, the greater part of late seventeenth-century political thought continued in prewar traditions, although it developed them to a new sophistication. That is to say, Hobbes's philosophic rigor was not widely congenial; argument from history and about the law remained prevalent, while the scholarly and analytic standards of both kinds of argument were elevated. Furthermore, most political thought remained Christian, and much Christian philosophy that was not centrally political focused on Hobbes as an enemy. (It is not strictly fair to regard Hobbes as anti-Christian; he went to great trouble to keep up his Christian credentials, and it is possible to conclude that he succeeded. In any event, he swept away ideas that most seventeenth-century people considered to be part of a Christian outlook: the idea that nature has dimensions of spirituality and intentionality, to which Hobbes seemed to oppose a mechanistic materialism; the idea that moral law and God's will have a straightforward and supereminent claim on human conscience, to which he opposed the state's claim to override individual judgment and to absorb the Church.)

In contrast to political thought that was essentially traditional, the mid-to-later seventeenth century developed some strands that were original but that differed from Hobbes's thought. As distinct from moral science, the beginnings of "social science" are discernible. In politics, the style of thinking of which Machiavelli was the great originator was absorbed in England—a concern, not with political *obligation*, but with the factual conditions under which various eventualities can be expected and under which such good ends as political stability can be attained. Machiavelli in his true colors (as opposed to the diabolic stage Machiavelli of the sixteenth century) contributed to the conservative Clarendon's subtle grasp of political history and to the original and influential work of James Harrington, the contemporary who came closest to a sociological explanation of the civil war and a theoretical constitution-maker whose preoccupation with stability and balance led to radical republican solutions. In another sphere, empirical natural science and commercial expansion cooperated in prompting a new interest in statistics, social description, and economic speculation.

Locke, who alone met Hobbes on his own ground, presents comparable problems of interpretation. In his major political work, he was more of a partisan spokesman, a Shaftesburian Whig, than Hobbes; in religion, he was at once the more convincing Christian and an important contributor to the liberal-tolerationist strain; in philosophy, he was an empiricist, a fundamental critic of the prevailing rationalism of the seventeenth century, of which Hobbes produced a version. On one level of his political thought, he both stated the liberal form of consensualism—the conditionality of the state as such and the right to resist it—and preserved for practical purposes something of the traditional faith in moral order independent of political subordination. But those accomplishments were only possible, only capable of a convincingness beyond commonplace pieties, because Locke was able to work on Hobbes's level of analysis, and indeed because he conceded part of Hobbes's case. Locke rethought the conception of man in "nature" (that is, in a stateless condition) so as to include property among the natural potentialities to be realized by political organization. (Hobbes gave a kind of meaning, albeit an inert one, to right and wrong in nature, but not to rights in things.) With the help of that and other amendments of Hobbes's picture of the pre- or extrapolitical condition, Locke got to an important distinction between man's primary commitment to organized society and a secondary commitment to mere government. The first commitment is indefeasible, the second is not. In other words, we must surrender individual judgment to a collectivity if we are to make anything of our moral promise (along Hobbes's lines), but the surrender is to the majority—to democracy or popular sovereignty. The majority has no moral title to alienate its sovereignty but rather a duty to erect a working government consonant with it, a supreme representative legislature being the chief feature. The duty to obey government, even a properly constituted one, is not absolute; appeal to the community against the government and resumption of original powers by the community cannot be ruled out. The only political duty that *is* absolute is the duty not to "drop out," not to stand on the abstract rights of mere nature. So we believe Locke is to be understood. The upshot is very different from Hobbes; the groundwork not so different. Although Locke was often understood simplistically, as Hobbes was, he left a far more sympathetic legacy to the eighteenth century, in politics as well as general philosophy. His bequest was second only to Newton's.

In an ironic sense, politics can serve as a point of entry to the later seventeenth century's achievement in science—politics, that is, in the sense of antipolitics. The collective life of science after the Restoration was focused in the Royal Society of London, which in turn descended principally from a group started at Oxford during the time of troubles. The Royal Society, which sponsored investigations and discussions and served as a clearinghouse for scientific reports from all over England and Europe, was broad in its interests. The boundaries of science and the sciences were less defined than they have since become, and the society's ideology, derived from Francis Bacon, promoted a wide-ranging sense of relevance. But two subjects were banned from the Royal Society's sessions: politics and religion. Reaction against the divisiveness of those concerns, and faith that men who differ over those matters can nevertheless reason together about others, is also evident in post-Restoration attitudes outside the scientific community. What from a latter-day point of view was reaction against failed revolution and sectarian squabbling was also in the spirit of the Royal Society's Jacobean patron: Francis Bacon. Bacon was a pragmatic royalist in politics; his chief hope in religion was that men might learn to study God in his underinvestigated works, instead of wrangling about his overinterpreted Scriptural Word, and that Christianity might bear the ethical fruits of cooperation and material betterment.

Bacon, one might say, was the most intentional and most successful revolutionary of the seventeenth century. The Royal Society consciously went about intellectual reform after his specifications; collaboration, the cumulation of data on many fronts, and experiment—requisites of scientific progress, in any case—were articles of faith in the most orthodox and organized sector of English science. Although important work was accomplished within that sector, the most important work, was actually done outside it, and that work proceeded from and toward a conception of the scientific enterprise at odds with Bacon's. For Isaac Newton, although a peripheral participant in the Royal Society, was temperamentally a "loner." His relations with the organized and ideological science of his day were tense—fruitfully tense, to be sure. The greatest of all physicists was too much a mathematician, and too subtle and singular a mind along the border between physics and philosophy, to satisfy the expectations of Bacon's disciples. The future belonged to Newton by the sheer force of ideas, but it took time and the overcoming of resistances for his physics to become classical for serious scientists (*and* to become the popular Newtonianism of the eighteenth century, which supposed the codification of nature's laws to have been accomplished). In the other direction, "the sheer force of ideas" provided the occasion for Newton: the revolution of the great crystal sphere of astronomy and physics from Copernicus to Kepler and Galileo. The local environment of English science, conditioned by English political and religious history and prophesied by an English lord chancellor, was sublunary. Yet, by pulling with Newton and against him, that environment accounts for him in part.

In an environment that put indiscriminate stock in experiment, Newton performed elegant and crucial experiments, notably in optics. His age believed that nature's workings could be explained—with patience and observation and more critical thought than the scholastics had been capable of; Newton advanced some exciting explanatory theories, such as the wave theory of the propagation of light. But he was not comfortable with explanatory theories; that discomfort points to his quarrel with his age. His most important achievement—the mathematical formulation of laws of motion applicable to heaven and earth, organized around the idea of universal gravitation—was *not* an explanatory theory. It was a mathematician's statement of what was the case, so far as the observed phenomena showed; gravitation was a construct for expressing the relationships that the formulae talked about, not a way of explaining *how* it is that apparently disconnected bodies influence each other. Contemporaries were properly disappointed in their expectations, if their expectations were proper. Even those whose empirical minds were skeptical of grandiose theorizing looked for mechanisms. Newton provided elegant mathematics, but to physics he seemed to furnish nothing new, save for what looked like a revival of the meaningless scholastic notion that disconnected bodies can act on each other by some occult power. Although he did not admit the last point, which is a mere misunderstanding, Newton accepted the basic charge. As he put it, "I do not frame hypotheses." He did not mean hypotheses in the operational sense, but explanatory theories, theories that go beyond describing the phenomena as economically as possible and are not confined to the operationalist role of directing the search for new observations. In a major dimension, Newton's philosophy of science was directed against the comprehensive explanation of nature worked out in a deductive, rationalistic style by René Descartes. In that aspect, it had common ground with the experimentalism of the English Baconians, as with such English criticisms of Descartes as Hobbes made within a variant rationalistic framework and Locke made into empiricism. But Newton went beyond those critiques, in the direction of an austere positivism: the belief that knowledge *is* the organization of quantifiable appearances, that man's aspiration to understand the world in any fuller or more comforting sense is overreaching.

Austere positivism perhaps, but over against it, for Newton, stood revealed religion. Like many seventeenth-century scientists, including ones who differed from him philosophically, Newton was an intense Christian intellectual. More days and hours of his life were devoted to the study of Biblical chronology than to physics and mathematics, and he thought seriously enough about theology to develop unorthodox opinions on some points. In a deeper sense, however, Newton's religious thrust was perhaps more orthodox or old-fashioned than were more standard blends of scientific enthusiasm and Christian concern. Other men, and none expressed this aspiration so well as Bacon, hoped to glorify and serve God by understanding his world. Newton gave the future its chief assurance of understanding, but he himself doubted the possibility. He looked out on a world whose reality defies our demand for intelligibility, however sharply we learn to observe the face presented to our experience and to measure and formulate what we see. For Newton, perhaps, that was to look out on a world where grace alone can satisfy our need for significance. Like Shakespeare, the greatest English poet, the greatest English scientist was not at one with the humanism that prevailed in different forms in both men's times. Whatever their unsearchable inward thought, the Christianity which so complicated the practical history of the century between them was in both men's time a living framework for intellectual doubt and counterweight to it.

Select Bibliography

Chapter One

The suggestions below are rigorously selective, attempting only to point to those works which are most recommended as direct complements to the text and starting points for further study. The contours of the text are accordingly followed.

There are excellent bibliographies for the sixteenth and seventeenth centuries. The most comprehensive are Conyers Read, *Bibliography of British History: Tudor Period, 1485–1603* (2nd ed., 1959) and Godfrey Davies, *Bibliography of British History: Stuart Period, 1603–1714* (2nd ed., 1970). The Conference on British Studies Bibliographical Handbooks are briefer but up-to-date and more than sufficient for most purposes. Two volumes in that series have been published: Mortimer Levine, *Tudor England, 1485–1603* (1968) and William L. Sachse, *Restoration England, 1660–1689* (1971). A volume on the earlier seventeenth century is forthcoming. Elizabeth C. Furber, ed., *Changing Views on British History* (1966) collects a useful series of articles on recent scholarship.

General books on the sixteenth and seventeenth centuries are numerous. We omit those at roughly the same level of detail as the present book and recommend the following as next steps to a more advanced, but still general level: G. R. Elton, *England Under the Tudors* (1955; repr. with further bibliography, 1962); G. M. Trevelyan, *England Under the Stuarts* (1904); Christopher Hill, *The Century of Revo-* lution, *1603–1714* (1961). Elton is an all-around book by a leading modern historian; the other two books need to be read together for a roughly equivalent treatment of the seventeenth century—Trevelyan for narrative, Hill for the generalizations of a major present-day historian whose predominant concerns are economic and cultural.

No general works are more rewarding than the volumes of the great *English Historical Documents* series (general editor D. C. Douglas), which, in addition to extensive selections from sources, have excellent introductions and bibliographies. Two volumes in the series covering parts of the sixteenth–seventeenth-century period have been published: C. H. Williams, *English Historical Documents, 1485–1558* (1967) and Andrew Browning, *English Historical Documents, 1660–1714* (1953).

For individuals of note, it is important to remember that the articles in the *Dictionary of National Biography*, which usually represent a very high standard of scholarship, are in most cases the best starting point.

For what "Renaissance" has meant to the following generations, see Wallace K. Ferguson, *The Renaissance in Historical Thought* (1948). For the essential character of humanism, see Hanna H. Gray, "Renaissance Humanism: The Pursuit of Eloquence," *Journal of the History of Ideas*, XXIV (1963).

No single volume quite covers the English Renaissance as the subject is conceived here, but see C. S. Lewis,

English Literature in the Sixteenth Century Excluding Drama (1954), a major interpretation of the cultural influence of humanism, which extends to the late sixteenth-century period discussed in Chapter Four below. H. A. Mason, *Humanism and Poetry in the Early Tudor Period* (1959), though a more personal and selective work, like Lewis deals with numerous aspects of the cultural influence of humanism. Elizabeth M. Nugent, *The Thought and Culture of the English Renaissance* (1956) is a broad anthology with introductions and bibliography.

For upper-class ideals, chivalric and humanistic, see Arthur B. Ferguson, *The Indian Summer of English Chivalry* (1960) and Elyot's *Governor* and the Hoby translation of Castiglione's *Courtier*, both conveniently available in Everyman editions. Lawrence Stone, *The Crisis of the Aristocracy, 1558–1641* (1965), though explicitly related to a later period, has extremely valuable material for the subjects discussed in this chapter—the structure of the ruling class and changes in its education and lifestyle; see especially chapter 12. John H. Gleason, *The Justices of the Peace in England, 1558–1640* (1969) and J. E. Neale, *The Elizabethan House of Commons* (1949), while primarily relevant for the governmental system discussed in Chapter Three below, have valuable material on the education and public aspirations of gentlemen.

For educational change in general, see Lawrence Stone, "The Educational Revolution in England," *Past and Present*, no. 28 (1964), and Mark H. Curtis, *Oxford and Cambridge in Transition, 1558–1642* (1959).

A general interpretation of the significance of Christian humanism is found in H. A. Enno van Gelder, *The Two Reformations of the Sixteenth Century* (1961). From the vast bibliography on Erasmus, we recommend as starting points Johan Huizinga, *Erasmus of Rotterdam* (1924), the best biography, and John P. Dolan, ed., *The Essential Erasmus* (1964) for a selection

of his writings, which are also represented in English translation by numerous other convenient editions. For the circle of English humanists around Erasmus, including Colet and More, Frederic Seebohm, *The Oxford Reformers* (1938) is something of a classic account. For More as a man, see R. W. Chambers, *Thomas More* (1935), the most important modern biography. William Roper, *The Life of Sir Thomas More, Knight* is a classic memoir by More's son-in-law. Among other editions conveniently available is Richard S. Sylvester and Davis P. Harding, eds., *Two Early Tudor Lives* (1962).

For "social humanism" in general, see Fritz Caspari, *Humanism and the Social Order in Tudor England* (1954) and Arthur B. Ferguson, *The Articulate Citizen and the English Renaissance* (1965). The two basic books on Tudor political theory—Christopher Morris, *Political Thought in England, Tyndale to Hooker* (1953) and the English portions of J. W. Allen, *Political Thought in the Sixteenth Century* (1928)—contain material on the social thought of humanism, though both extend much further. R. H. Tawney, *Religion and the Rise of Capitalism* (1926), the basic book on economic ethics in the early modern period, is highly relevant for the matters discussed in this chapter, although its focus is different and its scope larger.

Economic conditions in the background of "social humanism" are discussed in Peter Ramsey, *Tudor Economic Problems* (1963); Joan Thirsk, ed., *The Agrarian History of England and Wales*, vol. IV, *1500–1640* (1967); F. J. Fisher, "Commercial Trends and Policy in Sixteenth Century England," *Economic History Review*, X (1940); R. H. Tawney and Eileen Power, eds., *Tudor Economic Documents*, 3 vols. (1924). For economic regulation and philanthropy, see Margaret G. Davies, *The Enforcement of English Apprenticeship, 1563–1642* (1956), the best exemplary study of how regulation actually worked, and W. K. Jordan,

Philanthropy in England, 1480–1660 (1959).

On More's *Utopia,* see J. H. Hexter, *More's "Utopia": The Biography of an Idea* (1952) and Edward Surtz, *The Praise of Pleasure: Philosophy, Education, and Communism in More's Utopia* (1957). While *Utopia* itself is available in numerous convenient editions, James J. Greene and John P. Dolan, eds., *The Essential Thomas More* (1967) contains in addition a good introductory selection from More's other works.

Wolsey and early Henrician political history are discussed in A. F. Pollard, *Wolsey* (1929) and J. J. Scarisbrick, *Henry VIII* (1968), the most important book on the reign as a whole. George Cavendish, *The Life and Death of Cardinal Wolsey* is the classic contemporary account by a servant of Wolsey's (among various editions, published along with Roper's *More* in Sylvester and Harding, eds., *Two Early Tudor Lives, op. cit.*).

Chapter Two

There are many general treatments of the English Reformation, but two books have a preemptive claim on that level: A. G. Dickens, *The English Reformation* (1964) and Philip Hughes, *The Reformation in England,* 3 vols., (1951–54).

Among innumerable possible background approaches to the history of Protestantism, we recommend: Wilhelm Pauck, *The Heritage of the Reformation* (1950); John Dillenberger, ed., *Martin Luther, Selections from His Writings* (1961) and *John Calvin, Selections from His Writings* (1971); Heinrich Boehmer, *Road to Reformation: Martin Luther to the Year 1521* (Eng. ed., 1946); François Wendel, *Calvin: The Origins and Development of His Religious Thought* (Eng. ed., 1963). For the introduction of Protestantism into England, see William A. Clebsch, *England's Earliest Protestants, 1520–1535* (1964).

The divorce crisis and the unfolding of the political Reformation in England are discussed in Garrett Mattingly, *Catherine of Aragon* (1951) and J. J. Scarisbrick, *Henry VIII, op. cit.* Kenneth Pickthorn, *Early Tudor Government: Henry VIII* (1934) is a narrative with a constitutional emphasis, by which the succession of official acts can be well followed.

For this most central of subjects, it should be noted, the special works cited here are fully rivaled by such major general works as Elton's *England Under the Tudors, op. cit.,* and Dickens's *English Reformation, op. cit.* The main Reformation legislation can be read in many collections: for example, Carl Stephenson and Frederick G. Marcham, *Sources of English Constitutional History* (1937), the best all-purpose document book for English history, and G. R. Elton, *The Tudor Constitution* (1960).

For the dissolution of the monasteries, see David Knowles, *The Religious Orders in England,* vol. III (1959), which comprehends and points to the extensive prior work on this subject.

The Church under Henry VIII's management and the later years of his reign (besides the general books cited above, especially Scarisbrick's *Henry VIII*) is discussed in Lacey Baldwin Smith, *Henry VIII: The Mask of Royalty* (1971)—specifically on the end of the reign.

Justifications of the Henrician Reformation are treated in Christopher Morris, *Political Thought in England, Tyndale to Hooker, op. cit.*; J. W. Allen, *Political Thought in the Sixteenth Century, op. cit.*; Franklin L. V. Baumer, *The Early Tudor Theory of Kingship* (1940). Humanism in relation to the Henrician and Edwardian reformations is treated in W. Gordon Zeeveld, *Foundations of Tudor Policy* (1948) and James K. McConica, *English Humanists and Reformation Politics Under Henry VIII and Edward VI* (1965).

The following works treat major figures of the Reformation. There is an old biography of Thomas Cromwell, Roger B. Merriman, *The Life and Letters of Thomas Cromwell* (1902), but the most important modern work on him is at various places in the writings of G. R. Elton. Besides *England Under the Tudors, op. cit.,* and Elton's works listed under Chapter Three below, see "Thomas Cromwell," *History Today,* VI (1956), and "The Political Creed of Thomas Cromwell," *Transactions of the Royal Historical Society,* 5th ser., vol. VI (1956). Also, James A. Muller, *Stephen Gardiner and the Tudor Reaction* (1926); Lacey Baldwin Smith, *Tudor Prelates and Politics, 1536–1558* (1953); Jasper Ridley, *Nicholas Ridley* (1957); and *Thomas Cranmer and the English Reformation* (1962).

For Edward VI's reign in general, see W. K. Jordan, *Edward VI: The Young King* (1968) and *Edward VI: The Threshold of Power* (1970).

There is a technical literature on doctrinal aspects of the Protestantization and settlement of the English Church, the best recent example of which is Peter Brooks, *Thomas Cranmer's Doctrine of the Eucharist* (1965). The successive Prayer Books can be compared in various editions, including an Everyman. T. H. L. Parker, *English Reformers* (Library of Christian Classics, 1966) is a good anthology of Protestant theological and devotional writings.

The most important work on the politics of the Elizabethan settlement is J. E. Neale's. See his *Elizabeth I and Her Parliaments* under Chapter Three below, where his studies of the settlement are incorporated. See Chapter Three also for the beginnings of Puritanism.

On Mary Tudor, see H. F. M. Prescott, *Mary Tudor* (1940) and Wilhelm Schenk, *Reginald Pole: Cardinal of England* (1950).

For the persecution and Foxe, see William Haller, *Foxe's "Book of Martyrs" and the Elect Nation* (1963).

Chapter Three

For the Tudor inheritance of constitutional assumptions, consult the following: Sir John Fortescue, *The Governance of England* (standard ed., Charles Plummer, 1885)—also available in W. H. Dunham and Stanley Pargellis, eds., *Complaint and Reform in England, 1436–1714* (1938), a generally useful anthology; S. B. Chrimes, *English Constitutional Ideas in the Fifteenth Century* (1936); Kenneth Pickthorn, *Early Tudor Government: Henry VII* (1934)—not a narrative of the reign, but a constitutional analysis; and the basic works on Tudor political theory, Morris and Allen, *op. cit.* For Tudor constitutional history in general, one book is the indispensable guide: G. R. Elton, *The Tudor Constitution* (1960) —the key documents, with introductions

that add up to the best treatise on the subject.

A classic contemporary exposition of the English political system is found in Sir Thomas Smith, *De Republica Anglorum* (standard ed., L. Alston, 1906)— also available in Dunham and Pargellis, *op. cit.*

For Parliament, J. E. Neale's books represent much the most important body of work: *The Elizabethan House of Commons* (1949) and *Elizabeth I and Her Parliaments,* 2 vols. (1953–57).

On administrative history, see G. R. Elton, *The Tudor Revolution in Government* (1953). Around this important work, a considerable body of further literature has grown up, some of it critical of Elton's thesis, some of it elaboration, largely by Elton himself.

For a start, we recommend the controversial exchange represented by Henry Williams and G. L. Morris, "A Revolution in Tudor History?" *Past and Present*, no. 25 (1963), and G. R. Elton, "The Tudor Revolution: A Reply," *Past and Present*, no. 29 (1964).

For "law and order," or the techniques and success of governmental control over the community, the best starting point is chapter 5 ("Power") in Stone, *The Crisis of the Aristocracy, op. cit.*

It should be borne in mind that the inherited legal system underlay Tudor innovations and, with various adaptations, did most of the work of social control. For the organization of the system, see W. S. Holdsworth, *A History of English Law*, vol. I (new ed., with an up-to-date bibliographical preface by S. B. Chrimes, 1956). Tudor developments of the system and of the law it administered are authoritatively discussed in other parts of Holdsworth's long masterpiece, principally in volumes IV and V.

For the Star Chamber, see Thomas G. Barnes, "Star Chamber Mythology," *American Journal of Legal History*, V (1962).

There is no satisfactory introduction to the role of the privy council. One is best advised to pursue that subject in the first instance through the works of Elton and Holdsworth, *op. cit.* A masterful study of the king's council at the beginning of the Tudor period lays out the basis on which sixteenth-century innovations were built: William H. Dunham and Charles G. Bayne, *Select Cases in the Council of Henry VII* (Selden Society, 1958).

For the court, patronage, and the relationship between the Crown and the aristocracy, see Lawrence Stone, *The Crisis of the Aristocracy, op. cit.*, especially chapter 8, and Wallace T. MacCaffrey, "Place and Patronage in Elizabethan Politics," in *Elizabethan Government and Society*, eds. S. T. Bindoff, Joel Hurstfield, and Charles H. Williams (1961). For one crucial nexus of patronage and relations with the aristocratic community, see Joel Hurstfield, *The Queen's Wards* (1958) and H. E. Bell, *An Introduction to the History and Records of the Court of Wards and Liveries* (1953).

For Queen Elizabeth's reign in general, see J. E. Neale, *Queen Elizabeth I* (1954) and William Camden, *The History of the Most Renowned and Victorious Princess Elizabeth, Late Queen of England* (ed. with an important introd. by Wallace T. MacCaffrey, 1970), the major contemporary history. For the opening years of Elizabeth's reign, see Wallace T. MacCaffrey, *The Shaping of the Elizabethan Regime* (1968), and for the last years, Edward P. Cheyney, *History of England from the Defeat of the Armada to the Death of Elizabeth*, 2 vols. (1914–26). The Spanish Armada is treated in Garrett Mattingly, *The Armada* (1959).

The major figures of the "Elizabethan plateau" are discussed in Conyers Read, *Mr. Secretary Walsingham and the Policy of Queen Elizabeth*, 3 vols. (1925); *Mr. Secretary Cecil and Queen Elizabeth* (1955); *Lord Burghley and Queen Elizabeth* (1960); Lady Antonia Fraser, *Mary Queen of Scots* (1969).

For the Protestant religious front, or Elizabethan Puritanism, see Marshall Knappen, *Tudor Puritanism* (1939); Patrick Collinson, *The Elizabethan Puritan Movement* (1967); and the works on Puritanism cited under Chapter Four.

Chapter Four

General views of intellectual history around 1600 are found in E. M. W. Tillyard, *The Elizabethan World Picture* (1943); Patrick Cruttwell, *The Shakespearean Moment and Its Place in the Poetry of the Seventeenth Century* (1954); Hiram C. Haydn, *The Counter-Renaissance* (1950); Herschel C. Baker,

The Dignity of Man: Studies in the Persistence of an Idea (1947) and *The Wars of Truth: Studies in the Decay of Christian Humanism in the Earlier Seventeenth Century* (1952); Christopher Hill, *Intellectual Origins of the English Revolution* (1965).

For Shakespeare, there is only one starting point—the plays themselves—beyond which there is commentary without limit.

For Bacon, the text to start with is *The Advancement of Learning*, available in an Everyman edition. The best introduction to commentary on Bacon is Brian Vickers, ed., *Essential Articles for the Study of Francis Bacon* (1969).

For the Cokean mentality, see J. G. A. Pocock, *The Ancient Constitution and the Feudal Law* (1957). Changes in the conception and practice of history are discussed in F. S. Fussner, *The Historical Revolution: English Historical Writing and Thought, 1580–1640* (1962) and Levi Fox, ed., *English Historical Scholarship in the Sixteenth and Seventeenth Centuries* (1956). For direct study of Coke's career and contributions to the law, the best starting place is volume V of Holdsworth's *History of English Law, op. cit.*

Regarding the "New Anglicanism" and the Puritans, beyond the *Laws of Ecclesiastical Polity* themselves (Everyman edition of the first five books, all that was published in Hooker's lifetime, in 2 vols.), the best first step into Hooker is Izaak Walton's classic *Life* (conveniently available in the Oxford World's Classics edition of Walton's *Lives*). Charles M. and Katherine George, *The Protestant Mind of the English Reformation, 1570–1640* (1961) and John F. H. New, *Anglican and Puritan, 1558–1640* (1964) are placed together because they represent contrasting points of view on the question of whether there were profound differences between the two camps in the Church of England. Harry C. Porter, *Reformation and Reaction in Tudor Cambridge* (1958), because it deals with university history, gives the clearest existing picture of what academic theologians were arguing about at the end of the sixteenth century. Roland G. Ussher, *Reconstruction in the Church of England*, 2 vols. (1910), and Christopher Hill, *Economic Problems of the Church from Archbishop Whitgift to the Long Parliament* (1956) treat practical shortcomings of the Church, efforts to do something about them, and the bearing of these matters on Puritan-Anglican controversies. William Haller, *The Rise of Puritanism* (1938) is the most important single book for defining the Puritan tradition. It extends to 1640; one of its main contributions concerns the translation of Puritanism from the sixteenth century to the seventeenth. Everett H. Emerson, *English Puritanism from John Hooper to John Milton* (1968), an anthology with introductions, is an excellent guide to the Puritan tradition in the sixteenth and seventeenth centuries. For Puritanism and secular culture, one of the great books on Puritanism in general has the highest claim to attention: Perry Miller, *The New England Mind: The Seventeenth Century* (1939).

In addition to the well-known poems and the sermons of John Donne, see Izaak Walton's *Life* (Oxford World's Classics) and for a modern biography, R. C. Bald, *John Donne, A Life* (1970). For the remaining literary figures mentioned in the text, guidance beyond their works can be found in C. S. Lewis, *English Literature in the Sixteenth Century, op. cit.*, and the ensuing volume in the Oxford History of English Literature series, Douglas Bush, *English Literature in the Earlier Seventeenth Century* (1945).

James I's reign in general is treated in David H. Willson, *James VI and I* (1956). Samuel R. Gardiner, *History of England from the Accession of James I to the Outbreak of Civil War, 1603–1642*, 10 vols. (1883–84), the great history of early seventeenth-century England, is, despite its age, to many intents unsuperseded and of unparalleled completeness. G. P. V. Akrigg, *Jacobean*

Pageant (1962), despite the popular-sounding title, presents an excellent picture of James I's court and of the things that concerned the king most closely. Menna Prestwich, *Cranfield: Politics and Profits Under the Early Stuarts* (1966) gives the closest picture of "inside" politics. Cranfield is also the subject of an excellent study by R. H. Tawney, *Business and Politics Under James I: Lionel Cranfield as Merchant and Minister* (1958).

For Jacobean constitutional history, see J. R. Tanner, *Constitutional Documents of the Reign of James I* (1930), a thorough collection, with introductions; in effect, the best treatise. J. R. Tanner, *English Constitutional Conflicts of the Seventeenth Century* (1928) is much the best introduction to the constitutional history of the whole seventeenth century. J. P. Kenyon, *The Stuart Constitution, 1603–1688* (1966), sequel to Elton's *Tudor Constitution* in the same series, is, like Elton, an excellent guide via documents and introduc-

tions; less definitive, but only because seventeenth-century constitutional history is more complex. Holdsworth's *History of English Law,* vols. V and VI, *op. cit.,* is of great value for the seventeenth century.

One document collection more extensive than those generally cited here should be kept in mind in connection with seventeenth-century constitutional history: the volumes known as *State Trials,* ed. T. B. Howell. The title is narrower than the contents, for the collection includes full documentation for many proceedings of general historical interest. It is available in most libraries and affords one of the best opportunities for students of English history to go directly from a textbook to "the horse's mouth." For the political theory of a period when most political literature was closely tied to practical constitutional problems, see J. W. Allen, *English Political Thought, 1603–1644* (1938).

Chapter Five

For the whole history of the Revolution as it is conceived in this chapter, see Samuel R. Gardiner, *History of England . . . 1603–1642, op. cit.,* and its sequels: *History of the Great Civil War,* 4 vols. (1893), and *History of the Commonwealth and Protectorate,* 3 vols. (1894–1901). Gardiner also edited an excellent accompanying document book, *Constitutional Documents of the Puritan Revolution, 1625–1660* (1906). C. H. Firth, *The Last Years of the Protectorate,* 2 vols. (1909), in effect completes Gardiner's unfinished masterpiece. Selections from Clarendon's *History of the Rebellion* are conveniently available in the Oxford World's Classics (ed. G. Huehns, 1955)—full edition by W. D. Macray, 6 vols. (1888).

An explicit discussion of the historiography and interpretation of the Revolution can be found in Christopher Hill, "Recent Interpretations of the Civil

War," in *Puritanism and Revolution* (1956). It should be noted that the essays in this collection, besides the present one and another cited individually below, add up to a significant contribution to the substantive interpretation of the Revolution. J. H. Hexter, "Storm over the Gentry," in *Reappraisals in History* (1961), summarizes, supplies the bibliography for, and criticizes the most prominent modern controversy over socioeconomic explanation of the Revolution. Though their range is wider, other essays in *Reappraisals* are also relevant.

Puritanism in the social contexts behind the Revolution and as a source of "revolutionary ideology" is discussed in Christopher Hill, *Society and Puritanism in Pre-Revolutionary England* (1964) and Michael Walzer, *The Revolution of the Saints: A Study in the Origins of Radical Politics* (1965).

For constitutional history under

Charles I, see all the works cited under Jacobean constitutional history in Chapter Four, above, save for Tanner's document collection relating only to James I. Margaret Judson, *The Crisis of the Constitution* (1949), though it deals with the early seventeenth-century generally, is an excellent extended essay especially appropriate to the critical phase before the Long Parliament. D. L. Keir, "The Case of Ship Money," *Law Quarterly Review,* LII (1936), is much the best example of close analysis of a single judicial decision.

On Laud, see H. R. Trevor-Roper, *Archbishop Laud, 1573–1645* (1940). C. V. Wedgwood, *Thomas Wentworth, First Earl of Strafford, 1593–1641: A Revaluation* (1961), because it is a revaluation of the author's own earlier book on Strafford, published in 1935, is an unusual opportunity to see a historian's evolution. Also, H. F. Kearney, *Strafford in Ireland, 1633–41* (1961).

The Long Parliament and its immediate antecedents are treated in D. Brunton and D. H. Pennington, *Members of the Long Parliament* (1954) and Mary Keeler, *The Long Parliament, 1640–1641* (1954), biographical and statistical studies of the men who made up the assembly; Perez Zagorin, *The Court and the Country: The Beginning of the English Revolution* (1969); C. V. Wedgwood, *The Great Rebellion: The King's Peace, 1637–41* (1955).

For the war and Oliver Cromwell, see C. V. Wedgwood, *The Great Rebellion: The King's War, 1641–47* (1958). C. H. Firth, *Oliver Cromwell and the Rule of the Puritans in England* (1900) is at once a standard life of Cromwell and a good general narrative of the war and its aftermath. Thomas Carlyle, *Letters and Speeches of Oliver Cromwell,* 2 vols. (1845), although it contains editorial inaccuracies, presents a trip like no other trip through Cromwell's life and utterances, guided by the Victorian historian who rehabilitated him from a long period of detraction. Carlyle's imaginative sympathy for his hero is unapproachable by blander imaginations. See W. C. Abbot, ed., *The Writings and Speeches of Oliver Cromwell,* 4 vols. (1937–47) for the authoritative modern edition. Pym and the politics of the early war years are discussed in J. H. Hexter, *The Reign of King Pym* (1941).

For "Presbyterians," "Independents," and sects, there is no obvious step between general accounts of the Revolution and works on particular sectors of the politico-religious front. The first items that follow, however, would come indirectly to such an intermediate step, while the rest deal with particular groups. A. S. P. Woodhouse, *Puritanism and Liberty* (2nd ed., 1950), although primarily an edition of the Putney and Whitehall debates, also includes an introduction and an extensive anthology from a wide range of writers which come to the best treatise on the break-up of Puritan orthodoxy in political aspects. Also, William Haller, *Liberty and Reformation in the Puritan Revolution* (1955). Perry Miller, *Orthodoxy in Massachusetts 1630–50* (1933)—although the locus is not England, an excellent study of the intellectual stresses in one Puritan community, and American history is scarcely a category separable from English in the seventeenth century. W. K. Jordan's *The Development of Religious Toleration in England,* 4 vols (1932), is a monumental work tracing the idea of toleration through the sixteenth and seventeenth centuries. Volume III, the one that is directly in point for the mid-seventeenth century, presents the whole spectrum of religious thought through the crucial toleration issue. Perez Zagorin, *A History of Political Thought in the English Revolution* (1954) is about political thought in a broader sense than the immediately corresponding section of the text, but the spectrum it presents should be considered alongside the spectrum of politico-religious positions as we discuss it.

Milton's tracts, as the text suggests, are an excellent medium for studying the evolution of "Independency" out of the older Puritan orthodoxy. A particularly useful edition is J. Max Patrick, ed., *The Prose of John Milton* (1968). Two modern books are particularly useful for Milton's relation to Puritanism and practical politics: Don M. Wolfe, *Milton in the Puritan Revolution* (1941) and Arthur Barker, *Milton and the Puritan Dilemma, 1641–1660* (1942). A nineteenth-century book, David Masson, *The Life of John Milton, Narrated in Connection with the Political, Ecclesiastical, and Literary History of his Time*, 7 vols. (1859–94), might well be the most impressive "life and times" ever written.

For the deeper roots of spiritualism and sectarianism, going back to the Reformation, see George H. Williams, *The Radical Reformation* (1962) and Ernst Troeltsch, *The Social Teaching of the Christian Churches*, 2 vols. (1911; 1960). The latter develops a classic distinction between "Church-type" and "sect-type" branches of Protestantism.

On "Independents," see G. Yule, *The Independents in the English Civil War* (1958) and David Underdown, *Pride's Purge: Politics in the Puritan Revolution* (1971). Underdown's book analyzes factional divisions and incorporates his earlier work on "Independency," which is critical of Yule. On sects, see Louise Fargo Brown, *The*

Political Activities of the Baptists and Fifth Monarchy Men in England During the Interregnum (1912).

For Quakerism, consult William C. Braithwaite, *The Beginnings of Quakerism* (1912; 2nd ed., 1955) and see the classic *Journals* of George Fox.

The key texts about the Levellers are the Putney and Whitehall debates (Woodhouse ed.) and the writings collected in William Haller and Godfrey Davies, eds., *The Leveller Tracts, 1647–53* (1944) and Don M. Wolfe, *Leveller Manifestoes of the Puritan Revolution* (1944). For secondary accounts of the movement, see T. C. Pease, *The Leveller Movement* (1916); J. Frank, *The Levellers* (1955); and H. N. Brailsford, *The Levellers and the English Revolution* (1961). The element of historical mythology in Levelling is discussed by Christopher Hill, "The Norman Yoke," in *Puritanism and Liberty, op. cit.*

For the interregnum, beyond the general works cited above, the following are useful for special topics: H. R. Trevor-Roper, "Oliver Cromwell and His Parliaments," in *Essays Presented to Sir Lewis Namier*, eds. R. Pares and A. J. P. Taylor (1956); M. P. Ashley, *Financial and Commercial Policy Under the Cromwellian Protectorate* (2nd ed., 1962); G. D. Ramsay, "Industrial Laissez Faire and the Policy of Cromwell," *Economic History Review*, XVI (1946); E. W. Kirby, "The Cromwellian Establishment," *Church History*, X (1941).

Chapter Six

It is fair to say in general, without derogating from particular studies, that post-Restoration history has not received as much interesting treatment by modern scholars as Tudor and earlier seventeenth-century history. On the other hand, the kind of literature that is directly reflective of everyday life— prose literature in the full sense, perhaps one should say—only began to come into its own after the Restoration.

There is a way, therefore, in which the first step into the late seventeenth-century world can be via contemporary witnesses. It is not so easy to make that move for the earlier period; the assistance of historians is more necessary, as it is more available.

At the outset, then, let us recommend the two greatest English diaries: Samuel Pepys's (many editions, including abridgments, such as the Modern

Library's) and John Evelyn's, the definitive edition of which, by E. S. deBeer, 6 vols. (1955), is itself a major piece of Restoration scholarship. (Also available in a one-volume abridgment.) Daniel Defoe's *Journal of the Plague Year* is a historical novel by scientific standards, but the way to live through the great plague of 1665 in the first instance. John Aubrey's *Brief Lives* (best edition by Oliver L. Dick, 1955) is the gleanings of a professional anecdotalist, the only "Who's Who" to achieve the rank of literature and an incomparable portrait gallery. Looking to poems in an incipient age of prose, some of John Dryden's—most of all his famous political satire, *Absalom and Achitophel*—have an immediate topicality that is hard to find in earlier English literature. The comic dramatists of the Restoration play upon the social scene with a new kind of realism. For the post–1688 part of the period, bear in mind that such men as Joseph Addison and Jonathan Swift were writing about politics and mores. Present-day students may not at once remember that the most truly classic English work of literary history —Samuel Johnson's *Lives of the Poets*— includes the major writers before and just after 1700, the writers who were central to Johnson's own tradition, and about whom he wrote as men as well as poets.

On the other hand, explicit history told by contemporaries is not so abundant. Clarendon, however, continued to write about his post-Restoration experiences, principally in his autobiography, which in effect is a continuation of his *History*. (See the Huehns' edition, *op. cit.*, for extensive selections.)

Finally, before turning to modern works, it should be noted that the greatest Victorian history book and the most readable of all great histories deals with our last period: Thomas Babington Macaulay, *History of England from the Accession of James II*, 5 vols. (1849–61). (Available in many editions, including an Everyman.) The body of the book is a detailed treatment of James II and William III. The first three chapters, intended as background, are highly worthy of attention. Chapter 1 sketches in pre-Restoration history; chapter 2 is a good introduction to Charles II's reign; chapter 3, "The State of England in 1685," is *the* pioneering effort at what has come to be called social history and the foundation for other examples of the genre, including the one in this book. Macaulay also wrote a number of essays on seventeenth-century subjects, all of which are rewarding and easily available in various collections of his works.

For post-Restoration history in general, see G. N. Clark, *The Later Stuarts* (2nd ed., 1955); David Ogg, *England in the Reign of Charles II*, 2 vols. (2nd ed., 1955), and *England in the Reigns of James II and William III* (cor. ed., 1957); Andrew Browning, *English Historical Documents 1660–1714, op. cit.*

In the area of economic history, some of the works cited extend to the period before or the period after 1660–1714. There are advantages in concentrating one's reading in economic history around the pivotal late seventeenth century, when the decades before 1660 can be seen in perspective and the preindustrial eighteenth century in foreshadowing. Charles Wilson, *England's Apprenticeship, 1603–1763* (1965) is much the best guide to all aspects and to "perspective and foreshadowing." Also, H. J. Habakkuk, "English Landownership, 1680–1740," *Economic History Review*, X (1940). Eric Kerridge, *The Agricultural Revolution* (1967); cf. Joan Thirsk, ed., *Agrarian History of England and Wales, op. cit.* Kerridge opens the question of placing decisive agricultural change chronologically and explaining it, as across the whole sixteenth–eighteenth-century period. See also Ralph Davis, "English Foreign Trade, 1660–1700," *Economic History Review*, 2nd ser., vol. VII (1954), and "Merchant Shipping in the Economy of the Late Seventeenth Century," *Economic History Review*, 2nd ser., vol. IX (1956). E. F. Heckscher, *Mercantilism*,

2 vols. (rev. ed., 1955), is the great work on the assumptions and practices of the European economic system. And D. C. Coleman, "Labour in the British Economy of the Seventeenth Century," *Economic History Review*, 2nd ser., vol. VIII (1956).

Moving from economic history to social history built on "hard-boiled" economic and demographic foundations, see Peter Laslett, *The World We Have Lost* (1965); Lawrence Stone, "Social Mobility in England, 1500–1700," *Past and Present*, no. 33 (1966); and, for a contrasting view, William A. Speck, "Social Status in Late Stuart England," *Past and Present*, no. 34 (1966).

In the area of religion and ethics, the Restoration of the Church of England is discussed in Robert S. Bosher, *The Making of the Restoration Settlement: The Influence of the Laudians* (1951) and George R. Abernathy, *The English Presbyterians and the Stuart Restoration*, in *American Philosophical Society Transactions*, new series, vol. LV (1965). For the Puritan tradition, see Gerald R. Cragg, *Puritanism in the Period of the Great Persecution, 1660–88* (1957) and *From Puritanism to the Age of Reason* (1950); and William C. Braithwaite, *The Second Period of Quakerism* (1919). The second Cragg book cited just above is useful as a brief and fairly general approach to the large phenomenon of the emergence of liberal theology. There is no obvious book by which to pursue that subject more fully and in all aspects except for one old one, which, though added to and corrected by more recent specialized studies, is still worth keeping in mind: John Tulloch, *Rational Theology and Christian Philosophy in the Seventeenth Century*, 2 vols. (1872). Regarding practical Christianity, see R. H. Tawney, *Religion and the Rise of Capitalism, op. cit.*; Richard B. Schlatter, *The Social Ideas of Religious Leaders, 1660–88* (1940); and Dudley W. Bahlman, *The Moral Revolution of 1688* (1957). Paul A. Welsby, ed., *Sermons*

and Society: An Anglican Anthology (1970) extends from the Reformation through the nineteenth century and provides a convenient way to get an impression of the preachers of the Restoration period alongside preachers on social topics from other times.

Two books cited under Chapters Four and Five above—Tanner's *Constitutional Conflicts* and Kenyon's *Stuart Constitution*—are also the best general guides to constitutional history for the later seventeenth century. The successor to Elton and Kenyon in the same series, E. Neville Williams, *The Eighteenth Century Constitution, 1688–1815* (1960), covers the 1688–1714 period. The following deal with the English political system in comprehensive senses and focus in important ways on the late seventeenth and early eighteenth centuries: Betty Kemp, *King and Commons, 1660–1832* (1957); Clayton Roberts, *The Growth of Responsible Government in Stuart England* (1966); J. M. Plumb, *The Growth of Political Stability in England* (1967).

The topics of constitutional history, as well as straight political narrative and biography, can be approached for the earlier part of Charles II's reign through Dennis T. Witcombe, *Charles II and the Cavalier House of Commons, 1663–1674* (1966) and Maurice Lee, *The Cabal* (1965). For the Danby administration (and Danby's career as a whole), see Andrew Browning, *Thomas Osborne, Earl of Danby and Duke of Leeds, 1632–1712*, 3 vols. (1944–51).

The exclusion crisis is covered in J. R. Jones, *The First Whigs: The Politics of the Exclusion Crisis, 1678–1683* (1961) and K. H. D. Haley, *The First Earl of Shaftesbury* (1968). Parliament, political management, and party in broader contexts are treated in Andrew Browning, "Parties and Party Organization in the Reign of Charles II," *Transactions of the Royal Historical Society*, 4th ser., vol. XXX (1948); Douglas R. Lacey, *Dissent and Party Politics in England, 1661–1689* (1969); Keith G. Feiling, *History of the Tory*

Party, 1640–1714 (1924); Betty Behrens, "The Whig Theory of the Constitution in the Reign of Charles II," *Cambridge Historical Journal,* VII (1941). In John Carswell, *The Old Cause: Three Biographical Studies in Whiggism* (1954), only one of the lives deals with a figure from our period (Lord Wharton), but the book is useful for a sense of the Whig tradition over a long span of time.

For discussion of the events of 1688 and the years following, see G. M. Trevelyan, *The English Revolution, 1688–1689* (1938) and Gerald M. Straka, *Anglican Reaction to the Revolution of 1688* (1962), useful because it gets to the most typical perspective, that of people who could not accept the Revolution with complete comfort or justify it easily by liberal theories. Works focusing on the political world after 1688 include: Stephen B. Baxter, *William III and the Defense of European Liberty, 1650–1702* (1966), a biography covering William III's whole career; J. P. Kenyon, *Robert Spencer, Earl of Sunderland, 1641–1702* (1958), again, a biography of a man who was also important before 1688—on both sides of that divide, the type of the nonparty "operator"; Robert Walcott, *English Politics in the Early Eighteenth Century* (1956); G. M. Trevelyan, *England Under Queen Anne,* 3 vols., (1930–34)—Trevelyan's masterpiece; Geoffrey Holmes, *British Politics in the Age of Anne* (1967); Winston S. Churchill, *Marlborough, His Life and Times,* 4 vols. (1933–38).

So complex and problematic is Hobbes's meaning that no single interpretative study, of several excellent ones, can be recommended ahead of the others. The starting place for direct study of Hobbes is the *Leviathan* (best edition, with a significant introd., by Michael Oakeshott, 1957). See also Howard Warrender, *The Political Philosophy of Hobbes* (1957); J. W. N. Watkins, *Hobbes's System of Ideas: A Study in the Political Significance of Philosophical Theories* (1965); Maurice

M. Goldsmith, *Hobbes's Science of Politics* (1966); Leo Strauss, *The Political Philosophy of Hobbes: Its Basis and Genesis* (1936); Sterling P. Lamprecht, "Hobbes and Hobbism," *American Political Science Review,* XXXV (1940); Quentin Skinner, "The Ideological Context of Hobbes's Political Thought," *Historical Journal,* IX (1966). Samuel I. Mintz, *The Hunting of Leviathan* (1962) is the best study of Hobbes's contemporary opponents, concentrating on his extrapolitical works. Keith C. Brown, *Hobbes* (1965) presents a collection of articles.

As with Hobbes, so with Locke: there are many good studies, more than are listed here, and among them there is fruitful argument. Locke's two *Treatises of Government* are the obvious starting point. The edition by Peter Laslett (1960) has an introduction comprising important contributions to Locke scholarship. Locke's thinking in general is more accessible than Hobbes's, and his treatment of separate subjects more separate. See his *Reasonableness of Christianity* and *Letters on Toleration* for important documents in the history of liberal Christianity. His great *Essay Concerning Human Understanding* is relevant for that, among other subjects. Secondary works include the following: Maurice W. Cranston, *John Locke: A Biography* (1957); John W. Yolton, ed., *John Locke: Problems and Perspectives* (1969), a collection of essays, useful for getting a sense of current discussion of Locke; J. W. Gough, *John Locke's Political Philosophy* (1950); Willmore Kendall, *John Locke and the Doctrine of Majority Rule* (1941); Richard H. Cox, *Locke on War and Peace* (1960).

C. B. Macpherson, *The Political Theory of Possessive Individualism* (1962) deals in a connected way with Hobbes, the Levellers, Harrington, and Locke; strongest, in our judgment, on the Levellers and Locke.

Some of the strands of social thought other than the kind of political philosophy represented by Hobbes and

Locke may be pursued through the following works on Harrington, Machiavelli, and the republican tradition. Selections from Harrington's works are available in the Liberal Arts Library (ed. Charles Blitzer, 1955), and for the best secondary introduction, see Blitzer's *An Immortal Commonwealth: The Political Thought of James Harrington* (1960). Also Felix Raab, *The English Face of Machiavelli: A Changing Interpretation, 1500–1700* (1964); Zera S. Fink, *The Classical Republicans: An Essay in the Recovery of a Pattern of Thought in Seventeenth Century England* (1945); Caroline Robbins, *The Eighteenth Century Commonwealthman* (1959), which includes seventeenth-century background. For the antiquarian and legal traditions, see David C. Douglas, *English Scholars, 1660–1730* (2nd ed., 1951) and Sir Matthew Hale, *History of the Common Law* (repr., with introd. by Charles M. Gray, 1971). On economics, see William L. Letwin, *The Origins of Scientific Economics* (1963).

Scientific advancement made in England after the Restoration is discussed in Herbert Butterfield, *The Origins of Modern Science, 1300–1800* (2nd ed., 1957); Richard F. Jones, *Ancients and Moderns: A Study of the Rise of the Scientific Movement in Seventeenth Century England* (2nd ed., 1961); Robert K. Merton, *Science, Technology, and Society in Seventeenth Century England* (1970); Margery Purver, *The Royal Society: Concept and Creation* (1967); Richard S. Westfall, *Science and Religion in Seventeenth Century England* (1958); Frank Manuel, *A Portrait of Isaac Newton* (1968).

Kings and Queens of England

Important Kings Before the Norman Conquest

Bretwealdas
c.	477–491	Aelle, King of the West Saxons
c.	560–584	Caelwin, King of the West Saxons
	584–616	Aethelbert, King of Kent
c.	600–616	Raedwald, King of East Anglia
	616–632	Edwin, King of Northumbria
	633–641	Oswald, King of Northumbria
	654–670	Oswiu, King of Northumbria

King of Mercia
758–796   Offa

Kings of the West Saxons
802–839   Egbert
866–871   Aethelraed
871–899   Alfred
899–925   Edward the Elder

(Beginning in Egbert's time the West Saxon kings exercised authority over most of southern England, and Edward the Elder and his successors exercised a varying amount of control over the Scandinavian kingdoms in the north. In 954 this control became permanent and from then onward the kings of the West Saxons ruled all England.)

Rulers of England
959–975   Edgar the Peaceable
979–1016   Aethelraed the Redeless
1016–1035   Cnut
1042–1066   Edward the Confessor
1066   Harold Godwinson

Normans
1066–1087   William I
1087–1100   William II
1100–1135   Henry I
1135–1154   Stephen

Angevins-Plantagenets
1154–1189   Henry II

1189–1199	Richard I
1199–1216	John
1216–1272	Henry III
1272–1307	Edward I
1307–1327	Edward II
1327–1377	Edward III
1377–1399	Richard II

Lancastrians

1399–1413	Henry IV
1413–1422	Henry V
1422–1461	Henry VI

Yorkists

1461–1483	Edward IV
1483	Edward V
1483–1485	Richard III

Tudors

1485–1509	Henry VII
1509–1547	Henry VIII
1547–1553	Edward VI
1553–1558	Mary (I)
1558–1603	Elizabeth I

Stuarts

1603–1625	James I
1625–1649	Charles I
1649–1660	Commonwealth and Protectorate
1660–1685	Charles II
1685–1688	James II
1688–1702	William III and Mary (II)
1702–1714	Anne

Hanoverians

1714–1727	George I
1727–1760	George II
1760–1820	George III
1820–1830	George IV
1830–1837	William IV
1837–1901	Victoria
1901–1910	Edward VII
1910–1936	George V
1936	Edward VIII
1936–1952	George VI
1952–	Elizabeth II

Index